TEACHER'S BOOK 1

JACK C. RICHARDS DAVID BYCINA ELLEN KISSLINGER

NEW PERSON TO PERSON

COMMUNICATIVE SPEAKING AND LISTENING SKILLS

OXFORD UNIVERSITY PRESS

Oxford University Press
200 Madison Avenue
New York, NY 10016 USA

Walton Street
Oxford OX2 6DP England

OXFORD is a trademark of Oxford University Press.

ISBN 0-19-434679-X

Contributing Writer: Sue Brioux Aldcorn

Editorial Manager: Shelagh Speers
Editors: Kathy Sands Boehmer and Paul Phillips
Associate Editor: Robyn Flusser
Designer: Alan Barnett
Art Buyer: Stevie Pettus-Famulari
Production Manager: Abram Hall

Printing (last digit): 10 9 8 7 6 5 4 3 2

Printed in Hong Kong.

Illustrations by Sam Day, Karen Minot, Stephan Van Litsenborg, and William Waitzman

Cover design by Mark C. Kellogg

UNIT 5

FUNCTIONS	TOPICS	STRUCTURES	PRONUNCIATION FOCUS
Describing likes and dislikes, asking and giving opinions (preferences), agreeing and disagreeing	Vacations, activities, types of: sports, movies, books, music	Present simple: *I love it. / I can't stand it.* Short answers with *so* and *neither: So do I. / Neither do I. / Me neither.* Wh-questions: *What do you think of ...? / How do you like ...?* Yes/No questions: *Do you like ...?*	Comparison of the sounds [s] and [sh]

UNIT 6

FUNCTIONS	TOPICS	STRUCTURES	PRONUNCIATION FOCUS
Accepting and declining invitations, getting more information about invitations, setting the time and place, changing plans, adding to plans, showing preferences (review of likes and dislikes)	Shared interests (review), dating, getting together with friends, entertainment guides	*Could: Could we meet at the subway instead?* Have to: *I have to meet a friend. How about* + gerund: *How about going out for dinner?* Past progressive *have (got) to: I'm afraid I have to meet a friend. / I'd love it, but I've got to work.*	One word in a sentence is often more important than others and is stressed more heavily than the other words.

UNIT 7

FUNCTIONS	TOPICS	STRUCTURES	PRONUNCIATION FOCUS
Talking to salespeople, getting and giving help, locating items in a store, asking prices and colors, comparing things	Types of stores, refund/exchange policies, cash or charge, trying on clothes	*Can/Could: Can I help you (Could you help me) with something?* Count nouns: *a cup of coffee / a movie ticket.* Yes/No questions: *Do you have this in ...? / Do you carry this in ...?;* Determiners: *this/that/these/those.* Comparatives: *bigger/looser/brighter*	In American and Canadian English, *r* is pronounced after a vowel; e.g., *sweater.*

UNIT 8

FUNCTIONS	TOPICS	STRUCTURES	PRONUNCIATION FOCUS
Discussing the menu, asking about wants, specifying wants, offering service, ordering	Ordering food in restaurants, restaurant menus, service	Future forms: *will (have), going to (have), would care for / would like.* Contractions with *will* and *would: I'll have / I'd like.* Quantifiers *some, any, a piece of / an order of* + noun: *Anything else.*	Reduced form of *would you: wouldya.*

UNIT 9 PAGE 65

FUNCTIONS

Making small requests, making larger requests, asking for favors, complaining politely, requesting action, accepting an apology

TOPICS

Lending and borrowing things, seeking favors, resolving problems in hotels

STRUCTURES

Would you mind + gerund: *Would you mind lending me ...? Could I / you* + simple form: *Could I borrow ...? too* + adjective: *too hot.*

PRONUNCIATION FOCUS

Pronunciation of *can* and *can't*: *When can you help me? / I can't come over until 10 o'clock.*

UNIT 10 PAGE 73

FUNCTIONS

Giving, getting, and clarifying personal information; describing past experiences; discussing length of time

TOPICS

Childhood memories, school years, past accomplishments, personal history, work experience

STRUCTURES

Past simple: *I went to ... / I traveled for...* Past habitual: *used to.* Time expressions: *for a while / in (1974) / (years) ago / when / right after / after that / then*

PRONUNCIATION FOCUS

Reduced form of *Did you: did-juh*

UNIT 11 PAGE 81

FUNCTIONS

Asking about past experiences, asking for a description or an opinion, comparing places

TOPICS

Travel, unusual likes/dislikes

STRUCTURES

Present perfect: *Have you ever been ...?* Simple past: *What did you think of ...? How was it?* Comparatives: *Montreal is more exciting than Ottawa. / Montreal is the most exciting city in Canada.*

PRONUNCIATION FOCUS

Falling intonation with *Wh-*questions; e.g.,
Where did you go last night?

UNIT 12 PAGE 89

FUNCTIONS

Discussing future plans; discussing future wants, hopes and possible plans

TOPICS

Careers, hopes, and dreams; business trip itinerary

STRUCTURES

Future with *plan to / going to / planning to: What do you plan to do? / are you going to do? / are you planning to do?* Future with present progressive: *What are you doing after that? / I'm going back to school after that.* Expressing possibility: *I might go / I hope to go / hope I get (I'll get) / I'd like to go / I want to go.* Will vs. *going to: How long will you be there? / How long are you going to be there?*

PRONUNCIATION FOCUS

Stressed words in a sentence usually have a regular beat:
I'd like to see a movie.

COMPONENTS

New Person to Person, Book 1 consists of:

- **Student Book**

The Student Book contains 12 units, each unit made up of two lessons. Each lesson contains: a *Conversation, Give It a Try,* and *Listen to This.* Each unit ends with *Person to Person,* which gives students an opportunity to work together on task-based communicative activities using the functions taught in the unit. In addition, the *Let's Talk* activities at the end of the book allow students to further practice the main points of each unit. The types of practice range from controlled to free use of the language. Review activities at the back of the book also consolidate the functions of every three units.

- **Audiocassette/CD**

New Person to Person provides many opportunities to listen to native speakers. It has companion audiocassettes/CDs with recordings for:

1. *Conversation.* The conversation that opens each lesson in the unit is presented at a normal, natural speed. Accompanying comprehension questions and answers are provided in the Teacher's Book.

2. *Listen to This.* This listening selection includes conversations that will help students perform real-life listening tasks such as finding out about opening and closing times, getting directions, and listening to and writing down information on forms.

3. *Person to Person.* Most of these activities are listening-based as well.

The tapescripts are at the back of the Student Book. They should not be referred to unless necessary after students have heard a recording several times.

- **Teacher's Book**

The Teacher's Book presents step-by-step procedures for teaching each unit. Language Notes, Cultural Notes, and Pronunciation Notes are provided throughout in anticipation of areas that may cause difficulty for students. An *Optional Activity,* which may be photocopied for students, is also provided for each unit.

A Communicative Approach

Recent years have seen a de-emphasis on grammatical competence as the primary goal of language learning and a focus on communicative objectives instead. This has resulted in less attention to the rules of English grammar and grammatical accuracy, and more interest in the processes of communication and conversational fluency as a goal in conversation classes. For this reason, the focus of each unit in *New Person to Person* is not on grammar, but on conversational tasks or functions, such as talking about likes and dislikes, or asking permission.

Although grammatical competence is a component of conversational proficiency, there are additional skills specific to conversation. Some of the most important of these skills and abilities are discussed below.

Topics

To be able to converse, the learner must be familiar with a broad range of common topics that occur in everyday conversation. He/she needs to be able to respond to and initiate questions on the situations, events, and activities that are commonly referred to during social interaction with speakers of English. This means having sufficient vocabulary not only to be able to recognize what was said, but also to have something to say or add in response.

Speech Functions

When people meet they do more than exchange information. They use language to make social interaction possible. This involves the ability to carry out different kinds of conversational tasks and speech functions, such as to greet and acknowledge people, to open and close conversations comfortably, and to introduce and develop topics naturally. When we speak to people we not only *say* things, we *do* things: we describe events and feelings, make requests, and offer suggestions and recommendations, as well as respond and react to suggestions, requests, orders, and so on. These are the speech functions we use for conversation and which learners of English need to practice.

To illustrate the importance of language functions, let's take the example *will*. In grammar classes students learn that *will* has future meaning. However, *will* covers a variety of functions: prediction *(I think it will rain tomorrow.)*, warning *(Be careful or you'll fall.)*, offer *(I'll do it.)*, request *(Will you open the door?)*, threat *(Do that again and I'll scream!)*, and promise *(I'll take you out for dinner if you pass your exam.)*. If students aren't aware of these uses of *will*, they are likely to think that *will* is interchangeable with other future forms, resulting in inappropriate utterances. For example, they need to understand that *Are you going to open the door?* is not equivalent to *Will you open the door?* And the answer to *What are you doing after work?* cannot be *I'll go home.*

Just as a single structure can be used to express a number of functions, so can a given function be communicated by a range of grammatical forms. Consider how many ways advice can be given. We can use modals *(Maybe you should/ought to lie down.)*, questions *(Why don't you lie down?* or *Have you thought about lying down?)*, or the conditional *(If I were you, I would lie down.)*. In order to develop the necessary conversational and listening skills, extensive practice is needed, and this is what *New Person to Person* provides.

Unpredictable Forms

When we perform different kinds of speech functions, we usually take part in a series of exchanges. For example, I *invite* you to a movie. You *accept* the invitation and *inquire* where and when we will meet. I *suggest* a time and a place. You *accept* my suggestion or *suggest* an alternative. But although this sequence of functions can be predicted once the function of the first utterance in the series

is determined, the *actual words and phrases used* to express each function cannot be predicted. Conversational competence requires the listener to match and understand the meanings of different sentences and phrases according to where they occur within an exchange.

Appropriate Language

The degree of social distance between speakers influences the forms of address used, what is talked about, and how it is said. For each interaction, a speaker must decide what the relationship between the speaker and hearer is, then adjust his/her conversational choices accordingly. Thus, in speaking to a professor a student may ask, *Could I possibly speak with you for a minute?* and to a friend, *Hey, Bob, got a minute?*

As well as using language that is sufficiently polite or casual for the situation, we must also express speech functions according to the conventions of English. We can greet a person in English with *How are you?*, but although the expressions *Are you well?* and *How is your health?* are both English, they are not customarily used as greetings. A great deal of conversational language is, in this sense, idiomatic and conventional.

Mutually Created

Conversation is a two-way process. Participants share the responsibility of maintaining the flow of talk and making their contributions both comprehensible and relevant. Conversational competence thus involves the integration of grammatical skills with the other skills noted above, and practice in this is what *New Person to Person* provides.

The functions and topics included in *New Person to Person* Books 1 and 2 are based on a consideration of the communicative needs and related grammar skills required of students at the basic and intermediate levels. A complete list of the functions and topics appears in the Scope and Sequence on pages iii–v.

HOW A LESSON WORKS

Conversation

Each unit has two lessons. Each lesson begins with a taped conversation that includes examples of the functions to be studied in that lesson. Two subsections — Prelistening Questions and Vocabulary — can help prepare students to listen to the taped conversation.

Prelistening Questions

These questions are designed to stimulate students' interest and focus them on the topic of the conversation. Discussing the questions either in pairs, small groups, or as a class enables students to better make use of their knowledge of the topic as they listen to the conversation.

Vocabulary

The Teacher's Book suggests vocabulary items for presentation with each conversation. It is up to you to choose if and when to introduce them. You may wish to postpone the introduction of new vocabulary until after the students have heard the conversation once. This will encourage them to get the message from the whole conversation, rather than listen for individual words. Thus, students learn to keep listening even if they hear a word or two they don't understand.

When appropriate, provide a picture or example of the item being introduced. Alternatively, write the word on the board and present the definition given in the Teacher's Book. If time permits, ask students to make an original sentence with each new item. You may also wish to simply translate the word or expression, or allow the students to use a bilingual dictionary. In most instances, students will benefit more from using the context to understand the meaning.

Listening

Students should have several opportunities to hear the conversation. First, play the entire conversation without stopping. Then, play it again with frequent pauses during which students can repeat the lines. They will also read it afterward. As they do so, have them practice the "read and look up" technique:

One student looks at the text to be read aloud. When ready to speak, he/she looks at his/her partner and says a line (or part of a line). He/She then looks down at the page again for the next line, and again looks up while saying it. The reader's eyes should never be in the book while he/she is speaking. This will help students to role play more naturally. At the same time, it will improve their reading fluency by requiring them to take in phrases, rather than read word-by-word. Although students may resist this technique in the beginning, repeated practice will help them see how useful it is.

Time: approximately 20 minutes

Give It a Try

Every function heard in the conversation is presented separately in the *Give It a Try* section. This allows each function to be concentrated on individually. Follow the suggestions in the Teacher's Book for teaching pronunciation points where applicable. Culture, grammar, and usage notes are also provided to enable you to present the functions more effectively. The guided Practice activities give each learner an opportunity to practice the new functions with a partner or in a small group. They include practice with content in the Student Book and provide opportunities for students to use the same functions to practice talking about their own ideas and experiences.

Time: approximately 15 minutes for each numbered subsection

Listen to This

Both lessons in each unit end with a task-based listening section called Listen to This, which is designed to help students with real-life listening tasks. Following presentation of the recording, students listen again to check their own answers before comparing with partners or with the class. Each Listen to This section in the Teacher's Book contains answers to all the questions along with the suggested teaching procedure for that section.

Time: approximately 20 minutes

Person to Person

At the end of each unit, partners work together on a communicative task-based activity based on the functions in the unit. Each partner has information that the other needs to complete the activity, so it is necessary to give and receive information carefully. Students are separated into pairs, and each student either reads or listens to information for his/her part according to the instructions in the Student Book. Expressing personal opinions and ideas, along with active listening, is an important part of this section.

Optional Activities

One optional reproducible activity is provided per unit. Suggested teaching procedures and answers appear in the back of the Teacher's Book. In each unit, the *Optional Activity* is suggested where it best supports the order of presentation of the functions. However, you may decide to allow for time constraints, student progress, or other pedagogical considerations when presenting it. It is necessary to make copies of the *Optional Activity* for each student before class.

Time: approximately 15–25 minutes

Let's Talk

Each unit also has an additional activity, *Let's Talk,* which is presented at the back of the Student Book (teacher's notes appear at the end of each unit). It provides an opportunity to further practice the functions and vocabulary of the unit as the students use their imaginations to solve a task.

Time: approximately 15–20 minutes

Reviews

There are four *Reviews* in the Student Book. The first covers Units 1-3, the second covers the next three units, and so on. Each *Review* provides students an opportunity to practice the functions in a new grouped or paired task.

Time: approximately 15–25 minutes

ADDITIONAL CONSIDERATIONS

Grammar and Usage

New Person to Person is not meant to be a grammar text and should not be used as one. The authors assume that basic grammar has already been learned and that here the students need practice in using grammar in a natural, conversational setting. However, please note that grammar is carefully controlled so that, as far as possible, the major points of English grammar are reviewed in natural contexts. The units progress in grammatical difficulty, although they can be done out of sequence if the class can handle it. Language Notes, usually found in the *Give It a Try* sections, contain important grammar and usage explanations. A summary of the grammar points in each unit of the Student Book appears in the Scope and Sequence Chart on pages iii–v.

Pronunciation

Each unit highlights one pronunciation point, the *Pronunciation Focus.* In addition, other pronunciation points are highlighted in the Teacher's Book. By paying particular attention to these pronunciation points, you will give your students an awareness of those features of American English that will be most useful to them as both listeners and speakers. These pronunciation points are: sentence stress, intonation, rhythm, blending, and reduction.

- Sentence stress and intonation.

Speakers use stress and intonation to mark the words they want to highlight, to signal the end of a thought unit, and to indicate such things as whether that unit is part of a series or a completed thought, whether it is a statement, a *Wh-* question, a yes/no question, or a request.

Intonation Patterns

Speakers of English use various intonation patterns when conversing with others. Here are some examples:

request: Could I have your name, please?
statement: It's Paine.
Wh- question: How do you spell that?
series: It's P-A-I-N-E.
Yes/No question: Do you live in Chicago?

- Blending and reduction

Words that are not given strong stress are often said quickly, "swallowed," or otherwise altered. *What did he* becomes /*wuh-de*/, *Could you* becomes /*cu-juh*/, *did she* becomes /*che*/, and so on. This is because English is a stress-timed language. In contrast to many languages where speaking each syllable takes the same length of time, English requires *only* those syllables that are stressed to be said slowly. When listening to a rapid stream of speech, students of English sometimes find it hard to recognize even words that they know because they are unfamiliar with their unstressed (or reduced) forms. Part of communicative competence, then, is to be able to recognize reduced forms as well as grasp how

stress is used communicatively, such as to highlight important ideas. *New Person to Person* addresses these features of pronunciation throughout the Teacher's Book.

General considerations for teaching:
- To heighten students' awareness of the stress, tap out the rhythm or clap your hands, hitting the stressed syllables with greater force. This will also help students see that the rhythm is very even, which is why words get reduced.
- On the board, write intonation and stress patterns with examples.
- Emphasize the pronunciation point as you model the examples given in the Teacher's Book.
- Try to integrate pronunciation work with activities whenever possible. This will help students grasp that control of pronunciation is an essential part of communicative competence. However, during guided practice or role plays it is vital that students be encouraged to develop their fluency and not be interrupted. Pronunciation work should be done either during presentation of a conversation or function, or after the students have completed pair or group work.

Pair Work

New Person to Person is based on pair and small-group activities that maximize each student's opportunity to speak in class. Clear language models and guided activities enable pairs to work alone effectively. The elements of real communication are simulated in role plays and information-gap activities. While practicing, it is important to remind students that communication is much more than words; people say a lot with their faces, their gestures, their tone of voice.

As students practice in pairs or small groups, you can walk around the room and listen to them. In many instances, you will hear incorrect usage, hesitancy, unclear pronunciation, and other areas you may want to work on. It is important, however, not to interrupt the students during free practice. Note the areas that need work and assist the students afterward. Establish yourself as a resource. Encourage students to call on you when they need help.

The procedures mentioned throughout the Teacher's Book are only suggestions. Adapt them in accordance with your own preferences and the particular needs of your students. You will need to experiment to find what works best for your class, keeping in mind that extensive pair work will maximize class time.

COMPONENTS

Student Book, pages 1–8
Let's Talk 1, Student Book page 97
Cassette/CD
Optional Activity 1, page 127

OBJECTIVES

Functions: Meeting people, exchanging personal information, filling out forms (giving and getting information)

Topics: names, addresses, phone numbers, spelling for clarification, occupations (1)

Structures:

to be:
- I'm Mike Gates.
- I'm a student.

Wh- questions:
- What do you do?
- What are you studying?

Prepositions:
- I'm an engineer at IBM.
- I work in an office.
- She works for a trading company.

Indefinite/no article with occupations:
- I am a student.
- I am an engineer.
- I study business.
- I'm in sales.

Pronunciation Focus: In compound nouns, the first noun has heavier stress and higher pitch; for example, SAVINGS account

Listen to This: Listening for specific information: names and occupations; filling in a form

CONVERSATION 1
NICE TO MEET YOU.

Prelistening Questions

1. With books open, read the title of the conversation.

2. Direct students' attention to the photograph. Say: *This is a barbecue.* In pairs, have students describe what they see.

3. Ask students to speculate: *What happens at a barbecue? Who are these people? Do you think they know each other?* Elicit answers from several volunteers for each question. Maintain a rapid pace.

Culture Note: Barbecues are a very popular way to prepare meals in North America during the nice weather. Barbecues can be for family meals or for casual entertaining. Traditional foods that are barbecued include hot dogs, hamburgers, steak, and chicken. Men often cook at barbecues, even if they don't cook otherwise.

Language Note: The term *cookout* is often used instead of *barbecue* in some parts of the United States.

Vocabulary

Introduce these words and phrases now or after the students listen to the conversation.

burgers: short form for hamburgers

by the way: expression used to change the topic of a conversation

I'm starving: idiomatic way to say *I'm very hungry.*

Presentation

1. With books closed, play the recording or read the conversation at normal speed.

2. Ask the following general comprehension questions:
   - *What's the weather like?* (perfect)
   - *What's his first name?* (Mike)
   - *What's her first name?* (Barbara/Barb)
   - *What does she say to introduce herself?* (I'm Barb Johnson. Nice to meet you.)

3. Say: *Listen again. This time listen for what they do.* Play or read again, pausing for choral repetition.

4. Ask the following questions:
   - *What smells great?* (those burgers)
   - *What does Barb do?* (study medicine)
   - *Where?* (at Harvard)
   - *What does Mike do?* (He's an engineer.)
   - *Where?* (at IBM)
   - *Does he like being an engineer?* (yes)
   - *What's ready?* (the food)
   - *Who is starving?* (Barbara)

Elicit answers from various volunteers or have students tell their partners the answers.

5. Paired Reading. Have students read the conversation, switching roles.

Language Note: Point out to students that strangers often begin a conversation by talking about the immediate environment: the party, the weather, the room they are in. These are all considered safe conversational openers.

This is a barbecue.
What happens at barbecues?

Barb: Ummm. Those burgers smell great. It's a perfect day for a barbecue.
Mike: It sure is. I'm glad it didn't rain. My name's Mike Gates, by the way.
Barb: Oh, hi! I'm Barbara Johnson. Nice to meet you.
Mike: I'm sorry. What's your name again?
Barb: Barbara. But please, just call me Barb.
Mike: So Barb . . . what do you do?
Barb: I'm studying medicine.
Mike: Really? Where?
Barb: At Harvard. What about you?
Mike: I'm an engineer at IBM.
Barb: Oh, are you? That sounds interesting.
Mike: Yeah. I like it. Hey, it looks like the food is ready.
Barb: Good. I'm starving.

1. INTRODUCING YOURSELF

| ✦ My name's | Mike Gates. | | ✧ Hello. | My name's | Barb Johnson. |
| I'm | | | Hi. | I'm | |

Practice   Introduce yourself to your classmates.

2. GETTING THE NAME RIGHT

Notice how you can ask for and get clarification.

✦ Sorry, what's your *first* name again?
 I didn't | catch your | *first* | name.
  | get | *last* |

✧ It's | *Barbara*, but please call me *Barb*.
 | *Gates, Mike Gates.*

Practice   Introduce yourself to other classmates. This time ask the person to repeat his/her first, last, or full name.

3. ASKING SOMEONE'S OCCUPATION

✦ What do you do?	✧ I'm	a student.
		a computer analyst.
		an engineer.
Oh, are you?		

✧ How	about you?	✦ I work	for Citibank.
What			in an office.
			for a trading company.
Oh, do you?			

Practice   Ask your partner for his/her occupation. Ask other classmates.

GIVE IT A TRY

1. INTRODUCING YOURSELF

1. Direct students' attention to the function box. Give students time to read over the examples.

2. Model the examples; have students repeat chorally.

Pronunciation Note: Statement intonation. On the board, write the following statements and mark the intonation.

My name is Mike Gates.

Hi, I'm Barb Johnson.

Emphasize the stress placement as you model the examples.

Culture Note: Point out that smiling, shaking hands, and making eye contact are important when introducing oneself. Emphasize that the handshake should be firm, but not viselike.

3. Circulate in the classroom and demonstrate an appropriate introduction with various students. Have several pairs demonstrate for the class. Because many students are uncomfortable with hand shaking, ample time should be spent on this.

Practice

1. Divide the students into groups of about five or six students, depending on class size.

2. Group Work. Have students circulate within their groups and introduce themselves. Remind students to shake hands and make eye contact.

3. Ask several pairs to demonstrate for the class.

2. GETTING THE NAME RIGHT

1. Direct students' attention to the function box. Give students time to read over the examples. Say: *Sometimes we don't catch someone's name during an introduction.*

2. Model the examples; have students repeat chorally.

Pronunciation Note: Rising intonation to request repetition. On the board, write the following question:

What's your first name? (asking for repetition)

Point out that rising intonation is used here to signal a request for repetition. Contrast this with the normal intonation of a *Wh-* question:

What's your first name?

Language Note: It is important to point out that these questions are very commonly used by native speakers during introductions. It is definitely socially acceptable to seek clarification when an introduction is made.

3. Model the examples with several student volunteers.

Language Note: Names in English: *First name / Last name.* Explain the first name is also called the *given* name. It is the name parents choose and give to someone at birth. The last name is the *Family* name or *Surname.* It is the name shared by all the members of a family. On the board, write the following examples:

LAST NAME/FAMILY/SURNAME

Smith/Omura/Kim/Choi

FIRST NAME/GIVEN

John/Keiko/Eun-Joo/Hsui-Lin

Practice

1. Divide students into new groups of five or six students.

2. Group Work. Have students circulate within their groups and continue introducing themselves. This time have students ask each other to repeat their first, last, or full names.

3. Ask pairs of volunteers to demonstrate for the class.

Culture Note: Briefly explain that in the United States, people use first names right away when they meet someone of their own age or status. Point out to students that if they are unsure what to do, they should wait for the other person to suggest using first names, or suggest this themselves.

3. ASKING SOMEONE'S OCCUPATION

1. Direct students' attention to the function box. Give students time to read over the examples.

2. Model the examples; have students repeat chorally.

Pronunciation Note: Stress on the verb in short responses.

Oh, ARE you?

Oh, DO you?

Language Note: Emphasize the relationship between *I'm a student* and *Oh, ARE you?* and *I work for (Citibank)* and *Oh, DO you?* Point out the use of *for* as in *I work for (a company)* vs. *in* as in *I work in an office.*

Practice

1. Explain the activity. Ask the class for names of other occupations. Write a list on the board.

2. Pair Work. Have students take turns asking for each others' occupations. Tell students they can either answer truthfully or use one of the occupations listed on the board.

3. Group Work. Have students form small groups and continue asking about each other's occupations.

4. Ask pairs to demonstrate for the class.

OPTIONAL ACTIVITY 1: Match the Occupation.

See Teacher's Notes, page 123, and Activity Sheet, page 127.

4. ASKING FOR MORE INFORMATION

1. Direct students' attention to the function boxes. Give students time to read over the examples.

2. Model the examples; have students repeat chorally.

Pronunciation Note: intonation of *Wh-* questions. The intonation is like that of statements. The voice rises then falls on the last stressed syllable. Write the following questions on the board and draw the intonation lines:

What school do you go to?

What are you studying?

Move your hand along the intonation lines as you model the questions.

Culture Note: Americans usually use the word college to mean *college* or *university.* We commonly say a person is a *college student, in college,* or *going to college* whether the name of the school attended is, for example, *Barnard College* or *Columbia University.*

Language Note: Point out that we say: *I study business,* but *I'm in engineering.*

Practice

1. Explain the activity. Remind students to follow one of the models given.

2. Pair Work. Have students take turns interviewing each other about what they do.

Note: To make the activity more lively and interesting, encourage students to also make up occupations (either unusual, such as a sky diver, a hot-air balloon operator; or ordinary, such as a lawyer, a teacher).

3. Ask pairs to demonstrate for the class.

LISTEN TO THIS

1. Explain the activity. Give students time to look at the information given for the conversations.

2. Play the recording or read the conversations at normal speed as the students fill in the information they hear.

3. Play or read the conversations again as students check their answers.

4. Pair Work. Have students check their work by comparing what they wrote.

5. Ask volunteers for the answers.

Answers: Conversation 1: Man's name: *Bob Bradley,* Occupation: *a computer programmer;* woman's name: *June Owens,* Occupation: *a teller at the Bank of New York.* Conversation 2: Woman's name: *Kim Jackson,* She studies: *fine art,* She goes to: *Smith College;* Man's name: *John Hunt,* He studies: *law,* He goes to: *Princeton University.* Conversation 3: Man's name: *Mario Pirelli,* His company: *Coca-Cola;* Woman's name: *Mayumi Yamada,* Her company: *Sony Corporation*

6. Play or read the conversation again as a final check.

4. ASKING FOR MORE INFORMATION

✦ What do you do?	✧ What do you do?
✧ I'm a student.	✦ I'm *an engineer*.
✦ Really? What school do you go to ?	✧ Really? What company do you work for?
✧ (I go to) *Boston College.* *Seneca College.*	✦ I work for *Suzuki.* *a steel company.*
✦ What are you studying?	✧ What do you do there exactly?
✧ (I study) *Business.* (I'm in) *Engineering.* *Nursing.*	✦ I'm *a secretary.* in *Human Resources.* in *sales.*

Practice

Interview your partner and find out what he/she does. Use one of the models above.

LISTEN TO THIS

▭ Listen to these conversations and complete the information below.

Conversation 1

Man's name:.................................Bradley   Woman's name: ....Owens

Occupation: ....   Occupation: ....

Conversation 2

Woman's name:.........................Jackson   Man's name: ....Hunt

She studies:...   He studies:...

She goes to:...   He goes to:...

Conversation 3

Man's name:.....................................Pirelli   Woman's name: ....Yamada

His company: ....   Her company:...

CONVERSATION 2
COULD I HAVE YOUR NAME, PLEASE?

Where are the people?
What does the woman want to do?

Officer: Yes, can I help you?

Ms. Paine: I'd like to open a savings account.

Officer: Certainly. First we'll have to fill out a few forms. Could I have your name, please?

Ms. Paine: It's Paine, Sarah Paine.

Officer: And how do you spell your last name?

Ms. Paine: It's P-A-I-N-E.

Officer: Thank you. Next, is it Miss, Mrs., or Ms.?

Ms. Paine: I prefer Ms.

Officer: Fine. Now, could I please have your address, Ms. Paine?

Ms. Paine: 2418 Greystone Road.

Officer: Is that in Chicago?

Ms. Paine: Yes, that's right. The zip code is 60602.

Officer: OK, and please give me your telephone number.

Ms. Paine: It's 364-9758.

Officer: 364-9758. All right. And finally, Ms. Paine, what is your occupation?

Ms. Paine: I work at City Hospital. I'm a lab assistant.

Officer: Fine. I just need some ID, and we'll be all set.

Pronunciation Focus

In compound nouns, the first noun has heavier stress and a higher pitch. Listen and repeat.

SAVINGS account   TELEPHONE number
ZIP code   LAB assistant

Now practice the conversation.
Pay attention to compound nouns.

CONVERSATION 2
COULD I HAVE YOUR NAME PLEASE?

Prelistening Questions

1. With books open, read the title of the conversation.

2. Have students cover the conversation. Direct students' attention to the photograph. Read the prelistening questions to the class.

3. Pair Work. Have the students work together to use the photograph to answer the prelistening questions.

4. Elicit answers from several volunteers for each question. In addition, elicit from the class information about what personal details the students think are necessary to open a bank account. Specifically: *name, address, telephone number, occupation,* and *employer.* Although other details such as business telephone are usually necessary, this chapter only looks at those mentioned above.

Culture Note: In the United States, banks ask for someone's tax identification number when an account is opened. This is usually the same number as the person's social security number.

Vocabulary

Introduce these words and phrases now or after the students listen to the conversation.

Ms.: /*miz*/ is the feminine equivalent of the masculine title Mr. Unlike Miss or Mrs., it doesn't reflect a woman's marital status.

zip code: A number assigned by the post office to a town or section of a city. The number enables mail carriers to sort and deliver the mail efficiently.

lab assistant: someone who works in a laboratory at the hospital.

ID: a form of identification such as a driver's license or passport

to be all set: to have everything in order, ready, taken care of

Presentation

1. With books closed, play the recording or read the conversation at normal speed.

2. Ask the following general comprehension questions:
   - *What is the woman's name?* (Sarah Paine)
   - *What does she want to do?*
     (open a savings account)
   - *What does she have to do first?*
     (fill out a few forms)
   - *Where does she work?* (at City Hospital)

3. Say: *Listen again. This time listen for her address, her telephone number, her occupation, and the correct spelling of her last name.* Play or read the conversation again, pausing for choral repetition.

4. Ask the following questions:
   - *How do you spell her last name?* (P-A-I-N-E)
   - *What is her address?* (2418 Greystone Road)
   - *What city is that in?* (Chicago)
   - *What is the zip code?* (60602)
   - *What is her telephone number?* (364-9758)
   - *What is her occupation?* (She is a lab assistant.)
   - *What else does the bank officer need to open the account?* (some ID)

Elicit answers from various volunteers or have students tell their partners the answers.

5. Pronunciation Focus. Point out that in compound nouns, the first noun has heavier stress and a higher pitch. Model the examples; have students repeat chorally.

6. Paired Reading. Have students read the conversation again, switching roles. Circulate and make sure they pay attention to the compound nouns.

GIVE IT A TRY

1. NAMES

1. Direct students' attention to the function box. Give students time to read over the examples.

2. Model the examples; have students repeat chorally.

Pronunciation Note: Requests — rising intonation. Write the following question on the board and draw the intonation line:

Could I have your name, please?

Move your hand along the intonation line as you model the example.

3. Pair Work. Have students practice the examples, switching roles.

Practice 1

1. Explain the activity.

2. Pair Work. Have students take turns role-playing the situation in the bank.

3. Check by having several pairs demonstrate for the class.

Practice 2

1. Have students switch partners three more times and practice role-playing the bank situation. Maintain a rapid pace.

Note: One way to do this efficiently is to have the students stand up at their seats to do the role play. Tell them you will say: *Switch.* When they hear this, they should turn to their left and find a new partner.

2. Ask other pairs to demonstrate for the class.

Culture Note: Explain that to avoid confusion between letters we sometimes say *A as in apple,* or *B as in book* when spelling our name for someone. Have students try this using their own names.

2. ADDRESSES

1. Direct students' attention to the function box. Give students time to read over the examples.

2. Model the examples; have students repeat chorally.

Pronunciation Note: *Yes/no* question — rising intonation. Write the following question on the board and draw the intonation line.

Is that in Chicago?

Move your hand along the intonation line as you model the question.

3. Pair Work. Have students practice the examples in the function box, switching roles.

Language Note: Point out that *Could I have your address?* is an official-sounding expression. To find out the address of a classmate a student might ask *Where do you live?,* but should not say *Could I have your address?*

4. Explain how numbers are read in addresses. On the board, write the following addresses. Read them aloud; have students repeat chorally: *8 Main St.* = eight Main Street, *28 Main St.* = twenty-eight Main Street, *628 Main St.* = six twenty-eight or six two eight Main Street, *1628 Main St.* = sixteen twenty-eight or one six two eight Main Street. Write other examples on the board; have students repeat.

Culture Note: Point out that addresses on a street in North America typically follow a numerical order. In addition, the numbers on one side of the street are odd numbers, on the other side even numbers. For example, on a residential street the addresses might be 8, 10, 12, 14 (Rose St.) on one side of the street, 7, 9, 11, 13 (Rose St.) on the other side of the street. Ask students to explain how this compares to the system in their country.

Practice 1

1. Explain the activity. Remind students how we use prepositions in addresses. On the board, write: I live *at* 14 Main Street. (number + street) / I live *on* Main Street. (street only) / I live *in* San Francisco. (city) Model; have students repeat.

2. Pair Work. Have students take turns asking their partner's address.

Note: To have students practice this with western-style addresses rather than their own, first make a list on the board: *14 River St., 21 Downy St., 4130 Willow St.,* etc.

3. Check by having several pairs demonstrate for the class.

1. NAMES

✦ Could I have your name, please?

✧ It's *Paine. Sarah Paine.*
And how do you spell your | *last* | name?
| *first* |

✦ It's *P-A-I-N-E.*
It's *S-A-R-A-H.*

Practice 1 Role-play with your partner. You are a bank officer. Ask your partner his/her name and how to spell it.

Practice 2 Do the same with three other classmates.

2. ADDRESSES

✦ Where do you live?
Could I have your address?

✧ I live at *2418 Greystone Road.*

✦ Is that in *Chicago?*

✧ Yes, that's right.
No, it's in *River Grove.*

Practice 1 Ask your partner the name of his/her street and how to spell it. Confirm the city.

Practice 2 Ask other classmates.

3. TELEPHONE NUMBERS

What's your | telephone number?
Could I have your |

(It's) *364-9758.*

Practice 1 Ask your partner his/her telephone number. Repeat it and write it down.

Practice 2 Ask other classmates their names and telephone numbers. Make a list.

Role-play with your partner. Call the operator and ask for the number of one of the people on the list below. (All of them live in Toronto.) Write down the number he/she gives you. Then reverse roles. Now you are the operator and your partner calls you. Use the conversation below as a model.

Operator: Directory Assistance. What city, please?

Caller: Toronto. I'd like the number of Ms. Amanda Rhodes.

Operator: How do you spell the last name, please?

Caller: It's R-H-O-D-E-S.

Operator: Thank you. And could I have the address?

Caller: It's 418 Kingston Road.

Operator: The number is 987-0248.

Caller: 987-0248. Thank you very much.

Operator: You're welcome.

CALLER
Look at this side only.

NAME *Debbie Abel*
ADDRESS *9 Woodgate Rd*
PHONE NUMBER

NAME *Kate Bingham*
ADDRESS *784 Kingston Rd.*
PHONE NUMBER

NAME *Carolyn Bryans*
ADDRESS *12 Lakeside Place*
PHONE NUMBER

NAME *Carl Watson*
ADDRESS *1989 River St.*
PHONE NUMBER

OPERATOR
Look at this side only.

Abel, David, 724 Eastern Ave	867-5307
Abel, Debbie, 9 Woodgate Rd	455-4433
Bingham, Kate, 784 Kingston Rd	767-1690
Bingham, Sue, 621 Landmark Dr	321-5090
Bryans, Carolyn, 12 Lakeside Place	896-3427
Moore, Alex, 845 Cherry St	211-3952
Watson, Carl, 1989 River St	227-5486
Watson, Robert, 18 Palmgrove Blvd	987-2718

LISTEN TO THIS

Listen to the conversation. Fill in the form.

DARCY'S
DEPARTMENT STORE

CREDIT CARD APPLICATION FORM

NAME   TELEPHONE

ADDRESS

CITY   STATE   ZIP CODE
                    MA

OCCUPATION   EMPLOYER

BANK

Practice 2

1. Explain the activity. Tell students they are to circulate around the room and write down the addresses of other classmates. When they finish with one partner, they should circulate and look for another partner.

2. Class Work. Have students circulate and ask other classmates. Maintain a rapid pace.

Note: To encourage students to move quickly, this can be made into a game. Students can be timed. The student with the most (correct) addresses is the winner.

3. Check by asking pairs to demonstrate for the class.

3. TELEPHONE NUMBERS

1. Direct students' attention to the function box. Give students time to read over the example.

2. Model the examples; have students repeat chorally.

Pronunciation Note: *Wh-* question — intonation pattern. Write the following question on the board and draw the intonation line:

What's your telephone number?

Move your hand along the intonation line as you model the question.

3. Pair Work. Have students practice the examples in the function box, switching roles.

4. Point out that when giving a telephone number, we usually say each number individually with a pause after the first three numbers. Write several more telephone numbers on the board (*671-8902, 354-2219, 861-1756, etc.*). Model; have students repeat.

Practice 1

1. Explain the activity.

2. Pair Work. Have students take turns asking their partner's telephone number and writing it down.

Note: Point out that students who do not want to give out their real telephone number can make up a fictitious number instead.

3. Check by asking several volunteers for their partner's number.

Practice 2

1. Explain the activity. Divide students into groups of about eight to ten students.

2. Group Work. Have students circulate within their group and make a list of group members' names and telephone numbers.

3. Check answers by asking various students to tell the class a group member's number; for example *(Yuko), what is (Hiro's) telephone number?*

Practice 3

1. Give students time to read the directions.

2. Divide students into pairs. Tell students who are CALLERS to cover the OPERATOR'S side, and vice versa.

3. Model the conversation; have students repeat.

4. Pair Work. Have students practice the conversation, switching roles and asking about different people's telephone numbers. If old or toy telephones are available, encourage students to use them as well as gestures.

5. Ask pairs to demonstrate the role play for the class.

LISTEN TO THIS

1. Direct students' attention to the application form. Explain the activity. Check that students understand the following vocabulary: *credit card, zip code, chef.*

2. Play the recording or read the conversation at normal speed as the students fill in the form.

3. Play the recording or read the conversation again as the students check their answers.

4. Pair Work. Have students compare their answers.

5. Check answers by asking for the information: *What is her name?* (Jean Sands) *How do you spell her first name?* (J-E-A-N) Continue asking various students about the remainder of the form.

Answers: Name: *Jean Sands*, Address: *30 Jackson St.,* City: *Salem,* Zip code: *01970,* Telephone number: *654-1315,* Occupation: *chef,* Employer: *Bayside Hotel,* Bank: *East National Bank.*

6. Play or read the conversation again as a final check.

PERSON TO PERSON

Practice 1

1. Explain the activity. Divide the class into pairs and have pairs decide who will be Student A and who will be Student B.

2. Have students listen to the introduction. Then give them time to read the directions.

3. Direct students' attention to the disembarkation card. Give students time to read over it.

Note: Point out that a disembarkation card must be filled out by anyone entering the country.

4. To make sure students understand the directions, ask: *Who is going through Customs?* (a tourist) *Where?* (New York City) *Who interviews him?* (an immigration officer)

5. Play or read the conversation as the students fill in the form.

Answers: Surname: *Rosenzweig*; First name: *Albrecht*; Date of birth: *June 17, 1945*; Place of birth: *Austria*; Nationality: *Austrian*; Occupation: *Businessman*; Reason for travel in the United States: *visit brother;* Address in the United States: *238 East 82nd St., New York, New York*

6. Have students listen again and check their answers.

7. Pair Work. Have students compare their answers.

8. Call on volunteers for the answers.

Practice 2

1. Have students read the directions. Give students time to read over the information for their parts.

2. Pair Work. Have students practice the role play. Have students repeat, role-playing the part of someone different.

3. Check students' work by calling on various pairs to role-play the interviews.

Practice 3

1. Have students switch roles and read the directions for their parts.

2. Pair Work. Have students practice the role play.

3. Check their work by calling on various pairs to demonstrate for the class.

4. Expansion. Have several pairs role-play at the same time in order to simulate what it is actually like at an airport. Encourage students to use props and gestures.

LET'S TALK 1

Student Book, page 97.

1. Explain the activity. Ask students to read over the survey form. Check students' understanding of *survey* by asking volunteers to describe it in their own words.

2. Model the interviewer opener *Could I ask you a few questions, please?* Have students repeat. Elicit possible responses *(Sure / Yes, go ahead,* etc.).

3. Separate the students into pairs.

4. Pair Work. Have students interview their partners and fill out the form. Circulate and assist students with the names of occupations as needed.

Note: Let students use fictitious addresses and phone numbers if they don't want to give out actual information. If the class members are all students, encourage them to choose occupations they would like to have. For fun, students can choose outrageous or unusual occupations, as well.

5. Have students change partners, reverse roles, and fill out the form again.

6. Ask several pairs to conduct the interview in front of the class.

7. Ask several volunteers questions about their partners. If students chose outrageous or unusual occupations, the class can vote on which is the most outrageous or unusual.

PERSON TO PERSON

STUDENT A

(Student A looks at this page. Student B looks at the next page.)

▣ A tourist is about to go through Customs and Immigration in New York City. You will hear an immigration officer interviewing him.

Practice 1

Listen as the immigration officer helps the tourist. Fill out the form below as you listen.

DISEMBARKATION CARD

Surname: _____

First name: _____

Date of Birth: _____ Day / Month / Year _____

Place of Birth: _____

Nationality: _____

Occupation: _____

Reason for travel in the U.S.: _____

Address in the U.S.: _____

Compare your answers with your partner's.

Practice 2

You have just landed in San Francisco. Your partner is an immigration officer who is going to interview you. Role-play the part of the person below and answer the questions.

This is Ms. Yu-Fen Chan. She was born in Taipei, Taiwan, on September 10, 1951. She is a homemaker visiting her sister. Her sister lives at 63 Carpenter Street in San Francisco.

Practice 3

Now you are the immigration officer. Interview your partner and fill out the disembarkation card below.

DISEMBARKATION CARD

Surname: _____

First name: _____

Date of Birth: _____ Day / Month / Year _____

Place of Birth: _____

Nationality: _____

Occupation: _____

Reason for travel in the U.S.: _____

Address in the U.S.: _____

PERSON TO PERSON

STUDENT B

(Student B looks at this page. Student A looks at the previous page.)

📼 A tourist is about to go through Customs and Immigration in New York City. You will hear an immigration officer interviewing him.

Practice 1

Listen as the immigration officer helps the tourist. Fill out the form below as you listen.

DISEMBARKATION CARD ⭐ U.S. Customs

Surname: |_|_|_|_|_|_|_|_|_|_|_|_|_|_|_|_|_|_|_|_|_|_|_|_|_|_|

First name: |_|_|_|_|_|_|_|_|_|_|_|_|_|_|_|_|_|_|_|_|_|_|

Date of Birth: _____ / _____ / _____
            Day   Month   Year

Place of Birth: _____

Nationality: _____

Occupation: _____

Reason for travel in the U.S.: _____

Address in the U.S.: _____

Compare your answers with your partner's.

Practice 2

You are a customs officer at the San Francisco airport. Your partner is a tourist who is waiting to clear customs. As you interview him/her, fill out the disembarkation card below.

DISEMBARKATION CARD ⭐ U.S. Customs

Surname: |_|_|_|_|_|_|_|_|_|_|_|_|_|_|_|_|_|_|_|_|_|_|_|_|_|_|

First name: |_|_|_|_|_|_|_|_|_|_|_|_|_|_|_|_|_|_|_|_|_|_|_|

Date of Birth: _____ / _____ / _____
            Day   Month   Year

Place of Birth: _____

Nationality: _____

Occupation: _____

Reason for travel in the U.S.: _____

Address in the U.S.: _____

Practice 3

Now you are the tourist and your partner is the immigration officer. Role-play the part of the person below and answer the questions.

This is Jack Harrington. He was born in Sydney, Australia, on April 26, 1947. He is a banker on a business trip, and he is staying at the Sheraton Hotel.

COMPONENTS

Student Book, pages 9–16
Let's Talk 2, Student Book page 98
Cassette/CD
Optional Activity 2, page 128

OBJECTIVES

Functions: Describing your family, describing marital status, talking about children, asking about age, describing what someone looks like, describing clothing

Topics:
- names of family members: grandmother, grandfather, mother, father, daughter, son, aunt, uncle, niece, nephew, cousins
- names of colors: red, brown, white, blue, green, orange, yellow, pink, tan, purple, gray, black

names of identifying characteristics: tall/short, thin/heavy, long/short/medium-length, wavy/curly hair
fairly / pretty / kind of

Structures:
- Have you got / Do you have (any brothers or sisters?) / I've got / I have (a brother).
- Is he/she married? Yes, he is. / No, she isn't.
- How old is he/she? She's in her early (mid-, late) forties.
- What is he/she wearing? What does he/she have on?

Pronunciation Focus:
Reduced forms of unstressed words *to, and are,* and *do* in normal speech. Vowel reduced to [ə]; for example, *[want tə get]*

Listen to This: Matching pictures and descriptions; filling in charts

CONVERSATION 1
TELL ME ABOUT YOUR FAMILY

Prelistening Questions

1. With books closed, read the title of the conversation and the prelistening questions. Elicit an answer to each question from a student volunteer.

2. Pair Work. Have students open their books and take turns asking and answering the questions. Have them cover the photograph and the conversation first.

Note: These questions may be confusing for students as to whether you are talking about the nuclear family or the extended family. To clarify the difference, draw four circles on the board, label them *mother, father, son,* and *daughter* and write *nuclear* underneath. Above the circles add other circles, label them *grandmother, grandfather, aunt, uncle,* etc., and write *extended family.* Point out that when someone asks *How big is your family?* they usually mean the nuclear family. The term *relatives* can also be introduced at this time. Explain that *relatives* includes *grandmother, grandfather, aunt, uncle, cousins,* etc.; in other words, the extended family.

3. Ask the following questions: *Are families bigger or smaller now than 30 years ago? Why? Which size is better? Why?*

4. Direct students' attention to the photograph.

5. Pair Work. Have students describe what they see.

6. Class Work. Ask students to speculate: *Where are these people? Who are they? What is the man holding? Do you think these people know each other?* Elicit answers from several volunteers for each question. Maintain a rapid pace.

Vocabulary

Introduce these words and phrases now or after the students listen to the conversation.

business trip: a period of travel done for business purposes

lovely-looking (family): nice-looking; more commonly used by women than men

Presentation

1. With books closed, play the recording or read the conversation at normal speed.

2. Ask the following general comprehension questions:
   - *Where has he been?* (on a business trip)
   - *What are they talking about?* (their families / their children)

3. Say: *Listen again. This time listen for the names of their children and how old they are.* Play or read again, pausing for choral repetition.

4. Ask the following questions:
   - *How long has Jim been away from home?* (one month)
   - *How many children does Jim have?* (3)
   - *Who is the oldest?* (Judy)
   - *How old is she?* (24)
   - *How old is Jamie?* (21)
   - *How old is Julian?* (17)
   - *How big is Maria's family?* (3)
   - *Does she have a son or a daughter?* (a son)
   - *What is his name?* (Tim)

Elicit answers from various students or have students tell their partners the answers.

5. Paired Reading. Have students read the conversation, switching roles.

CONVERSATION 1
TELL ME ABOUT YOUR FAMILY.

How big is your family?

What family members usually live together?

What do you consider a big family?

Announcer: National Flight 294 to Miami is delayed due to severe weather conditions. Please stand by for additional information.

Maria: Oh no! I hate these long delays!

Jim: I know. I can't wait to get home. I've been on a business trip for a month. I really miss my family.

Maria: A month is a long time to be away. Do you have any children?

Jim: I have three. Two boys and a girl. Would you like to see a picture?

Maria: Oh, how nice! Now, who's this?

Jim: This is Judy, my oldest. She's twenty-four.

Maria: Is she married?

Jim: Yes, she is. And these are my two sons, Jamie and Julian.

Maria: How old are they?

Jim: Jamie is twenty-one. He's in college now. Julian is seventeen, and that's my wife, Beth, next to my daughter.

Maria: Well, you certainly have a lovely-looking family.

Jim: Thank you. So, tell me about your family.

Maria: My husband and I have a son, Tim.

1. DESCRIBING YOUR FAMILY

◆ Tell me about your family.
Do you have | any brothers or sisters?
Have you got |

◇ I have | a brother | but *no sisters.*
I've got | | and *a sister.*

I live with *my parents and my grandparents.*
I'm *an only child.*

grandmother	nephew
grandfather	cousin
mother	
father	
daughter	
son	
aunt	
uncle	
niece	

Practice 1

Ask your partner if he/she has any brothers or sisters. Your partner will ask you. Then, ask another classmate.

Practice 2

Student A: You are Amy. Answer your partner's questions about your family. Then reverse roles.
Student B: Your partner is Amy. Ask questions about her family. Then reverse roles.

Practice 3

Now, quickly draw your family tree. Tell your partner who the people are. Your partner will tell you about his/her family.

2. DESCRIBING MARITAL STATUS

◆ Are you married? Is he/she	◇ Yes, I am. he/she is.	◇ No, I'm not. he/she isn't.
		I'm single. He/she's separated. divorced. widowed.

Practice 1

Ask your classmates if they are married. If everyone is single, choose a marital status.

Practice 2

Ask your partner about the members of Amy's family. Then reverse roles.

GIVE IT A TRY

1. DESCRIBING YOUR FAMILY

1. Direct students' attention to the function box. Give students time to read over the examples.

2. Model the examples; have students repeat.

Pronunciation Note: Rising intonation at the end of *yes-no* questions. The voice begins to rise on the last stressed syllable of the question and continues to rise. On the board, draw the following intonation line.

Move your hand along the line as you model the examples in the function box.

Language Note: Point out that *Do you have* and *Have you got* are interchangeable, but *Do you have* is more commonly used in American English. Explain that *only child* is a term used for someone who has no sisters or brothers.

3. Direct students' attention to the box listing family members. Model the names; have students repeat chorally.

Language Note: Point out that English, unlike some other languages, does not have highly defined terms for family relations; for example, the second daughter of my younger brother is simply called *niece* in English. Ask volunteers if this contrasts with their own language.

4. Model the questions and answers in the function box, substituting *nieces/nephews, sons/daughters,* etc.

Language Note: Point out that *mom* and *dad* are informal for *mother* and *father. Mommy* and *Daddy* are used by young children. *Grandma* and *grandpa* are often used instead of *grandmother* and *grandfather.* Ask students to explain the various names for *mother* and *father* and *grandmother* and *grandfather* in their culture.

Practice 1

1. Explain the activity.

2. Pair Work. Have students take turns asking and answering questions about their families.

3. Have students change partners and continue asking and answering the same questions.

4. Ask several pairs to demonstrate for the class.

Practice 2

1. Direct students' attention to the pictures. Explain that they show Maria's family tree. Give students time to study the pictures.

2. To check understanding, ask: *Does Maria have any sisters?* (yes) *Does she have any brothers?* (one) *Does Carol have any children?* (Yes, two)

3. Divide the students into pairs. Read the directions.

4. Pair Work. Have students take turns asking and answering questions about Maria's relatives, using the information in the family tree. Circulate and help students as needed.

Language Note: As you listen, you may decide it is appropriate to interrupt the students and introduce other terms such as *in-law* (*brother-in-law, sister-in-law,* etc.)

5. Ask pairs to demonstrate for the class.

Practice 3

1. Explain the activity. Give students time to draw their family trees. Circulate and help students as needed.

2. Pair Work. Have students take turns describing their families.

3. Ask several volunteers to describe their families for the class. Encourage them to use gestures and point to their drawings as they talk.

Note: With large classes, this can also be done as a small group activity.

2. DESCRIBING MARITAL STATUS

1. Direct students' attention to the function box. Give students time to read over the examples.

2. Model the examples; have students repeat.

Pronunciation Note: Rising intonation. Once again, draw the intonation line on the board. Demonstrate with the examples in the function box.

Language Note: A person who is *separated* is no longer living with a spouse, but is not divorced.

3. Ask pairs to model asking and answering the questions in the function box for the class.

Practice 1

1. Explain the activity.

Note: If you already know that everyone is single, have them choose a different marital status for this activity.

Culture Note: Point out that the question *Are you married?* is not socially appropriate with someone you've just met or hardly know. It is safer to ask about where a person works or what a person's hobbies are.

2. Divide the class into groups of about eight students. The actual number will depend on total class size.

3. Have students prepare an interview sheet by dividing a piece of paper into five columns and writing the headings *married, single*, etc. at the top. Model this on the board.

4. Group Work. Have students circulate within their groups and write down each person's marital status.

5. Have a volunteer from each group report the marital status of those in the group. Ask: *How many people are married, single,* etc. Compile, or have a student compile, the information on the board using the columns you drew earlier.

Practice 2

1. Give students time to read the directions. To check understanding, ask: *Is Carol married?* (yes) *Who is she married to?* (John) Continue: *Is Barbara married?* (No)

Language Note: The term *single* is often used nowadays to describe either a man or a woman who is unmarried. *Single* is often considered a neutral term, whereas the terms *bachelor* (an unmarried man), and *spinster* or *old maid* (an unmarried woman) have various connotations.

2. Pair Work. Have students ask and answer questions about Maria's family, switching roles.

3. Ask volunteers to demonstrate for the class.

3. TALKING ABOUT YOUR CHILDREN

1. Direct students' attention to the function box. Give students time to read over the examples.

2. Model the examples; have students repeat chorally.

Pronunciation Note: Rising-falling intonation in a series of clauses. Each clause ends with a rising tone, except for the last clause, which ends with a rising-falling tone.

On the board, write the following statement and intonation line:

the oldest is twenty-four, the second-oldest is twenty-one, and the youngest is seventeen.

Move your hand along the intonation line as you model the example.

Practice

1. Explain the activity. Students can either talk about their own families or the family in the picture.

2. Pair Work. Have students practice the conversation, switching roles.

3. Call on pairs to perform for the class. Encourage students to use gestures and to hold pieces of paper to represent photographs of their families.

LISTEN TO THIS

1. Direct students' attention to the pictures. Explain the activity. Give students time to look at the pictures.

2. Pair Work. Have students speculate who the people are in each of the pictures. Ask volunteers for their opinions.

3. Play the recording or read the conversation at normal speed as the students number the pictures 1–4, according to the order that the narrator speaks about them.

4. Check understanding by asking: *Which is number one, which is number two*, etc.

Answers: 1. b, 2. d, 3. a, 4. c

5. Give students time to read the questions.

6. Play or read the conversation as students answer the questions.

7. Play or read the conversation again as students check their answers.

8. Pair Work. Have students check each other's work by asking and answering the questions.

9. Ask volunteers for the answers.

Answers: *1.* two sons; *2.* yes, no grandsons, two granddaughters; *3.* Her nephew is nineteen. Her nieces are seventeen and fifteen. Her nephew plays with the city symphony orchestra. Her nieces are in high school.

10. Play or read the conversation again if needed.

3. TALKING ABOUT YOUR CHILDREN

◆ Do you have | any children?
Have you got |

◇ No, I don't.
(Yes.) I have | three children, two boys and a girl.
I've got | a daughter.

◆ How old | are they?
| is she?

◇ The oldest is twenty-four. The second oldest is twenty-one,
and the youngest is seventeen.
My son is three and my daughter is six months old.

Practice

Try the conversation above with a partner. Talk about the pictures or your own family.

LISTEN TO THIS

Ellen is showing her friend some pictures from her 50th birthday party.
Number the pictures 1-4 as she talks about each one.

Now listen again and answer these questions.

1. How many children does Ellen have? ....

2. Does she have any grandsons? .... granddaughters? ....

3. How old is her nephew? ....
   How old are her nieces? ....
   What do they do? ....

CONVERSATION 2
WHERE ARE THEY?

You can't find your friend.
What do you describe first? Height? Hair? Clothes?

Clerk 1: Oh, darn. Where are they?

Clerk 2: Who?

Clerk 1: I went to get this CD for a woman and her husband. Now I can't find them.

Clerk 2: What do they look like?

Clerk 1: Well, she's fairly tall with curly red hair. He's tall with short blond hair. They look like they're in their late thirties.

Clerk 2: Hmm. I don't see anyone like that. What are they wearing? Do you remember?

Clerk 1: Yeah. He's wearing a red sweatshirt and blue jeans. She's wearing a white skirt and a purple sweater.

Clerk 2: A white skirt and a purple sweater? Hey, wait! I think I see them in the classical section.

Clerk 1: You're right. . . Sir! Madam! I have that CD you're looking for.

Pronunciation Focus

In normal speech, words like *to*, *and*, *are*, and *do* are unstressed and the vowel is reduced to [ə]. Listen.

Word	Reduced pronunciation
to	want to get
and	woman and her husband
are	What are they wearing?
do	What do they look like?
them	I see them over there.

Now practice the conversation. Pay attention to the unstressed words.

CONVERSATION 2
WHERE ARE THEY?

Prelistening Questions

1. With books closed, read the prelistening questions. Talk about the idea of distinguishing or identifying features. For example, to say: *my friend is medium height with dark hair* may not be very helpful, whereas to say *she has long dark hair and is wearing a yellow baseball hat* is more specific and useful.

2. Pair Work. Have students each describe someone who is sitting near them as their partners guess who is being described.

3. Direct students' attention to the photograph in the book. Check that the conversation is covered. Ask students to describe what they see.

4. Class Work. Ask the following questions:
   - *What kind of store is this?*
   - *What kinds of music does the store sell?*
   - *What are the sales clerks doing?*
   - *Who is in the classical section?*

Elicit answers from volunteers. Maintain a rapid pace.

Vocabulary

Introduce these words and phrases now or after the students listen to the conversation.

darn: an expletive, like *oh, shoot!,* that is acceptable in public

wavy: slight curls, curls that aren't very tight

late thirties: around thirty-eight or thirty-nine years old. *Early thirties* is thirty-one to thirty-three and *mid-thirties* is about thirty-four to thirty-seven.

Hmm: a conversation filler used to signal someone is thinking or looking around.

Presentation

1. With books closed, play the recording or read the conversation at normal speed.

2. Ask the following general comprehension questions:
   - *Who is the clerk looking for?*
   - *Why? Does he find them??*

3. Say: *Listen again. This time listen for what the man and the woman look like.* Emphasize that when people are describing someone, they often stress the identifying feature (for example, an *orange golf* shirt).

4. Play or read the conversation again, pausing for choral repetition.

5. Ask the following questions:
   - *Is the woman tall or short?* (fairly tall)
   - *What color is her hair?* (red)
   - *Is it straight?* (No, it's curly.)
   - *Is the man short?* (No, he's tall.)
   - *What color is his hair?* (blond)
   - *How old are they?* (in their late thirties)
   - *What color is the man's sweatshirt?* (red)
   - *What color are his jeans?* (blue)
   - *What is the woman wearing?* (white skirt and purple sweater)

Elicit answers from various volunteers or have students tell their partners the answers.

6. Pair Work. Have students take turns describing the man and the woman.

7. Pronunciation Focus. Explain the reduced forms of unstressed words *to, and, are,* and *do* in normal speech. Point out how the vowel is reduced to [ə] Model the examples. Model again; have students repeat chorally.

8. Paired Reading. Have students read the conversation again, switching roles. Circulate and make sure they pay attention to the unstressed words.

GIVE IT A TRY

1. ASKING ABOUT AGE

1. Direct students' attention to the function box. Give students time to read over the examples.

2. Model the examples; have students repeat chorally.

Pronunciation Note: For the questions, stress follows the typical stress-time rhythm of English; for example, *How old is he?* For the responses, the stress is normally placed on the qualifier: *pretty young,* or on the modifier: *mid-teens.* On the board, draw the following intonation lines.

Move your hand along the intonation lines as you model the examples in the function box.

Language Note: Explain that *fairly, pretty,* and *kind of* all have roughly the same meaning of *somewhat.* (*He was fairly tired, not extremely tired, It was fairly late, but not very late.*)

3. Pair Work. Have students practice the examples in the function box, switching roles.

Language Note: Point out that *How old is he?* is too direct in formal or business situations. The indirect question: *May I ask how old she is?* or *About how old would you say she is?* is considered more polite and is thus preferable. The question *How old are you?* is generally not asked. If it is asked, a polite response is *I'd rather not say.*

Practice

1. Explain the activity. Emphasize that they are only expected to make their best guess about the ages of the famous people, unless they happen to know them.

2. Model the example using *(Tom Cruise in his thirties).* Model again; have students repeat chorally.

3. Pair Work. Have students take turns asking and answering questions about famous people, using the model in the book.

4. Check by having two pairs demonstrate for the class.

Note: Point out that *He/she* and *in his/her* can be omitted by Student B. In other words, to say only: *Pretty old, early eighties, I think* is acceptable.

5. Expansion. Bring to class or ask students to bring pictures of people from magazines or the newspaper. Have students work in pairs to describe who they see, using the model in the book.

2. ASKING FOR A DESCRIPTION

1. Direct students' attention to the function boxes. Give students time to read over the examples. Present pictures or photographs of people with these characteristics.

2. Model the examples; have students repeat chorally.

Language Note: There are many words in English that mean *not fat* (*slender, trim, lean, thin, skinny*), but they have different connotations depending on the situation. *Slender, trim,* and *lean* are all usually compliments. They convey a sense of someone not being fat and of taking care of oneself. *Thin* is usually neutral, but can be negative if someone has been ill recently. *Skinny* usually means underweight. It can be used as a compliment for someone who has recently dieted, or an insult for someone who wants to be bigger (He's too skinny; he won't make the football team.). *Fat, heavy, stocky, sturdy, solid, and chubby* are some of the ways to express the opposite of *thin. Sturdy* and *solid* are polite ways of saying *heavy* or *slightly overweight. Chubby* is used for children.

3. Pair Work. Have students practice the examples in the function box, switching roles.

Practice

1. Explain the activity. Model the example. Model again; have students repeat chorally.

2. Pair Work. Have students take turns describing and guessing who is being described. Encourage students to work at a rapid pace and to describe as many family members as possible.

3. Ask several pairs to demonstrate for the class.

4. Expansion. Have students take turns describing members of the class, using the example in the book.

1. ASKING ABOUT AGE

◆ How old is	he?
	she?

✧ Pretty	young.	He's in his	(mid-) teens.
Fairly	old.	She's in her	(early) seventies.
Kind of			(late) forties.

Practice

Think of three famous people, for example an actor, a singer, an athlete, or a politician. Ask your partner the ages of these people. Use this model:

A: How old is ....?
B: He/she's pretty old/young. (In his/her)....................., I think.

2. ASKING FOR A DESCRIPTION

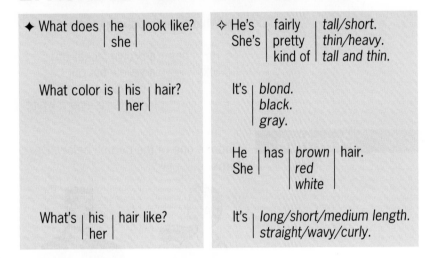

◆ What does	he	look like?
	she	

✧ He's	fairly	tall/short.
She's	pretty	thin/heavy.
	kind of	tall and thin.

What color is	his	hair?
	her	

It's	blond.
	black.
	gray.

He	has	brown	hair.
She		red	
		white	

What's	his	hair like?
	her	

It's	long/short/medium length.
	straight/wavy/curly.

Practice

Look at Amy's family on page 10 again. Describe one of them to your partner. Your partner will guess who you are describing.

Example:
Student A: She has shoulder-length, straight blond hair.
Student B: That's Barbara.

3. DESCRIBING PEOPLE

✦ What is he/she wearing?

✧ He's wearing | *jeans and a red sweatshirt.*
a blue suit.
black pants and a green sport shirt.

She's wearing | *a white skirt and a purple blouse.*
a tan uniform.
a pink summer dress.

red orange yellow green blue purple

pink gray black white brown tan

✦ What does he/she have on?

✧ He | has | *a brown jacket on.*
She | | *a yellow hat on.*
a red raincoat on.
pink shorts and a white T-shirt on.

Practice

Choose one of the people below. Describe his/her clothing to your partner. Take turns.

LISTEN TO THIS

🔲 Three people all say they witnessed the same crime. Listen as they describe the suspect to a police detective. Fill in the chart below.

	Height	Weight	Age	Hair	Clothing
Witness 1					
Witness 2					
Witness 3					

Look at the chart. What do *you* think the suspect looked like?

3. DESCRIBING PEOPLE

1. Direct students' attention to the first function box. Give students time to read over the examples.

2. Model the examples; have students repeat chorally.

3. Direct students' attention to the names of colors. Point out that the modifiers *light* and *dark* are commonly used with colors; for example, *light blue, dark green*.

Pronunciation Note: Review of English as a stress-timed language. The stress in English is very regular and words have to be compressed to maintain a regular rhythm. On the board, write:

She's wearing a tan uniform.

Clap your hands according to the stress pattern as you model the statement. Next write:

She's wearing a light tan uniform.

Model this, following the same procedure. Emphasize to the students that the stress pattern remains the same; that is, *tan* and *light tan* need to be spoken in the same amount of time. Present additional examples, adding more modifiers. This can be done in a humorous, playful way while demonstrating a very important pronunciation point.

4. Direct students' attention to the second function box. Follow the procedure above.

Practice

1. Explain the activity. Give students time to look at the pictures. Check vocabulary by asking: What kind of sweater is the man in the second picture wearing? (V-neck) What kind of shoes? (loafers). Write the vocabulary on the board. Spot-check any other items the students might not know.

2. Pair Work. Have students take turns describing the people in the pictures. Encourage the partners to seek clarification; for example: Do you mean a red sport shirt? What else is she wearing? Circulate and help students with vocabulary as necessary.

3. Ask several pairs to demonstrate for the class. Explain any vocabulary that seems problematic.

LISTEN TO THIS

1. Direct students' attention to the chart. Explain the activity. Check students' understanding of the following vocabulary: *to witness, crime, a suspect, a police detective*.

2. Play the recording or read the conversations at normal speed as the students fill in the chart.

3. Play the recording or read the conversations again as the students check their answers.

4. Pair Work. Have students compare their answers.

5. Check answers by asking: *What did Witness 1 say about the suspect's height?* (She said he was short.) *What did Witness 2 say about the suspect's age?* (He said he was 20.) Continue asking about the remainder of the chart.

Answers:

Witness 1: *short, thin, early thirties, light brown hair, medium length, curly, blue and red golf shirt, shorts, knee socks*

Witness 2: *pretty tall, thin, twenty, blond, wavy and short, blue golf shirt with red stripes, brown shorts, black socks*

Witness 3: *tall, pretty thin, late teens, brown curly hair, medium length, blue shirt, brown pants*

6. Pair Work. Have students look at the chart and note where the descriptions match. Ask students to decide what the suspect looked like.

7. Ask volunteers to present their conclusions to the class. Have the class try to reach a consensus as to what the suspect looked like by having them vote on particular characteristics; for example, *How many people think he was tall?*

OPTIONAL ACTIVITY 2: How Are They Different?
See Teacher's Notes, page 123, and Activity Sheet, page 128.

PERSON TO PERSON

Practice 1

1. Divide the class into pairs and have students decide who will be Student A and who will be Student B.

2. Have students listen to the introduction. Then give them time to read the directions.

3. Ask questions to make sure students understand the activity. Ask the Student A group: *Where is your partner going?* (to the airport) *Why?* (to pick up three friends of yours) *What will your partner ask you?* (what they look like) *What should you do?* (Answer, but don't give any extra information.) Ask the Student B group: *What are you going to do?* (Go to the airport to pick up three friends of your partner.) *What are you going to ask your partner?* (to describe the friends) *What should you do?* (Continue asking questions until you can identify each person, then write the name under the correct picture.)

4. With a student volunteer, model the example. Model again, have students repeat chorally.

5. Remind students that they can use stress to emphasize identifying features. On the board, write: *long hair; long, dark hair; long, dark, wavy hair.* Model each sentence, exaggerating the stress. Have students repeat chorally.

6. Pair Work. Have students complete the activity.

7. Ask volunteers to identify their partner's friends for the class.

Practice 2

1. Have students read the directions for Practice 2. Follow the same procedure for Practice 1, omitting step 5.

2. Expansion: Group Work. Divide the class into small groups. Have students take turns describing someone from another group. Have the group members ask questions and decide who is being described.

LET'S TALK 2

Student Book, page 98.

1. Explain the activity. Check students' understanding of *award* by giving examples (for the best teacher, for the student who scored highest on a big exam, etc.).

2. Give students time to read the directions and the chart.

2. Model the opener *I can't tell you who it is, but I can answer questions.* Have students repeat.

3. Divide the class into groups of four. Have students fill in their names at the tops of their chart.s

4. Have each student fill in one column about his or her person.

5. Group Work. Have group members take turns asking each other for parts of the description of the person each student is thinking of. Tell students to mark the information in their own charts. After students have completed their charts, have them each write down who is being described (under Person's name). Ask students to compare answers and discuss any part of the descriptions they disagree with.

Note: Give students a few example questions to help them get started *(What sex is the person, (Yuko)?, What color hair does the person have, (Shigeo)?*

Note: This activity can be done two ways: students can complete one description at a time or students can complete the whole chart and then guess all of the people at the same time.

6. Ask volunteers to report who group members were thinking of.

PERSON TO PERSON

STUDENT A

(Student A looks at this page. Student B looks at the next page.)

Practice 1

Your partner is going to the airport to pick up three friends of yours. Your partner will ask you for their descriptions. Answer his/her questions, but don't give any extra information.

Ask your partner to pick up Angela, Nadine, and Miki.

Example:
Student A: Could you pick up Angela at the airport?
Student B: Sure. What does she look like?

Continue answering questions until your partner can identify the person.

Practice 2

Now, you are going to the airport to pick up three friends for your partner. Ask questions until you can identify each person. Write the name under the correct picture.

PERSON TO PERSON

STUDENT B

(Student B looks at this page. Student A looks at the previous page.)

You are going to the airport to pick up three friends for your partner. Ask your partner for their descriptions. He/she will answer your questions, but will not give you any extra information.

Example:
Student A: Could you pick up Angela at the airport?
Student B: Sure. What does she look like?

Continue asking questions until you can identify each person. Write the name under the correct picture.

Now, ask your partner to pick up Andy, Greg, and Ian. Answer his/her questions.

COMPONENTS

Student Book, pages 17–24
Let's Talk 3, Student Book page 99
Cassette/CD
Optional Activity 3, page 129
Review (Units 1–3), Student Book page 100

OBJECTIVES

Functions: Asking for location of an item, describing/identifying things, describing uses, ordering descriptive adjectives

Topics: shapes, rooms of a house, furniture, "what's it made of," uses

Structures:

- Do you know where (my suitcase) is?
- What's it made of? / What's it used for?
- It's/They're made of (metal). It's/They're used for (cutting).
- It is + adjective: It's big/small. It's round/flat/oval.
- It's a long, narrow, flat thing.
- Prepositions of place: on the (table) / in the (cabinet) / in front of / behind / next to / to the left (right) / under

Pronunciation Focus: Linking of final consonants to words beginning with a vowel sound: *come on / does it*

Listen to This: Listening for specific information; listening for descriptions

CONVERSATION 1
DO YOU KNOW WHERE IT IS?

Prelistening Questions

1. Have students open their books and cover the conversation.

2. Direct students' attention to the photograph. Read the title of the conversation and the prelistening questions.

3. Pair Work. Have students take turns asking and answering the questions.

4. Elicit answers from several volunteers for each question.

5. Ask the following questions:

- *Do you think he usually cooks dinner? Why / Why not?*
- *Do you think he knows how to cook? Why / Why not?*
- Have students use information in the photograph to support their answers.

Culture Note: In North America, more men are cooking now than in the past. There are several reasons for this. There has been an increase in the number of families where both husband and wife work full time and in single-parent families headed by men. Some men look at cooking as a hobby or a type of relaxation. Men who are single or students often learn to cook as well. Barbecuing has traditionally been considered the man's territory as far as cooking is concerned, although increased use of gas grills has made this less true nowadays.

Vocabulary

Introduce these words and phrases now or after the students listen to the conversation.

by the way: used to change topics in a conversation

olive oil: a type of cooking oil

Presentation

1. With books closed, play the recording or read the conversation at normal speed.

2. Ask the following general comprehension questions:

- *What is he doing?* (cooking dinner)
- *What is he making?* (a surprise)
- *Does he want any help?* (No)

Elicit answers from various volunteers.

3. Say: *Listen again. This time listen for what he needs to cook dinner, and where these things are located.* Play or read the conversation again, pausing for choral repetition.

4. Ask the following questions:

- *What is the first thing he needs?* (olive oil)
- *Where is it?* (in the cabinet over the sink)
- *What else does he need?* (a big pot)
- *Where is it?* (in the drawer under the oven)
- *What time does she want to eat?* (whenever it is ready)
- *What can she do to help him?* (stay out of the kitchen)

Elicit answers from various students or have students tell their partners the answers.

5. Paired Reading. Have students read the conversation, switching roles.

Who are these people?
What is the man doing?
Do men in your culture like to cook?

Michelle: What are you doing?

Dominic: I'm cooking dinner tonight.

Michelle: That's great. Thank you. What are you making?

Dominic: A surprise. By the way, where do we keep the olive oil?

Michelle: It's in the cabinet over the sink.

Dominic: In the cabinet over the . . . I've got it. Thanks. And . . . do you know where the big pot is?

Michelle: It's in the drawer under the oven.

Dominic: OK. I'm ready. Now, what time do you want to eat?

Michelle: Whenever it's ready, but what can I do to help?

Dominic: Just stay out of the kitchen!

1. ASKING WHERE THINGS ARE

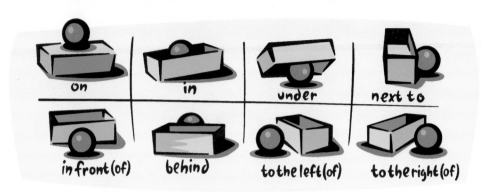

on   in   under   next to

in front (of)   behind   to the left (of)   to the right (of)

◆ Where | is | the *sugar bowl?*
         | are | the *coffee cups?*

◇ It's | on the *kitchen table.*
   They're | in the *cabinet to the left of the refrigerator.*

Practice 1

You are at a friend's house helping to make dinner. You don't know where anything is. Ask your partner about five of the following things. Then reverse roles. The answers are in the picture.

blender	mugs	plates
toaster	glasses	silverware
coffee maker	cooking pots	sugar
kettle	cups and saucers	rice

Practice 2

Now ask about objects in the classroom.

GIVE IT A TRY

1. ASKING WHERE THINGS ARE

1. Direct students' attention to the function box. Give students time to read over the examples.

2. Model the examples; have students repeat chorally.

Pronunciation Note: Stress in NOUN-NOUN constructions. With NOUN-NOUN constructions such as sugar bowl and coffee cups, stronger stress is usually given to the first word (or first part of each compound word). For example, *sugar bowl, coffee cups, kitchen table, cookie jar.*

3. On the board, write the above NOUN-NOUN phrases. Model; have students repeat chorally. Elicit other examples *(teapot, coffeemaker, breadbasket).*

4. Direct students' attention to the pictures of the ball. Read the caption aloud for each picture; have students repeat chorally.

5. Pair Work. Have student take turns pointing to different pictures and telling each other the location of the ball.

Note: For additional practice, a drill can be done using simple realia in the classroom (*a pen and a book, a pencil and a notebook,* etc.). Place (*the pen*) in different locations in relationship to (*the book*). Randomly ask one student to say the preposition *(next to)* and another student to make a statement *(The pen is next to the book)*. Have the rest of the class repeat chorally.

Practice 1

1. Explain the activity. Give students time to study the picture.

2. Pair Work. Have students ask and answer questions about five things in the kitchen, then switch roles. Circulate and assist with additional vocabulary as necessary.

3. Ask several pairs to demonstrate for the class.

Practice 2

1. Explain the activity. Tell students to switch partners.

2. Pair Work. Have students ask and answer questions about five things in the classroom, then switch roles. Assist with vocabulary as necessary.

3. Expansion: Game. One student thinks of an object in the room. Other students ask questions about it until they guess what it is *(Is it next to the dictionary? Is it in front of the bookshelf?)*. This can be done as a whole-class activity or in small groups, depending on class size.

2. ASKING WHERE THINGS ARE — MORE POLITELY

1. Direct students' attention to the function box. Give students time to read over the examples.

2. Model the examples; have students repeat chorally. Demonstrate *hanging over the back of the chair* using a jacket, backpack, or other realia available in the classroom.

Pronunciation Note: Review of rising intonation for *yes/no* questions. The voice begins to rise on the last stressed syllable of the question and continues to rise. On the board, write the following questions:

> *Do you know where my suitcase is?*
> *Do you know where my jeans are?*

Draw a rising intonation line. Move your hand along the line as you model the questions. Have students repeat.

Language Note: Point out that when asking for someone's help in finding something, we often use the more polite form *Do you know where...?* This is especially important when we can't assume that the other person knows where it is. To draw students' attention to the difference in word order between the direct and indirect question forms, write the following on the board:

> *Where is my suitcase? Do you know where my suitcase is?*
> *Where are my jeans? Do you know where my jeans are?*

Model the questions; have students repeat chorally.

3. Direct students' attention to the pictures. Read the caption aloud for each picture; have students repeat chorally.

4. Pair Work. Have student take turns pointing to the pictures and telling each other the location of the ball or the jacket. Make sure students understand the difference between *hanging on* and *hanging over* by asking a volunteer to demonstrate for the class using realia available.

Practice 1

1. Explain the activity. Pair students with members of the opposite sex if possible.

2. Emphasize that the answers are in the picture. Give students time to study the picture.

3. Pair Work. Have students role-play Dominic asking Michelle where five things he needs for the weekend are located.

Practice 2

1. Explain the activity. Have students continue working with the same partner.

2. Pair Work. Have students role-play Michelle asking Dominic where five things she needs for the weekend are located.

Note: For both Practices 1 and 2, students can repeat the role play, using other items on the list.

3. Expansion. In pairs, have students make lists of other items in the room, then give them to another pair to use to do the role play again.

LISTEN TO THIS

1. Explain the activity. Give students time to read the questions. Make sure students understand that for each of the four conversations they are to answer both questions.

2. Play the recording or read the conversations at normal speed as the students answer the questions.

3. Play or read the conversations again for students to check their work.

4. Pair Work. Have students check their work by taking turns asking and answering the questions about each conversation.

Answers: 1. a) *scissors,* b) *ginger ale,* c) *a book,* d) *computer disks* 2. a) *beside the telephone,* b) *in the fridge / on the bottom shelf behind the juice,* c) *on the coffee table under the newspaper,* d) *on the middle shelf between the paper and the computer games*

Language Note: Point out that *fridge* is a short form for refrigerator that is used in casual conversation.

5. Ask various students for the answers.

6. Play or read the conversations again as a final check.

2. ASKING WHERE THINGS ARE – MORE POLITELY

◆ Do you know where my | suitcase is?
| jeans are?

◇ It's | in the corner between the dresser and the wall.
They're | hanging over the back of the chair.

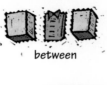
between

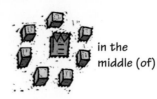

in the middle (of)

on the corner (of)

in the corner (of)

hanging on

hanging over

Practice

Michelle and Dominic are going away for the weekend.

Student A: You are Dominic. Ask Michelle where the following things are:
your watch, sandals, and *pajamas.*
Student B: You are Michelle. Ask Dominic where the following things are:
your purse, necklace, and *sunhat.*

Take turns. Continue asking about other items.

LISTEN TO THIS

🔊 Listen to the four short conversations and answer the following two questions for each.

1. What is the speaker looking for?
a)...
b)...
c)...
d)...

2. Where is the thing he/she is looking for?
a)...
b)...
c)...
d)...

CONVERSATION 2
WHAT DOES IT LOOK LIKE?

Where is this man?
What do you think is wrong?
Do you ever forget the name of an object?
What do you say?

Pronunciation Focus

Notice how final consonants are linked to words beginning with a vowel sound.

come on   the tip of my tongue

does it   color is

Find other linked consonants like this in the conversation and mark them. Then practice the conversation. Pay attention to linked sounds.

Luis:	Teresa?. . . I can't find the what-do-you-call-it.
Teresa:	What can't you find?
Luis:	You know. The thing.
Teresa:	What thing?
Luis:	Oh, come on. . . you know! It's on the tip of my tongue.
Teresa:	What does it look like? Maybe I can help you find it.
Luis:	It's a long, narrow, flat thing. It's made of plastic.
Teresa:	OK. What color is it, and what's it used for?
Luis:	It's red. You use it for drawing straight lines.
Teresa:	Luis! You mean the ruler! It's in the box behind the telephone.
Luis:	Oh, yeah. I knew that all along. I was just testing you.

CONVERSATION 2
WHAT DOES IT LOOK LIKE?

Prelistening Questions

1. Have students open their books and cover the conversation.

2. Direct students' attention to the photograph. Read the title of the conversation and the prelistening questions.

3. Pair Work. Have students take turns asking and answering the questions.

4. Elicit answers from several volunteers for each question. Have students support their answers by describing details in the picture. *(This man is in his office. He's trying to find something, but he can't. Look at his messy desk.)*

Language Note: The prelistening questions can bring up phrases that are commonly used by English speakers when they are looking for a word. There is a wide range of phrases including: *the what-do-you-call-it, the thing-a-ma-jig, the thing.* Explain that attributes can also be given: *you know, the thing that's small, and long, that has ink in it, that you can write with (a pen).* Explain that students can use the expressions *What do you call this/that in English? How do you say that in English?* as well.

Vocabulary

Introduce these words and phrases now or after the students listen to the conversation.

It's on the tip of my tongue: an idiom meaning *I can almost remember something, but not quite.*

narrow: opposite of wide

to draw: to put down on paper with a pen, pencil, etc.

to test: to check understanding or knowledge of

Presentation

1. With books closed, play the recording or read the conversation at normal speed.

2. Ask the following general comprehension questions:
   - *What is the problem?* (Luis can't find something.)
   - *Does Teresa know where it is?* (Yes)

3. Say: *Listen again. This time listen for what the object looks like.*

4. Play or read the conversation again, pausing for choral repetition.

5. Ask the following questions:
   - *Is the object long or short?* (long)
   - *Is it wide or narrow?* (narrow)
   - *Is it flat?* (Yes)
   - *Is it made of wood?* (No, it's made of plastic.)
   - *What color is it?* (blue)
   - *What do you use it for?* (to draw straight lines)
   - *What is it in?* (a box)
   - *Where is the box?* (behind the telephone)

Elicit answers from various volunteers or have students tell their partners the answers.

6. Check students' understanding of the last line. Ask: *Why does Luis say, "I knew that all along"?* Make sure students understand that this is a playful cover-up for the fact that he could not remember the name of a very common object.

7. Pronunciation Focus. Explain how final vowels are linked to words beginning with a vowel sound. Model the examples; have students repeat chorally and individually.

8. With books open, play or read the conversation again as students find other linked consonants in the conversation and mark them.

9. Paired Reading. Have students read the conversation, switching roles. Remind them to pay attention to the linked sounds.

GIVE IT A TRY

1. DESCRIBING THINGS (1)

1. Direct students' attention to the function box. Give students time to read over the examples.

2. Model the examples; have students repeat chorally. Show these shapes and sizes either by drawing them on the blackboard or by using objects in the classroom.

Pronunciation Note: Stress on content words. Stress is placed on what is being queried: *What SIZE is it? What SHAPE is it?* In the response, *It's (They're)* is reduced and the content word is stressed. *It's BIG. They're ROUND.* Write the examples on the board marking the stress. Model; exaggerating the stress. Have students repeat.

3. On the board, write: *rectangular/rectangle, triangular/triangle.* Point out the shift in stress. Model; have students repeat.

4. Pair Work. Have students practice the conversational exchanges, switching roles.

5. For additional practice, point to different objects in the room and ask: *What size is it? What shape is it?* etc. Elicit answers from various students.

Practice

1. Explain the activity. Divide the students into pairs.

2. Model the example. Model again; have students repeat their parts.

3. Pair Work. Have students take turns describing the boxes, and guessing which one is being described. Circulate and help with vocabulary as needed.

4. Check by having several pairs demonstrate for the class.

1. DESCRIBING THINGS (1)

✦ What size is it?	✧ It's	big/small. long/short. narrow/wide.
✦ What shape is it?	✧ It's	round/a circle. square/a square. rectangular/a rectangle. triangular/a triangle. oval/an oval. flat.
✦ What does it look like?	✧ It's a long, narrow, flat thing.	

Practice

Choose one of the boxes below. Describe it to your partner. Your partner will guess which one you are describing.

Example:
Student A: There is a big, red, round ball. There is a small, blue triangle in front of the ball.
Student B: It's number 1.

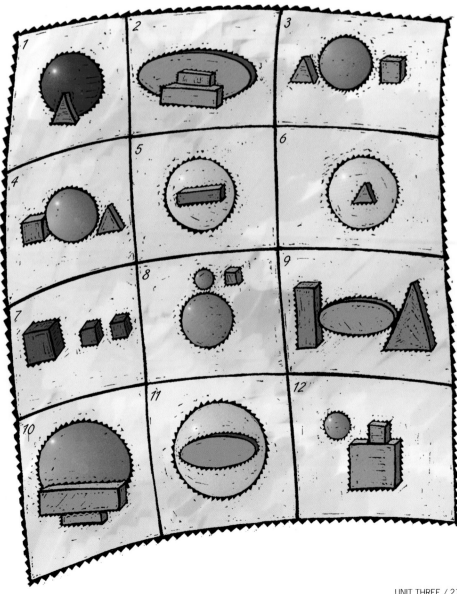

2. DESCRIBING THINGS (2)

◆ What's it What are they	made of?	✧ It's They're	made of	*wood.* *metal.*

Practice

You and your partner have ten minutes to think of as many objects as you can. Write them down and compare your lists with your classmates.

Objects made of
wood:..
plastic:...
metal: ....
cloth:..
glass:..
paper:...
leather:...

3. DESCRIBING USES

◆ What	is it are they	used for?	✧ A *knife* is *Scissors* are	used for *cutting.*

Practice

Choose two of the objects below and describe them for your partner to identify. Then reverse roles.

Example:
A: It's long and narrow and it's made of metal.
B: What's it used for?
A: It's used for cutting.
B: It's a knife.

LISTEN TO THIS

▭ A group of people from long ago are describing their inventions to each other. Listen to the description, and name the object each speaker invented.

Speaker 1 .... Speaker 5 ....
Speaker 2 .... Speaker 6 ....
Speaker 3 .... Speaker 7 ....
Speaker 4 .... Speaker 8 ....

2. DESCRIBING THINGS (2)

1. Direct students' attention to the function boxes. Give students time to read over the examples.

2. Model the examples; have students repeat chorally.

Pronunciation Note: Blended sounds: *It's made of* /Itzmade uv/ and stress on content words (materials): *It's made of WOOD*. The first part of the sentence is blended and reduced /Itzmade uv/ and the final word is stressed.

3. Pair Work. Have students practice the examples in the function box, switching roles.

Practice————————————

1. Explain the activity. Divide the students into pairs.

2. Pair Work. Have students work together to list objects made of the materials listed.

3. Group Work. Have two pairs compare their lists.

4. Ask volunteers to tell the class what is on their lists. Have each volunteer talk about one material. Tell the rest of the class to listen carefully and add to their lists anything they hadn't included.

Language Note: Questions regarding the difference between *made of* and *made from* might come up. A simple explanation is that *made from* asks for the source of the material; for example, plastic is made from petroleum, tofu is made from soybeans, sake is made from rice. In other words, the material has been transformed in some way.

3. DESCRIBING USES

1. Direct students' attention to the function box. Give students time to read over the examples.

2. Model the examples; have students repeat chorally.

Pronunciation Note: Review of stress on content words. *What's it USED for? A KNIFE is for CUTTING*. Write the examples on the board, marking the stress. Model; have students repeat.

Practice————————————

1. Explain the activity. Model:

    A: *It's long and narrow and it's made of metal.*

    B: *What's it used for?*

    A: *It's used for cutting.*

    B: *It's a knife.*

Repeat with a student volunteer.

2. Pair Work. Have students take turns describing and identifying the objects in the pictures.

3. Ask several pairs to demonstrate for the class.

OPTIONAL ACTIVITY 3: What Is It? *See Teacher's Notes, page 123, and Activity Sheet, page 129.*

LISTEN TO THIS

1. Give students time to read the directions. To stimulate interest and get students thinking about what to listen for, do one or two examples using the names of other common household items: *a toaster, a hair dryer, a washing machine*. Describe the item and ask volunteers to identify it.

2. Play the recording or read the descriptions at normal speed as the students write down the name of each object.

3. Play the recording or read the descriptions again as the students check their answers.

4. Pair Work. Have students compare their answers.

5. Check answers by asking: *What is Speaker 1's invention?* (the wheel) *What is Speaker 2's invention?* (a ballpoint pen) Continue asking about the remainder of the inventions.

Answers: Speaker 1: *wheel*, Speaker 2: *ballpoint pen*, Speaker 3: *refrigerator*, Speaker 4: *gloves*, Speaker 5: *broom*, Speaker 6: *compact disc*, Speaker 7: *light bulb*, Speaker 8: *a blanket*

6. Play or read the descriptions again as a final check.

7. Expansion. For additional practice in listening for specific information, have the students listen to each description again as you stop the recording and give students time to take notes. In pairs, have students use their notes to describe the inventions. Alternatively, have students work in pairs to write descriptions of other inventions, then exchange them with another pair who will guess what the inventions are.

PERSON TO PERSON

Practice 1

1. Explain the activity. Divide the class into pairs and have students decide who will be Student A and who will be Student B.

2. Have students listen to the introduction. Then give them time to read the directions.

3. Play or read the conversation as students check the items Bruce/Ron will bring to the apartment.

4. Play or read again as students check their answers.

Answers: Bruce: CD player, speakers, TV, coffee table, floor lamp; Ron: sofa, wall unit, end tables, easy chairs, lamps

Practice 2

1. Have students read the directions.

2. Pair Work. Have students tell each other what Bruce/Ron is bringing and decide where these things will be put in the room.

3. Have each student draw the things in the room according to what the partners decide.

Practice 3

1. Pair Work. Have students work with their partners to compare their drawings. Circulate and help them describe the differences.

2. Group Work. Have pairs present their drawings to each other and discuss the differences.

3. If time permits, ask several students to present their drawings to the class. Alternatively, ask several groups to present their optimal arrangement.

LET'S TALK 3

Student Book, page 99.

1. Give students time to read the directions. Check student understanding of the following vocabulary: *interior* *design, to decorate, to furnish, a model apartment.* On the board, help students make a list of living-room-furniture vocabulary: *sofa, (floor) lamp, throw rugs, curtains, wall-to-wall carpet, coffee table, end table,* etc.

2. Model the opener *Which room do you want to talk about first?* Have students repeat.

3. Separate the students into pairs.

4. Pair Work. Have students work together to decorate and furnish the apartment. Circulate and assist with vocabulary as needed.

5. Ask several pairs to present their designs to the class. Encourage them to use the floor plan as they talk.

REVIEW (UNITS 1–3)

Student Book, page 100.

1. Give students time to read the situation and the directions. Check understanding by asking: *Where have you just moved? Do you know anyone there? Who do you call? What do you agree to do?* Elicit answers from several volunteers.

2. Model an example opener: *This is* (your name) *speaking. My cousin* (his/her name) *said I should call you.* Have students repeat.

3. Separate the students into pairs.

4. Pair Work. Have students work together to write the telephone conversation. Encourage students to refer to Units 1, 2, and 3 for help.

Note: Based on Units 1, 2, and 3, possible topics for the conversation include: finding out each other's occupations, or asking about each other's families. Remind students that they aren't supposed to know each other, so each partner will have to give a description of himself/herself. The art (interior of a coffee shop) is given so that students can practice prepositions. Supply students with the line: *Let's meet at the Cafe Coco. I'll be at the table in the corner / in front of the window,* etc.

5. Group Work. Have two pairs form a group. Ask pairs to take turns performing their conversations.

6. Ask one or two pairs to perform for the class.

(Student A looks at this page. Student B looks at the next page.)

Bruce and Ron are two American students who are entering their second year of college. They decided to rent an apartment this year instead of living in a college dormitory.

Practice 1

Listen to the conversation and check (✔) the items that Bruce will bring to the apartment.

Practice 2

Briefly describe the items that Bruce is bringing to the apartment. Your partner will describe the items that Ron is bringing. Together, decide where these things will be put in the room. Draw them in the room below.

Practice 3

Compare your room with your partner's. Do they look the same? What's different?

(Student B looks at this page. Student A looks at the previous page.)

▱ Bruce and Ron are two American students who are entering their second year of college. They decided to rent an apartment this year instead of living in a college dormitory.

Practice 1

Listen to the conversation and check (✔) the items that Ron will bring to the apartment.

Practice 2

Briefly describe the items that Ron is bringing to the apartment. Your partner will describe the items that Bruce is bringing. Together, decide where these things will be put in the room. Draw them in the room below.

Practice 3

Compare your room with your partner's. Do they look the same? What's different?

COMPONENTS

OBJECTIVES

Functions: Talking about days and dates, talking about time: opening and closing / starting and finishing times, asking for and giving directions

Topics: getting around the city, calendar, time (days, months)

Structures:

- Prepositions of time: It's *on* Monday. / It's *in* October. / It starts *at* 8:00. / It opens *at* 10:00 A.M.
- Imperative with directions: Go up two blocks and turn right. / Go up this street and take a left.
- Modals in polite requests: Could you tell me where the post office is?
- Prepositions of place: across from the post office / between the bakery and the drugstore / around the corner /at the end of the block / in the middle of the block
- Transitions (next, then): Next go to the library, then go to the bank to cash a check.

Pronunciation Focus: Stress placement on words that carry important meaning in a sentence. *Do you know where the police station is?*

Listen to This: Listening to match pictures and descriptions; filling in charts

CONVERSATION 1
SEE YOU THEN!

Prelistening Questions

1. With books closed, read the prelistening question.
2. Pair Work. Have students take turns asking and answering the question.
3. Elicit answers from several volunteers. Develop this into a whole-class discussion about how birthdays are celebrated. The discussion can be broken down by sex, age, family customs, and cultural practices. Some birthdays are more important than others; discuss at what age people can drive, vote, and be considered an adult in the students' cultures.
4. Have students open their books and cover the conversation.
5. Direct students' attention to the photograph. Ask students to speculate:

- *Who are the people?*
- *What are they talking about?*
- *What is their relationship?*
- *What month is it?*

Have students use information in the picture to support their answers.

Vocabulary

Introduce these words and phrases now or after the students listen to the conversation.

Carnegie Hall: a famous concert hall in New York City

Hold on: idiom that means *just a second / wait a second.* Used to catch someone's attention.

fabulous (idea): *great, terrific* (idea)

half past eleven: an alternative way to say eleven thirty (11:30)

Presentation

1. With books closed, play the recording or read the conversation at normal speed.
2. Ask the following general comprehension questions:

- *Is Greg doing anything for Sheila's birthday?* (Yes)
- *What are they going to do?* (go to a concert)
- *What does their friend* (Karen) *want to do after the concert?* (meet for coffee and birthday cake / go to a cafe)

3. Say: *Listen again. This time listen for more details about Sheila's birthday and what they are going to do.* Play or read the conversation again, pausing for choral repetition.
4. Ask the following questions:

- *When is Sheila's birthday?* (Friday, the twenty-third)
- *Where is the concert?* (at Carnegie Hall)
- *What time does the concert start?* (eight o'clock)
- *Why can't Karen meet Greg and Sheila before eight o'clock?* (She has to work.)
- *What time does the concert end?* (half past eleven)
- *Where does Karen want to meet after the concert?* (Cafe Alfredo)
- *What time does the cafe close?* (It's open until at least 1:00.)
- *Does Greg decide to meet her?* (Yes)

Elicit answers from various students or have students tell their partners the answers.

5. Paired Reading. Have students read the conversation, switching roles.

What do you do on your birthday?

Karen: Greg, when is Sheila's birthday? Is it this week?

Greg: Yeah, it's this Saturday, the twenty-eighth.

Karen: I'd really like to see her on her birthday. Are you two doing anything?

Greg: Well, yes, we have tickets to a concert at Carnegie Hall.

Karen: What time does it start?

Greg: It starts at 8:00.

Karen: Hmmm... I'm afraid I can't make it by then. I have to work late on Saturday. Hold on... I have an idea. What time does the concert end?

Greg: Pretty late. Probably around half-past eleven.

Karen: Well, how about going to the Cafe Alfredo for some coffee and birthday cake after the concert? I'll meet you there.

Greg: Well, what time does the cafe close?

Karen: It's open until at least 1:00. Come on, admit it... it's a fabulous idea.

Greg: OK, OK, Karen. We'll see you then!

1. DAYS AND DATES

◆ When	is your *birthday*? is your *anniversary*? is the *party*?	◇ It's on	Monday. October 13.
		It's in	October.

Practice

Find out when your classmates' birthdays are. Do any of your classmates share the same birthday?

2. STARTING AND FINISHING TIMES

◆ When What time	does the *concert*	start? end?	◇ It	starts *at 8:00 (sharp)*. ends *about 10:15*.

Practice

Student A
Ask your partner when three of the following events start and finish: movie, concert, opera, ballet, baseball game. Then reverse roles. Your partner will ask you about three events. Use this conversation as a model:

A: What time does the....................start?

B: ....

A: And when does it end?

B: ....

Student B
Use the entertainment guide below to find the starting times. Ending times are two hours later for the movie and concert; three hours later for the opera, ballet, and baseball game. Use this conversation as a model:

A: ....?

B: At eight o'clock (sharp).

A: ....?

B: At about ten.

AROUND TOWN

The Arts
Opera and Ballet

Carmen
at the Metropolitan Opera House—7:30

Swan Lake
American Ballet Theater—7:30

Concerts

Philadelphia Symphony Orchestra at Lincoln Center—**8:00 PM**

Movies

Demi Moore, Patrick Swayze, and Whoopie Goldberg. The romance of the decade, **6:45 PM**

Pretty Woman
Julia Roberts, Richard Gere. A real Cinderella story, **7:45 PM**

Sports

BASEBALL
New York Mets vs. Montreal Expos, **3:00 at Shea Stadium**

CHARITY TENNIS
This year's Wimbledon winners play to raise money for disabled children. 1 PM—7PM

GIVE IT A TRY

1. DAYS AND DATES

1. Direct students' attention to the function box. Give students time to read over the examples.

2. Model the examples; have students repeat.

Pronunciation Note: Sentence stress. Stress is given to content words (nouns, verbs, adjectives, adverbs) and to *Wh-* questions. These words are said louder and held longer. The other words in the sentence (auxiliary verbs, articles, pronouns, and prepositions) are generally not stressed. They are usually reduced and spoken quickly. Write the following on the board, marking the stress:

> *When is your birthday?*
> *It's in October.*

Exaggerate the stress as you model the examples.

Language Note: In response to the question *When is your birthday?* we can reply *it's (on) October thirteenth, it's the thirteenth (if the month is already known), it's the thirteenth of October.* When using the ordinal number only, the preposition *on* is optional. Point out that we say *on* a date (*October thirteenth*), but we say *in* a month (*October*).

3. Ask volunteers to model the examples.

Practice

1. Explain the activity.

2. Divide students into groups of about six students, depending on class size.

3. Group Work. Have students ask and answer about when their birthdays are.

4. Ask one volunteer from each group to write their birthdays on the board, or report them orally. Ask the rest of the class to check if anyone shares the same birthday.

5. Expansion. Have several students go to the library or use reference materials to find out the birthdays of famous people. They can then report the information to the class by having other classmates ask them questions:

> *When is (Tom Cruise's) birthday? / It's ...*

2. STARTING AND FINISHING TIMES

1. Direct students' attention to the function box. Give students time to read over the examples.

2. Model the examples; have students repeat.

Pronunciation Note: Sentence stress, continued. (See 1. Days and Dates.) On the board, write the following, marking the stress:

> *When does the concert start? It starts at 8:00.*

Exaggerate the stress as you model the examples.

Language Note: Point out that *8:00 sharp* means exactly at eight o'clock.

Culture Note: Discuss what it means to be on time. Some cultures place a high value on promptness, some expect a guest to arrive 30 to 45 minutes past the time stated on an invitation. In North America, people are generally expected to be prompt. Arriving late can be considered a sign of disrespect.

3. Ask pairs to model the examples for the class.

Practice

1. Divide the students into pairs. Give students time to read the directions and model conversation for their parts. To check understanding, ask Student B: *If a movie starts at 7:00 P.M., what time does it end? If a baseball game starts at 1:00 P.M., when does it end?*

2. Model each example with a student volunteer.

3. Pair Work. Have students practice conversations about three events, then switch roles and continue.

4. Ask pairs to demonstrate for the class.

Note: Point out that the questions *When does it end (start)?* and *What time does it end (start)?* are interchangeable.

OPTIONAL ACTIVITY 4: Alibi. *See Teacher's Notes, page 123, and Activity Sheet, page 130.*

3. OPENING AND CLOSING TIMES

1. Direct students' attention to the function box. Give students time to read over the examples.

2. Model the examples; have students repeat chorally.

Pronunciation Note: Review of sentence stress. It is important to help students realize that the stress is placed on those content words that are essential to conveying the meaning. Exaggerate the stress and (reduce the other words) as you model the examples:

Could you please tell me when the store opens? etc.

Language Note: Point out that we usually use the indirect question form *(Could you please tell me…?)* when asking for information over the telephone.

Practice

1. Explain the activity. Model the conversation. Use gestures to indicate calling the post office and writing down the opening and closing times.

2. Model again, this time with a student volunteer.

3. Direct students' attention to the list of places and their opening and closing times. Have students quickly scan for information: *(Yuko), can you please tell me when the Medical Clinic opens? (Hiro), could you tell me what time Rexall Drugs closes?* Continue, maintaining a rapid pace.

4. Pair Work. Have students role-play the conversation, switching roles.

5. Call on pairs to perform for the class. Encourage students to use gestures and props.

Note: This role play will be much more effective if students use a telephone.

6. Expansion. Bring copies of the entertainment section from a local English language newspaper. In pairs, have students prepare lists of *What time…* questions. Have students find new partners and take turns asking the questions they have prepared.

LISTEN TO THIS

1. Explain the activity. Give students time to read over the places and events they will hear information about.

2. Play the recording or read the conversations at normal speed as the students listen and fill in the blanks.

3. Play or read the conversations again as students check their answers.

4. Pair Work. Have students compare their answers by asking and answering questions about the information given. Model the following to help them get started: *Can you tell me what time the City Park Swimming Pool opens? 10 A.M. / Could you tell me when it closes? 10 P.M.*

Answers: a) *City Park Swimming Pool opens: 10 A.M., closes: 10 P.M.* b) *Casablanca starts: 7:15, ends: 9:00. Breakfast at Tiffany's starts: 9:30, ends: 11:30. Theater doors open: 6:45.* c) *Rock 'n' roll concert starts: 8:00 P.M. ends: around midnight; Box Office opens: 10:00, closes: 8:00*

5. Ask pairs to ask and answer the questions for the class.

6. Play or read the conversations again as a final check.

3. OPENING AND CLOSING TIMES

| ✦ Could you | (please) tell me | when | *the store* | opens? |
| Can | | what time | | closes? |

Role-play calling the places below to find out their opening and closing times. Take turns. Follow this model:

A: (calls the post office on the telephone)

B: Post office.

A: Hello. Could you tell me what time you open?

B: We open at 9:00.

A: And when do you close?

B: At 5:30.

A: Thank you.

Here is the information you need:

Post Office	9:00 a.m.	–	5:30 p.m.
Citibank	9:00	–	5:00
Medical Clinic	9:30	–	8:00
Museum of Modern Art	11:00	–	6:00
Rexall Drugs	10:00	–	7:00
Macy's	10:00	–	9:30

LISTEN TO THIS

You are going to listen to information about when places open and close and when events start and end. Listen and fill in the blanks.

	Open / Start	Close / End
a) City Swimming Pool		
b) Casablanca		
Breakfast at Tiffany's		
Theater doors		
c) Rock 'n' roll concert		
Box office		

CONVERSATION 2
HOW DO I GET THERE?

Have you ever lost anything important? What did you do?

Have you ever gotten lost? What did you do?

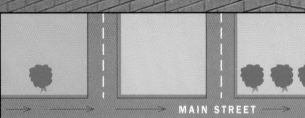

Pronunciation Focus

Words that carry stress in sentences are usually the words that carry important meaning in the sentence. Listen to the stressed words.

Do you know where the police station is?

No, I don't. I'm not from around here.

Now listen to the conversation again and mark the stressed words. Then practice the conversation.

Keith: Excuse me, do you know where the police station is?

Woman: No, I'm sorry. I don't. I'm not from around here.

Keith: OK, thanks anyway.

Anna: Hi, Keith! How's it going?

Keith: Not too good. I lost my wallet, and it had all my ID and credit cards in it.

Anna: Oh, no!

Keith: So, how do I get to the police station from here?

Anna: It's easy. Go up Main Street about three blocks. When you get to Oak Street, turn left. It's right next to the post office. You can't miss it.

Keith: OK. Go up this street and turn left at Oak. It's beside the post office.

Anna: That's it.

Keith: Thanks, Anna.

Anna: No problem.

CONVERSATION 2
HOW DO I GET THERE?

Prelistening Questions

1. With books closed, read the prelistening questions.
2. Pair Work. Have students take turns asking and answering the questions.
3. Elicit answers from several volunteers. Develop this into a whole-class discussion of strategies people can use when they are lost.
4. Have students open their books and cover the conversation.
5. Direct students' attention to the photographs. Ask students to speculate:
   - *What is the problem?*
   - *What do you think he has lost?*
   - *What is he asking?*
   - *Do you think she can help him?*

Elicit answers from several volunteers.

6. Direct students' attention to the map. Explain that they will use this to follow the directions given in the conversation. Give students time to briefly study the map.

Culture Note: The idea of using *blocks* is difficult for students who come from countries where either blocks are not laid out in a regular way or where people tend to use landmarks rather than blocks and street names in directions. Many students will benefit from spending a few minutes looking at the map and calculating various distances in blocks before listening to the conversation. You might also point out that landmarks are often given in directions in North America as well. *(Go two blocks, you'll see a bank on your left.)*

Vocabulary

Introduce these words and phrases now or after the students listen to the conversation.

thanks anyway: the appropriate response if a request cannot be granted (instead of *Thank you)*

How's it going?: casual alternative to *How are you doing?*

No problem: casual alternative to *You're welcome!*

Presentation

1. With books closed, play the recording or read the conversation at normal speed.
2. Ask the following general comprehension questions:
   - *What is the man looking for?* (the police station)
   - *Why?* (He lost his wallet.)
   - *Does the first woman know where the police station is?* (No)

   Does the second woman? (Yes)

Language Note: Point out the contrast in the expressions he uses to ask for directions depending upon whether or not he knows the person he is asking *(Excuse me, do you know where...?* vs. *So how do I get to...?)*

3. Say: *Listen again. This time listen for how to get to the police station.*
4. Play or read the conversation again, pausing for choral repetition.
5. Ask the following questions:
   - *What should he do first?* (go up the street three blocks)
   - *At Oak Street what should he do?* (turn left)
   - *What is the police station next to?* (the post office)

Elicit answers from various volunteers or have students tell their partners the answers.

6. Pair Work. Have students take turns using the map to explain how to get to the police station.

Culture Note: Point out that it is very common to repeat the directions in order to confirm them.

7. Pronunciation Focus. Explain that words which carry stress in sentences are usually words that carry important meaning in the sentence. Model the example sentences, exaggerating the stress:

   Do you know where the police station is?
   No, I don't. I'm not from around here.

8. With books open, play or read the conversation again Have students mark the stressed words.
9. Paired Reading. Have students read the conversation, switching roles. Circulate and make sure they are paying attention to the stress.

GIVE IT A TRY

1. DESCRIBING LOCATIONS

1. Direct students' attention to the function box. Give students time to read over the examples.

2. Model the examples; have students repeat chorally.

Pronunciation Note: Intonation of introductory expressions. Each of the introductory expressions: *Excuse me, Sure, Thank you,* and *Sorry* is given rising-falling intonation. Draw attention to the intonation on these expressions as you model the examples. Also review rising intonation for yes-no questions:

Do you know where the hardware store is?

Language Note: *Could you tell me where...?* is a polite way of asking directions of strangers. In describing where something is located, we often point out a landmark or reference point: *It is across from the library. It is next to the fire station,* etc.

3. Pair Work. Have students practice the exchanges, switching roles.

Practice

1. Explain the activity. Divide the students into pairs. Give students time to read their parts and study the map.

2. Pair Work. Have students take turns asking about and giving the locations of the places on their lists. Tell students to continue with other places on the map if they have time.

3. Expansion. In pairs, have students make a map of the area around the school or some other area the students know well and mark the location of five places. In addition, have them make a list of those five places. Then have them exchange their map and list with another pair who will use them, following the procedure as above.

2. GIVING DIRECTIONS

1. Direct students' attention to the function box. Give students time to read over the examples.

2. Model the examples; have students repeat chorally.

Pronunciation Note: Intonation for politeness. Rising tone is used on the *Wh-* word and on the last stressed syllable to indicate politeness:

Which way is the camera store?

Where is the closest post office?

Language Note: Point out that *just past (the Paris restaurant)* means *right after* or *immediately after (the Paris restaurant).* We can also say *just before / just after.* The expressions *go up / go down (the street)* are difficult for many students. They seem to be used interchangeably. Point out that a speaker will usually gesture in the direction of *up* or *down* (*the street*) as the directions are given. Sometimes a speaker will also use the expressions in conjunction with a well-known landmark; for example, *go up the street toward downtown / toward the river / away from the post office.*

3. Pair Work. Have students practice the examples, switching roles.

Culture Note: Since directions are usually given with gestures, it is very important to use gestures while modeling the exchanges. Make sure students use gestures throughout the practice as well.

4. Direct students' attention to the art. Model the directions for each picture; have students repeat chorally.

Pronunciation Note: Stress, rhythm, and intonation. To review these pronunciation features, tap out the patterns as you model the directions.

5. Pair Work. Have students practice the examples in the function box, substituting different places and locations: *How do I get to the (drugstore) from here? It's up this street on the left. / It's in the middle of the block just past the Paris restaurant,* etc. Circulate and assist as needed.

6. Ask several pairs to demonstrate for the class.

1. DESCRIBING LOCATIONS

✦ Excuse me. | Do you know where the *hardware store* is?
| Could you tell me where the *hardware store* is?

✧ Sure. It's *on Elm Street,* | *across from the post office.*
| *between Eleventh and Twelfth Avenues.*

✦ Thank you.

✧ Sorry. I'm not sure.
✦ Thanks, anyway.

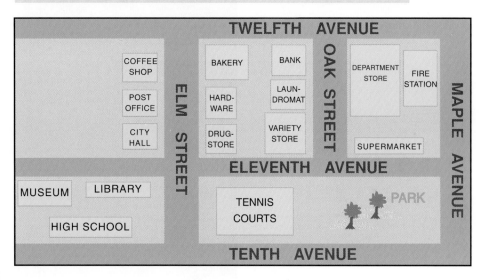

Practice

Ask your partner about the location of these places on the map. If you can't find the place, say that you don't know where it is.

Student A asks about:

1. city hall   3. camera store
2. laundromat   4. fire station

Student B asks about:

1. supermarket   3. post office
2. video store   4. park

2. GIVING DIRECTIONS

✦ Excuse me. | Which way is the | *camera store?*
| How do I get to the | *camera store* from here?

✧ It's down this street | on the *right.*
| just past the *Paris restaurant.*
  Go up *two* blocks, and turn *right.*
  Go up this street, and take the *second left.*

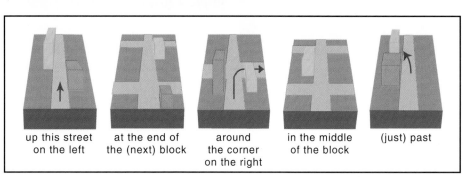

up this street   at the end of   around   in the middle   (just) past
on the left   the (next) block the corner of the block
                                   on the right

Look at the map below. Ask your partner how to get to the following places.
Student A starts out from location A (stadium).
Student B starts out from location B (bus station).

A wants to get to:

1. Citibank
2. Grace Hospital
3. Empire Cleaners
4. A-1 Car Rental

B wants to get to:

1. Bill's Variety Store
2. Spirit Women's Wear
3. St. Stephen's Church
4. Chinese Garden Restaurant

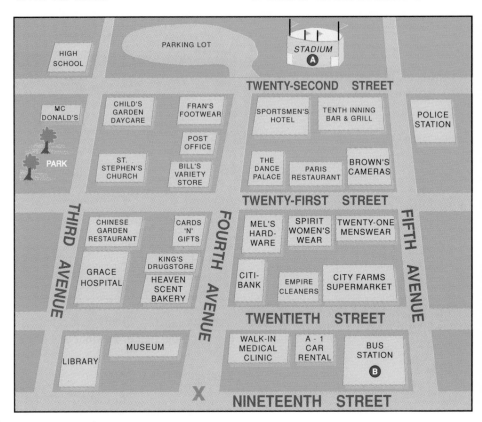

Ask your partner where you can do these things. Your partner will answer using the map above.

1. cash a traveler's check
2. fill a prescription
3. have some French food
4. buy a shirt and tie

5. get some film developed
6. buy a hammer and nails
7. buy some stamps
8. see a doctor without an appointment

Example:
Student A: Where can I buy a donut?
Student B: You can buy a donut at the bakery.

LISTEN TO THIS

Start at Point X on the map above. Listen to the conversation and follow the directions. Then write down where each person is going.

Location 1 ....
Location 2 ....
Location 3 ....
Location 4 ....

Practice 1

1. Explain the activity. Divide the students into pairs. Have them decide who is Student A and who is Student B.
2. Have them read the directions for their parts. To check understanding, ask a student from each part: *Where do you start from?* (Student A: stadium; Student B: bus station.). Have them find these locations on the map.
3. Pair Work. Have students take turns asking for and giving directions to the places on their lists. If time permits, have students switch roles and repeat.
4. Ask several pairs to demonstrate for the class.

Practice 2

1. Give students time to read the directions.
2. Ask a pair to model the example.
3. Check students' understanding of the vocabulary by asking: *What do you need a prescription for? What kinds of things can you buy at a hardware store / a variety store / Macy's?*

Culture Note: It is important to take some time to make sure students understand the different types of stores and that no appointment is needed in a walk-in clinic; otherwise, they cannot complete the exercise.

4. Pair Work. Have students practice asking and giving directions, then switch roles and repeat. Encourage students to continue with their own ideas of other errands they could do based on the stores located on the map.
5. Ask several pairs to demonstrate for the class.

LISTEN TO THIS

1. Explain the activity. Make sure students locate Point X on the map. Remind them that in each conversation, they start at Point X. Encourage students to trace the routes on the map as they listen to the directions.
2. Play the recording or read the conversations at normal speed as the students listen and write down where each person is going.
3. Play or read the conversations again as students check their answers.
4. Pair Work. Have students check their work by comparing what they wrote.

Answers: Location 1: *Fran's Footwear,* Location 2: *McDonald's,* Location 3: *Spirit Women's Wear,* Location 4: *Police Station*

5. Ask volunteers for the answers.
6. Play or read the conversations again as a final check.
7. Expansion. Have students make up their own destinations and continue practicing in pairs.

PERSON TO PERSON

Practice 1

1. Explain the activity. Divide the class into pairs and have students decide who will be Student A and who will be Student B.

2. Have students listen to the introduction. Then give them time to read the directions. To check vocabulary, discuss what is in a first aid kit.

Note: Students can either start at X for each errand or start at X for the first errand and then use places visited as subsequent starting points. Answers will vary according to procedure followed.

3. Model an opener to help students get started: *I need to (buy a bicycle helmet) today. / Go straight, ...*

4. Pair Work. Have students complete the activity. Circulate and check that they fill in the name of each location.

5. Check the directions for each errand by asking various pairs to role-play for the class.

Practice 2

1. Have students read the directions.

2. Follow the procedure for Practice 1.

LET'S TALK 4

Student Book, page 101.

1. Give students time to read the directions. Check students' understanding of the directions by asking: *Who is coming to your city? Why? What have you been asked to do?* Check vocabulary: *exchange program, dorm*

Note: *Your city* means the city in which the classes are being held. When paired, the students can use a major city that both partners are familiar with.

2. Model the opener *Let's think of as many places as we can. Then we can choose some and arrange the schedule.* Have students repeat.

3. Separate the students into pairs.

4. Pair Work. Have students work together to plan the schedule. Circulate and assist with vocabulary as neeeded.

Note: Remind students that if they plan free-time activities, they must be able to give the foreign students directions from the school to where they are going.

5. Group Work. Have two pairs compare their schedules. Alternatively, call on pairs to present their schedules to the whole class. Have students discuss each other's suggestions and timetables.

6. Expansion. In small groups, have students role-play presenting the schedule to the foreign students. Two students can present the schedule, while the others listen and seek clarification as needed.

(Student A looks at this page. Student B looks at the next page.)

Practice 1

Your partner will tell you about four errands he/she has for today. Decide which places your partner has to visit and give him/her directions using the map below.

Practice 2

You have four errands to do today. Tell your partner about all four. He/she will give you directions on the map below. As you arrive at each location, write the name. Your errands are:

cash a check   get your coat cleaned
get a library card   get some computer paper

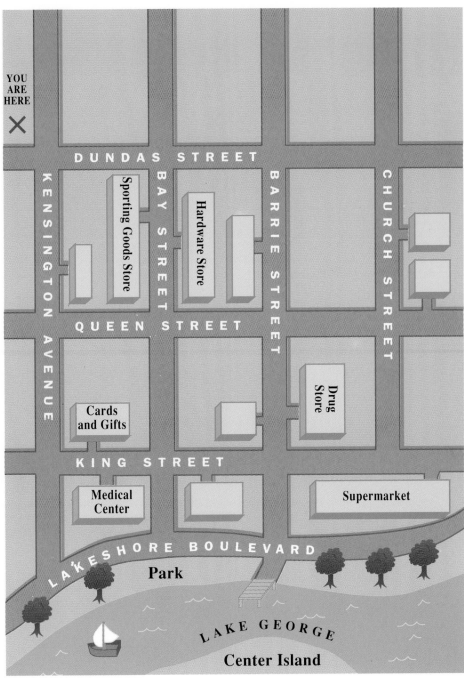

PERSON TO PERSON

STUDENT B

(Student B looks at this page. Student A looks at the previous page.)

Practice 1

You have four errands to do today. Tell your partner about all four. He/she will give you directions on the map below. As you arrive at each location, write the name. Your errands are:

buy a bicycle helmet   buy a birthday card
buy a first-aid kit   see the eye doctor

Practice 2

Your partner will tell you about four errands he/she has for today. Decide which places your partner has to visit and give him/her directions using the map below.

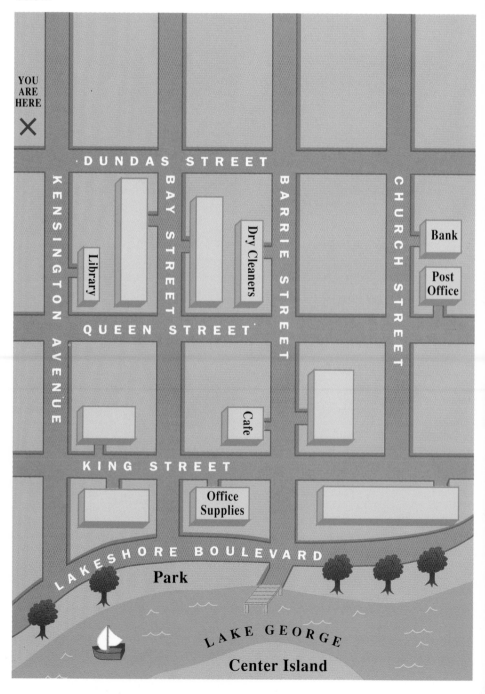

COMPONENTS

Student Book, pages 33–40
Let's Talk 5, Student Book page 102
Cassette/CD
Optional Activity 5, page 131

OBJECTIVES

Functions: Describing likes and dislikes, agreeing and disagreeing, asking and giving opinions (preferences)

Topics: vacations, activities, types of: sports, movies, books, music

Structures:
- Simple present: I love it. / I can't stand it.
- Short answers with *so* and *neither:* So do I. / Neither do I. / Me neither.
- Question words: What do you think of the people? / How do you like the city?
- *Yes/No* questions: Do you like the city? / Do you like Thai food?

Pronunciation Focus: Comparison of the sounds [s] and [sh]

Listen to This: Listening for people's opinions; listening for whether two people agree or disagree

CONVERSATION 1
HOW DO YOU LIKE THE CITY?

Prelistening Questions

1. With books closed, read the title of the conversation and the prelistening questions. Elicit an answer to each question from a student volunteer.

2. Pair Work. Have students take turns asking and answering the questions. Circulate and assist with vocabulary as needed.

3. Class Work. Ask other volunteers to answer the questions Make sure students give reasons for why they do or do not like big cities. Make a list on the board of things to do in big cities.

Note: If the class is held in a big city, have students list specific things to do there.

4. Have students open their books and cover the conversation. Direct students' attention to the photograph. In pairs, have them describe what they see.

5. Class Work. Ask students to speculate:

- *Where are these people?*
- *Who are they?*
- *What have they been doing?*

Elicit answers from several volunteers for each question. Maintain a rapid pace.

Vocabulary

Introduce these words and phrases now or after the students listen to the conversation.

So, what do you think?: short form of *What do you think of* (something)? Used in conversation when the topic is obvious from the context.

Let's go American: used to express *Let's do it American style.* Can be used with different nationalities; for example, *Let's go Italian. I really like pizza.*

Presentation

1. With books closed, play the recording or read the conversation at normal speed.

2. Ask the following general comprehension questions:

- *Where are they?* (New York)
- *Do they like it?* (Yes)
- *What don't they like?* (the traffic)
- *What are they going to do next?* (eat dinner)

Elicit responses from various students or have students tell their partners the answers.

3. Say: *Listen again. This time listen for what each of them likes in New York and where they are going to eat.* Play or read again, pausing for choral repetition.

4. Ask the following questions:

- *What does she like?* (the stores and the shopping)
- *What does he like?* (the museums)
- *Where does she decide to eat?* (McDonalds)
- *Is that OK with him?* (Yes)

Elicit responses from various students or have students tell their partners the answers.

5. Paired Reading. Have students read the conversation, switching roles.

CONVERSATION 1
HOW DO YOU LIKE THE CITY?

Do you like big cities?
What can you do in big cities?

Marta: So, what do you think? How do you like New York?

Paul: I'm having a great time. I love it. I'm glad we came.

Marta: Yeah. I really like the stores and the shopping.

Paul: I love the museums, too.

Marta: But the traffic is pretty bad.

Paul: Yeah. I hate all this traffic. It's really noisy.

Marta: Listen, it's almost dinnertime. There are lots of restaurants around here. What do you want to try? Italian? Greek? Japanese? Thai?

Paul: I can't stand making decisions. You choose!

Marta: OK. Let's go American. Where's the nearest McDonald's?

1. TALKING ABOUT LIKES AND DISLIKES

◆ How do you like │ the *city?*
What do you think of │ the *people?*

◆ Do you like │ the *city?*
│ *New York?*

✧ I love │ it.
I really like │

✧ It's │ OK.
│ all right.

✧ I can't stand it.
I hate it.
I don't like it (at all).

Practice 1

Ask your partner if he/she likes the following things. Add three more of your own and ask about them.

If you don't know anything about the thing or activity, answer like this:

Student A asks about:

1. classical music
2. dogs
3. Mexican food
4. action movies
5. swimming
6. ....
7. ....
8. ....

Student B asks about:

1. playing golf
2. jazz
3. shopping for clothes
4. discos
5. watching TV
6. ....
7. ....
8. ....

GIVE IT A TRY

TALKING ABOUT LIKES AND DISLIKES

1. Direct students' attention to the function box. Give students time to read over the examples.
2. Model the questions; have students repeat chorally.
Language Note: Point out that *What do you think of…?* and *How do you like…?* are both used to ask for someone's opinion and cannot be answered with *yes* or *no*. In contrast, *Do you like…?* can be answered with *yes* or *no*, although an opinion or reason is usually expected.
Pronunciation Note: The intonation patterns of *What do you think of…* and *Do you like…?* are different. Write the following on the board; mark the intonation patterns for each:

> *What do you think of...?*
> *Do you like...?*

The first question follows the pattern of rising, then falling intonation on the last stressed syllable. The second question follows the pattern of rising intonation of *yes/no* questions. Move your hand along the intonation lines as you model the examples in the function box.
3. Direct students' attention to the responses in the function boxes.
4. Model the responses; have students repeat chorally.
Pronunciation Note: Point out that stress is placed on the content word in each of these responses:

> *I LOVE it.*
> *I HATE it,* etc.

Emphasize the stress as you model the examples.

Language Note: Point out that *I can't stand it* or *I hate it* are very strong statements. Milder ways to express dislike are: *I really don't like it* or *I'm not crazy about it / I'm not wild about it.* The expressions *It's all right* and *It's not bad* show neutrality and a lack of enthusiasm for something.
5. Practice a few exchanges with various students. Possible questions: *What do you think of (Tokyo)? Do you like (pizza)? How do you like (the park near here)?*

Practice 1

1. Give students time to read the directions.
2. Divide the students into pairs and assign parts.
3. Model the three examples, using a different response with each; have students repeat chorally for their parts. Model again; ask individual students to respond.
4. Give students time to read over the lists of things they are to ask about and to add three more things to the lists.
5. Pair Work. Have students take turns asking each other about the things or activities on their lists. Circulate and help as needed.
6. Ask several pairs to demonstrate for the class.

Practice 2

1. Give students time to read the directions.

2. To check understanding, ask: *What do you think of watching TV, (Hiroko)? How are you going to mark that?* (with a check) *(Hiroko), ask (Shigeo) if he likes big cities. How are you going to mark his answer?* (Write in his name or initials.)

3. Give students time to mark their own likes and dislikes and to add two ideas of their own.

4. Group Work. In groups of three, have students take turns asking each other about their likes and dislikes.

5. Spot-check by asking students information about other group members: *(Mayumi) does (Yasuhiro) like pets?*

Practice 3

1. Explain the activity. To check understanding of *in common with,* select two students you know have several things in common. Say: *(Yuko) and (Tomu), you have several things in common. You both live in (Tokyo), you are both (18 years old), and you both like to (play tennis).*

2. Give students time to look at their charts and decide who they have the most in common with.

3. Pair Work. Have students work with new partners to report what they found out.

Note: Remind students to watch out for the third person marker when reporting the likes and dislikes of the people they interviewed. *(I don't really like pets* vs. *He doesn't really like pets,* etc.)

4. Ask volunteers to report to the class: *(Hiro) and I both love big cities, but we can't stand flying.*

5. If time permits, compile students' answers on the board: *How many people love big cities? Raise your hands. How many people can't stand flying?,* etc. Have a student volunteer compile the answers or do it yourself.

6. Discuss the information on the board and see if the class has a certain personality; for example, *We are a class that loves big cities, doesn't really like to watch TV, and can't stand politicians.*

LISTEN TO THIS

1. Explain the activity. Give students time to read over the topics they will listen for.

Note: Point out that *to go out after work* means to go somewhere together either as friends or on a date.

2. Play the entire recording or read the conversation at normal speed as the students listen for general understanding. Do not have them write at this time.

3. Ask the following questions: *What are they going to do first?* (eat dinner) *What are they going to do after dinner?* (go bowling) Elicit responses from volunteers.

4. Play or read the conversation again as students fill in their answers.

5. Play or read the conversation a third time for students to check their answers.

6. Pair Work. Have students compare their answers.

7. Ask volunteers for the answers.

Answers: Chinese food, Mary: *Doesn't really like it*; Stan: *loves it.* Hamburgers, Mary: *wants (likes)*; Stan: *will be OK.* Musicals, Mary: *loves*; Stan: *hates.* Documentaries, Mary: *can't stand*; Stan: *wants to see.* Bowling, Mary: *likes it*; Stan: *likes it*

8. Play or read again as a final check if needed.

Look at the list of things below. Mark your own likes and dislikes with a check (✔). Ask two other people about their likes and dislikes. Write in their names or initials.

?	love	like	OK	don't really like	hate/can't stand
Big cities					
Pets					
Flying					
Watching TV					
Smokers					
Politicians					
Studying English					

Look at your chart. Decide which person you have the most in common with. Now, work with a classmate that you haven't spoken to yet. Report to each other what you found out.

▭ Mary and Stan have decided to go out after work. They're talking about what to do. Write their opinions about the following topics.

	Mary	Stan
Chinese food		
hamburgers		
musicals		
documentaries		
bowling		

What are these people planning to do?
Which activities do you like?

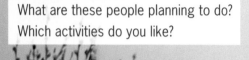

Pronunciation Focus

Listen and practice these words.

with [s]	with [sh]
sea	shore
sun	ocean
sand	fishing

Now practice the conversation.
Pay attention to the sounds [s] and [sh].

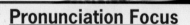

Tom: This one looks great! I love the seashore.

Ellen: So do I. The sun...the sand...the ocean!

Tom: And listen to this! What do you think of sailing, swimming, windsurfing, and fishing?

Ellen: Oh, Tom! They sound fantastic. I really like all those things.

Tom: Yeah...me, too.

Ellen: Well, except fishing. To be honest, I hate fishing, but I love all the others.

Tom: Hey! Look at this! We can stay in a big hotel or we can stay in a little cabin by the beach.

Ellen: You know, I really don't like those big hotels.

Tom: Neither do I. Let's stay in a cabin. It'll be much nicer right beside the ocean.

CONVERSATION 2
I LOVE THE SEASHORE.

Prelistening Questions

1. Have students cover the conversation. Direct students' attention to the photograph. Ask students to speculate:
- *What are these people planning to do?* (take a vacation / go to the seashore)
- *What are some of the activities there?* (sailing, swimming, snorkeling, fishing, etc.)

Elicit answers from several students.

2. Pair Work. Have students continue talking about where these people are thinking of going and the activities available there. Circulate and help with vocabulary.

3. Ask the class: *Which activities do you like?* Elicit answers from various students.

Vocabulary

Introduce these words and phrases now or after the students listen to the conversation.

seashore: the beach

windsurfing: water sport done by one person on a board with a sail

to be honest: to tell the truth

cabin: a small house that is usually simple and modest

Presentation

1. With books closed, play the recording or read the conversation at normal speed.

2. Ask the following general comprehension questions:
- *Where are they thinking of going?* (to the seashore)
- *Where are they going to stay?* (in a cabin)

3. Say: *Listen again. This time listen for what they like and dislike.*

4. Play or read the conversation again, pausing for choral repetition.

5. Ask the following questions:
- *What activities do they both like?* (sailing, swimming, and windsurfing)
- *What activity does she hate?* (fishing)
- *Where can they stay?* (in a big hotel or in a cabin)
- *Does she like big hotels?* (No)
- *Does he?* (No)
- *Why do they want to stay in a cabin?* (It'll be nicer right beside the ocean.)

Elicit answers from various volunteers or have students tell their partners the answers.

6. Pronunciation Focus. Explain what the focus is. On the board, write the examples with [s]: *sea, sun, sand,* and with [sh] *shore, ocean, fishing.* Model; have students repeat chorally.

7. With books open, play or read the conversation again. Tell students to pay attention to the sounds [s] and [sh].

8. Paired Reading. Have students practice the conversation, switching roles.

GIVE IT A TRY

1. AGREEING AND DISAGREEING WITH LIKES AND DISLIKES

1. On the board, list several things or activities: *pizza, science-fiction books, cleaning my room,* etc. Point to *pizza.* Say: *Pizza. I love it. / Really? So do I. / You do? I don't.* Continue modeling the first set of examples, using your list on the board.

2. List several more items. Model again; have students repeat chorally.

Note: The function boxes are set up in three sets so that students can easily see the relationship between the verb / presence of a negative and the appropriate short answer.

3. Ask the class: *What are some things you don't like?* Elicit responses from various volunteers. Model the next set of examples, following the procedure above.

Note: Have students repeat individually if time permits.

4. Say to the class: *Think of something you can't stand.* Elicit responses from volunteers and make a list on the board. Model the next set of examples, following the procedure above.

Pronunciation Note: How stress conveys meaning. The stress and intonation patterns here are based on what is old information and what is new. We say:

I LOVE PIZZA.

The stress is on both the verb and the object to convey this new information to the listener. However, we say:

I LOVE it.

Here the stress is only on *love* because the topic (pizza) is already known and the focus is on the speaker's feelings about it. With the expressions to show agreement: *Really? So do I. / Me neither,* and disagreement: *You do? I don't. / Really? I like it,* stress is placed on the content words that convey the agreement or disagreement.

5. Pair Work. Have students practice the examples, switching roles. Circulate and check intonation and stress.

Note: It is very important for students to understand the importance of stress here. It is worthwhile to spend a little extra time practicing these patterns.

Practice 1

1. Explain the activity. Direct students' attention to the art. Ask students to look at the body language and facial expressions in each picture. For the first picture ask: *Do they agree or disagree? How do you know?* Elicit comments from several students.

2. Pair Work. For each picture, have students decide whether the people agree or disagree. Then have students role-play the conversations, switching roles.

3. Check by having various pairs demonstrate each conversation for the class.

Culture Note: Point out to students that it is socially acceptable to disagree in English-speaking countries as long as the topic is neutral and the disagreement is conveyed politely. To develop this further, point out that in a conversation between people who do not know each other very well, people try to steer toward safe topics (such as movies or types of food) and away from topics where there might be disagreement; for example, politics.

Practice 2

1. Explain the activity. Give students time to work alone to list two things they like, two things they don't like, etc.

2. Pair Work. Have students take turns telling each other about their likes and dislikes and responding with an appropriate short answer.

3. Ask pairs to demonstrate for the class.

4. Call on students one at a time to state a like or dislike. Ask other students to agree and disagree. This can also be done as a chain. The student who disagrees then makes a new statement that others respond to. Maintain a rapid pace.

OPTIONAL ACTIVITY 5: What Do You Think Of...? *See Teacher's Notes, page 124, and Activity Sheet, page 131.*

1. AGREEING AND DISAGREEING WITH LIKES AND DISLIKES

	AGREE	DISAGREE
✦ I love it. I like them. I hate it.	✧ Really? So do I. Me, too.	✧ You do? I don't. Really?
✦ I don't like them.	✧ (No.) Neither do I. Me neither.	✧ You don't? I do.
✦ I can't stand it.	✧ (No.) Neither can I. Me neither.	✧ You can't? │ I like it. Really?

Practice 1

With your partner, decide whether the people below agree or disagree. Role-play their conversations. Then reverse roles.

Practice 2

Tell your partner two things you like, two things you don't like, two things you can't stand, and so on. Your partner will respond with a short answer.

2. STATING PREFERENCES

✦ I like *swimming*, but I don't like *diving*.
He likes *classical music*, but he can't stand *opera*.

Practice 1

Look at the lists below. Add three more choices in each category.

SPORTS	FOOD	MOVIES	MUSIC	ACTIVITIES	CHORES
baseball	Italian	musicals	rap	shopping	dusting
golf	French	comedies	jazz	eating out	vacuuming
soccer	Chinese	romance	classical	reading	laundry
volleyball	Indian	horror	heavy metal	listening to music	washing dishes
basketball	Japanese	action	rock 'n' roll	watching TV	cooking
_____	_____	_____	_____	_____	_____
_____	_____	_____	_____	_____	_____
_____	_____	_____	_____	_____	_____

Practice 2

Form small groups. Choose a category and talk about something that you like and don't like. Take turns until everyone has had a turn.

Example:
First Student: I like baseball, but I don't like volleyball.
Second Student: I love cooking, but I hate washing dishes.

LISTEN TO THIS

▭ You are going to hear short conversations about likes and dislikes. Sometimes the speakers agree; sometimes they disagree. Check (✔) AGREE or DISAGREE as you listen to each one.

	Agree	Disagree
1.		
2.		
3.		
4.		

2. STATING PREFERENCES

1. Direct students' attention to the function box. Give students time to read over the examples.

2. Model the examples; have students repeat chorally.

Pronunciation Note: Contrastive stress and intonation. The intonation pattern is as follows:

I like SWIMMING, but I don't like DIVING.

He likes CLASSICAL MUSIC, but he can't STAND OPERA.

In the first statement, primary stress is on *swimming* and *diving;* secondary stress is on *don't*. In the second statement, stress is placed on *classical music* and *opera*. The voice rises more on *opera*, however, to emphasize the contrast between the two types of music. Emphasize this contrastive stress as you model the examples.

3. Ask volunteers to make other examples; have the class repeat chorally. Alternatively, do this as a chain. One student makes a statement and cues the next student to continue by saying his/her name at the end of the statement. For example, the first student says: *I like pizza, but I don't like hamburgers. (Yuko).* The second student, (Yuko), continues: *I like hamburgers, but I don't like ice cream (Hiro).* The third student, (Hiro), continues: *I like ice cream, but I can't stand frozen yogurt.* If students have difficulty continuing, tell them they can change the topic as follows: *I like frozen yogurt, but I don't like playing golf.*

Note: Having students cue each other encourages active listening in a whole-class activity.

Practice 1————————————

1. Explain the activity. To help students add more choices, ask volunteers for one or two examples from each category.

Note: The category *Chores* might be difficult for students. Ask students to describe some of the tasks around the house; give them the appropriate vocabulary as needed.

2. Give students time to add their own choices to each category. Circulate and help with vocabulary as needed.

Practice 2————————————

1. Explain the activity. Model the example; have students repeat chorally and individually.

2. Divide the students into small groups.

3. Group Work. Have students take turns choosing a category and talking about things from it that they like and don't like.

4. Ask volunteers to report to the class what they found out in their groups: *(Yasu) likes classical music, but he doesn't like jazz.*

LISTEN TO THIS

1. Explain the activity. Emphasize to the students that they are to focus on whether the speakers agree or disagree; it is not necessary for them to catch every detail of the conversations.

2. Play the recording or read the conversations at normal speed as the students mark their answers.

3. Play the recording or read the conversations again for the students to check their answers.

4. Pair Work. Have students compare their answers.

5. Check as a class by asking: *In Conversation 1, do the speakers agree or disagree?* Continue asking about the other conversations.

Answers: Conversation 1: *disagree*, Conversation 2: *agree*, Conversation 3: *disagree*, Conversation 4: *agree*

6. Expansion. For vocabulary development, play the conversations again one at a time; point out the following vocabulary. Conversation 1: *to be honest* (used to preface a disagreement or a comment the speaker doesn't know how the listener will receive); Conversation 2: *Sounds perfect* (like *Sounds great,* but stronger; Conversation 3: *You're kidding* (common idiomatic expression to express disagreement and the feeling of "I'm really surprised you think that way"); Conversation 4: Ask what the speakers' relationship is. *(Husband and wife)* How do you know? *(….dear, the kids)*

PERSON TO PERSON

Practice 1

1. Divide the class into pairs and have pairs decide who will be Student A and who will be Student B.

2. Have students listen to the introduction. Then give them time to read the directions. Ask the class if they know of any films made by these three filmmakers. Write their answers on the board.

Note: Spending a few minutes having students briefly describe the movies they know is a worthwhile activity. It will stimulate interest and help them focus on the discussion they are going to hear.

3. Give students time to quickly read over the topics they are to listen for.

4. Play or read the conversation as the students mark their answers.

Answers: a) *Fellini,* b) *Bergman,* c) *Kurasawa: man likes / woman dislikes,* d) *Horror movies: man dislikes / woman likes,* e) *Heavy metal music: woman dislikes / man dislikes (implied),* f) *Classical music: man likes / woman likes,* g) *Comedy movies: man likes / woman likes (somewhat)*

5. Have students listen again to check their answers.

Practice 2

1. Have students read the directions for their parts.

2. Pair Work. Have students discuss the man's and woman's opinions.

3. Check by calling on various students to present the man's and woman's opinions.

Practice 3

1. Give students time to read the directions. Make sure students understand that they are to take turns describing the movies, then decide which one the man and woman should go see. Remind them that they should base their decision on what the man and woman like and dislike.

2. Check students' understanding of the following vocabulary: *kidnapped, insane, composer, scar, victim.*

3. Pair Work. Have students complete the activity.

4. Check their work by calling on various pairs to explain to the class which movie they chose and why.

LET'S TALK 5

Student Book, page 102.

1. Give students time to read the directions. Direct students' attention to the travel posters. Briefly discuss each poster. Help students brainstorm on the possible activities at each place. Assist with vocabulary as needed *(the Eiffel Tower, Arche De Triomphe, the Moulin Rouge, Hollywood, the Golden Gate Bridge, beach, surfers, hiking, golfing, trail, moose).*

2. Model the opener *What's there to do in Paris?* Have students repeat. Elicit possible responses: *We can go to (the Eiffel Tower), There's the (Moulin Rouge),* etc.

3. Separate the students into pairs.

4. Pair Work. Have students work together to plan their vacations. Circulate and assist with vocabulary as needed.

Note: This activity can also be done in small groups with the members reaching a consensus on where to go and what to do.

5. Ask volunteers to explain to the class where they will go and what they will do. Encourage classmates to ask questions and seek clarification as needed.

PERSON TO PERSON

(Student A looks at this page. Student B looks at the next page.)

📼 You are going to hear a discussion between a man and a woman about movies and music. They refer to three famous filmmakers—Fellini, Bergman, and Kurosawa.

Practice 1

Listen to the conversation and check the man's likes and dislikes.

	Likes	Dislikes
a) Fellini		
b) Bergman		
c) Kurosawa		
d) Horror movies		
e) Heavy metal music		
f) Classical music		
g) Comedy movies		

Practice 2

Without turning the page, discuss the man's and woman's opinions with your partner.

Practice 3

Describe the following movie to your partner. Your partner will describe a movie to you. Decide which movie the man and woman should go to see.

The Phantom of the Opera—A beautiful French opera singer is kidnapped by an insane composer who lives beneath the Paris Opera House. This man with a terrible scar has killed before. Will she be his next victim?

PERSON TO PERSON

STUDENT B

(Student B looks at this page. Student A looks at the previous page.)

You are going to hear a discussion between a man and a woman about movies and music. They refer to three famous filmmakers—Fellini, Bergman, and Kurosawa.

Practice 1

Listen to the conversation and check the woman's likes and dislikes.

	Likes	Dislikes
a) Fellini		
b) Bergman		
c) Kurosawa		
d) Horror movies		
e) Heavy metal music		
f) Classical music		
g) Comedy movies		

Practice 2

Without looking at the previous page, discuss the man's and woman's opinions with your partner.

Practice 3

Your partner will describe a movie to you. Then, describe the following movie to your partner. Decide which movie the man and woman should go to see.

Love and Death—This is Woody Allen's funniest film. He makes fun of love and death, politics, and serious foreign films. There is a lot of beautiful classical music by Prokofiev.

COMPONENTS

Student Book, pages 41–48
Let's Talk 6, Student Book page 103
Cassette/CD
Optional Activity 6, page 132
Review (Units 4–6), Student Book page 104

OBJECTIVES

Functions: Accepting and declining invitations, getting more information about invitations, setting the time and place, changing plans, adding to plans, showing preferences (review of likes and dislikes)

Topics: shared interests (review), dating, getting together with friends, entertainment guides

Structures:
- *Could*: Could we meet at the subway instead?
- *Have to*: I have to meet a friend.
- *How about* + gerund: How about going out for dinner?
  How about meeting at 7:15?
- What kind of party? Where is it?
- I'd love to. That's a great idea. Why not? That's a good idea.
- I'm afraid I have to meet a friend. I'd love it, but I've got to work.
  Maybe we can do it some other time.

Pronunciation Focus: Word Stress. One word in a sentence is often more important than others and is stressed more heavily than the other words.

Listen to This: Listening for specific information

CONVERSATION 1
HOW ABOUT COMING WITH US?

Prelistening Questions

1. With books closed, read the title of the conversation and the prelistening questions. Elicit an answer to each question from a student volunteer.

2. Group Work. Have students discuss the questions. Circulate and assist with vocabulary as needed.

Note: The second question has to do with parents' rules for dating as well as more general social rules.

3. Class Work. Ask volunteers to answer the questions. Mention that in North America there is tremendous variation in rules. For example, some people start dating in their very early teens, while others can only go on group activities at that age.

4. Have students open their books and cover the conversation. Direct students' attention to the photograph. In pairs, have them describe what they see.

5. Class Work. Ask students to speculate:
- *Who are these people?*
- *How do they know each other?*
- *What are they talking about?*

Elicit answers from several volunteers for each question. Maintain a rapid pace.

Note: Students can also review describing people by briefly telling each other what the people in the photograph look like.

Vocabulary

Introduce these words and phrases now or after the students listen to the conversation.

How's it going: a casual way to say *How are you?* usually used with peers

Do you mean…?: expression used to seek clarification

a bunch (of us): idiomatic way to say a *fairly large group* (of people)

Presentation

1. With books closed, play the recording or read the conversation at normal speed.

2. Ask the following general comprehension questions:
- *What's Kenji doing tomorrow night?* (going to dinner at a Thai restaurant)
- *Does Debbie want to go?* (Yes)

3. Say: *Listen again. This time listen for more details about what they are going to do.* Play or read the conversation again, pausing for choral repetition.

4. Ask the following questions:
- *Where is the Thai restaurant located?* (on University Avenue)
- *What is the name of the restaurant?* (The Bangkok)
- *Who's going there?* (a bunch of their friends)
- *Why is Kenji going to call the restaurant?* (to make reservations)
- *What time can Debbie go?* (any time after 6:00)
- *When is Kenji going to call her?* (tonight)
- *Why is he going to call her?* (to tell her the time)

Elicit answers from various students or have students tell their partners the answers.

5. Paired Reading. Have students read the conversation, switching roles.

Language Note: Point out that the expressions *Do you mean…?* and *That's the (one)* are very commonly used in seeking clarification of and confirming information. If time permits, present other examples: *Do you know the bookstore near the corner? Do you mean The World Bookstore? That's the one. / Have you heard about the new dance club in town? Do you mean the Up Beat? Yeah, that's the one.* Ask students to create other examples based on information where they live.

Culture Note: Making reservations usually requires calling a restaurant and saying the time you want to come and the number of people in the group. For reservations, the group is referred to as *a party.* The restaurant asks: *How many people are in your party?* The response is: *I'd like a reservation for a party of (four).* If you cannot make it to the restaurant for your reservation, it is important to call and cancel it.

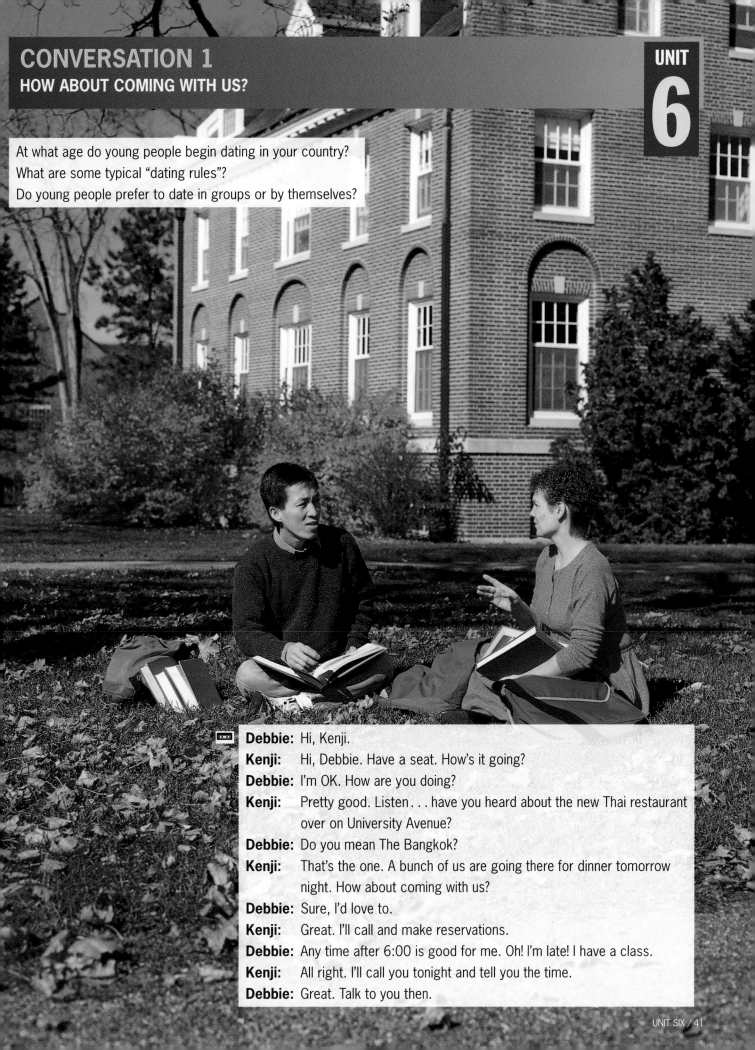

At what age do young people begin dating in your country?

What are some typical "dating rules"?

Do young people prefer to date in groups or by themselves?

Debbie: Hi, Kenji.

Kenji: Hi, Debbie. Have a seat. How's it going?

Debbie: I'm OK. How are you doing?

Kenji: Pretty good. Listen... have you heard about the new Thai restaurant over on University Avenue?

Debbie: Do you mean The Bangkok?

Kenji: That's the one. A bunch of us are going there for dinner tomorrow night. How about coming with us?

Debbie: Sure, I'd love to.

Kenji: Great. I'll call and make reservations.

Debbie: Any time after 6:00 is good for me. Oh! I'm late! I have a class.

Kenji: All right. I'll call you tonight and tell you the time.

Debbie: Great. Talk to you then.

1. ACCEPTING INVITATIONS

✦ Do you feel like	going out for dinner	Saturday?
What about		tonight?
How about		

✧ Sure.	I'd love to.
OK.	That's a great idea.
	Why not?
	That's a good idea.

Practice

Invite your partner to do the following things. Your partner agrees. Find out if he/she feels like:

1. going out for dinner next Friday
2. seeing a movie Sunday afternoon
3. going for coffee
4. playing tennis
5. going camping

Add some ideas of your own.

2. DECLINING INVITATIONS

✦ Do	you	want to	have lunch tomorrow?
Would		like to	

✧ Oh,	I'm sorry. I can't.	I have to	meet a friend.
	I'm afraid	I've got to	

✦ That's too bad. Maybe next time.

Practice

Invite your partner to do the following things. He/she is busy and makes an excuse. Then reverse roles. Add ideas of your own to each list.

Invitations

1. go to a party tonight
2. see a movie Friday night
3. go golfing on Sunday
4. go shopping on Saturday
5...
6...

Excuses

1. work late
2. meet a friend
3. visit my parents
4. go to a meeting
5. ....
6. ....

GIVE IT A TRY

1. ACCEPTING INVITATIONS

1. Direct students' attention to the function box. Give students time to read over the examples.

2. Model the examples; have students repeat.

Pronunciation Note: Review of question and statement intonation. The intonation rises on the *yes/no* question; it rises, then falls for the statement. On the board, write the following and mark the intonation:

> *Do you feel like going out for dinner Saturday?*
> *Sure. That's a great idea.*

Move your hand along the intonation lines as you model the examples.

Language Note: *Do you feel like …? What about …?* and *How about…?* all mean *Do you want to …?* Emphasize that all three take a gerund: *Do you feel like <u>swimming</u>? How about <u>having pizza</u>? What about <u>seeing a movie</u>?* Write the examples on the board and underline the gerunds. Elicit other examples from the class.

Practice

1. Give students time to read the directions and the list of activities.

2. Pair Work. Have students take turns making and accepting invitations to do the activities listed.

3. Ask several pairs to demonstrate for the class.

4. Ask students for other activities they could also do. Make a list on the board.

5. Pair Work. Have students switch partners and continue.

Language Note: The expression *go for (a) (coffee)* is often used when an informal invitation for a specific food or drink is made. The use of the indefinite article is tricky here. Sometimes, it is optional: *go for (a) pizza / (a) coffee.* However, we say: *go for a Coke / go for a drink.* When the invitation includes the name of a meal, the article is not used: *go for lunch/breakfast/dinner.*

2. DECLINING INVITATIONS

1. Direct students' attention to the function box. Give students time to read over the examples.

2. Model the examples; have students repeat.

Pronunciation Note: Blending of *want to* and *have to* and practicing reduced forms. *Want to* and *have to* change to /*wanna*/ and /*hafta*/ in spoken English. The regular rhythm of English causes the speaker to reduce other words as well. On the board, write the following; mark the stress:

> *Do you want to have lunch tomorrow?*

Model the question, exaggerating the rhythm. Point out how the first part of the question is reduced and that primary stress falls on the content words at the end of the question (*lunch tomorrow*). On the board, write: *I have to meet a friend.*

Repeat the procedure, emphasizing the stress and reductions.

Language Note: *Would you like to …?* is more polite than *Do you want to …?* They must both be followed by the simple form of the verb. On the board, write the expressions + VERB to serve as a prompt during the practice.

Culture Note: When declining an invitation, it is important to give a reason so as not to sound too harsh. Vague, but acceptable excuses are: *I'm already busy. / I already have plans.* To show enthusiasm or friendliness, we might say: *I'd really like to, but I'm busy.*

3. Pair Work. Ask pairs to model asking and declining the invitations for the class.

Practice

1. Explain the activity. Give students time to briefly skim their lists and add ideas of their own.

2. Pair Work. Have students practice making and declining the invitations.

3. Class Work. Call on a pair to do the first invitation. Model what they say, emphasizing the rhythm. Have the class repeat chorally. Continue with the next two invitations.

4. Pair Work. Have students reverse roles and repeat. Circulate and help students with the rhythm.

3. GETTING MORE INFORMATION

1. Direct students' attention to the function box. Give students time to read over the examples.

2. Model the examples; have students repeat.

3. Pair Work. Ask pairs to model asking and responding to invitations for the class.

Pronunciation Note: Review of rising intonation on *yes/no* questions:

Would you like to go to a party this Saturday?

Blended and reduced forms */itza/*:

It's a birthday party.

Culture Note: It is acceptable to ask a good friend questions such as *Who's going?* or *What are you wearing?* For someone you do not know well, you can ask *How many people will be there? What will people be wearing?* It is important to first show agreement (*Sounds good*), then ask follow-up questions; otherwise, the speaker runs the risk of sounding as though his/her interest or participation is contingent on who else is doing it.

Practice

1. Explain the activity. Give students time to read the information and fill in the blanks with their own ideas/information.

2. Review the following vocabulary. *A potluck dinner:* This is a party to which each guest brings something to eat. The host or hostess might assign each guest a category such as salad, bread, or dessert; otherwise, the guest can bring whatever he or she chooses. This type of party is often easier to host and provides guests an opportunity to experience different styles of cooking. *My place:* a term used to refer to the place where a person lives, such as a house, an apartment, or a condominium.

Culture Note: The Blue Jays and the Yankees are two popular teams in North America. The Blue Jays are from Toronto, Ontario in Canada, and the Yankees are from New York. When we talk about baseball teams, the definite article, *the*, is necessary: *The Blue Jays.*

Language Note: *It's up to you* is a commonly used expression that means *you can decide.*

3. Pair Work. Have students take turns inviting their partners to and getting more information about the events listed. Circulate and help as needed.

4. Ask pairs to demonstrate for the class, using their own ideas and information.

LISTEN TO THIS

1. Explain the activity. Give students time to read over the information in the book.

2. Play or read the conversations as students finish each sentence.

3. Play or read again as students check their answers.

4. Pair Work. Have students compare their answers by reading them aloud to each other.

5. Ask volunteers for the answers.

Answers:

1. Ted and Diane
   a) Diane wants to go dancing.
   b) Ted wants to go out to listen to some music.
   c) Club Blue Note serves mostly fancy salads and light things.
   d) The prices at the club are very good.

2. Ben and Oscar
   a) Ben invites Oscar to a baseball party.
   b) Oscar can't go because he has to go to the airport to pick up his brother-in-law.
   c) Oscar can go after he gets back from the airport.
   d) Oscar will bring something to drink.
   e) They will order pizza for dinner.

6. Play or read the conversation again as a final check if necessary.

3. GETTING MORE INFORMATION

✦ Would you like to | go to a party this Saturday?
Do you want to |

✧ Sounds good. | What kind of party?
| Where is it?
| Who's going?

✦ It's a birthday party/potluck dinner.
It's at my place/Dave's.
Some people from work/school.

Practice

Invite your partner to the following events. Your partner will ask for extra information. Take turns. Fill in the blanks with your own ideas/information.

Event	Information requested	Information
1. potluck dinner	What can I bring?	It's up to you.
2. baseball game	Who's playing?	Blue Jays and Yankees
3. dinner	What time?	8 o'clock
4. go for a drive	Where?	in the country
5. see a movie	Which movie?	....
6. go swimming	....	....
7.	....	....
8.	....	....

LISTEN TO THIS

🔈 You are going to hear two conversations. Listen and finish each sentence.

1. Ted and Diane

a) Diane wants to ....

b) Ted wants to ....

c) Club Blue Note serves mostly...........................and ....

d) The prices at the club are ....

2. Ben and Oscar

a) Ben invites Oscar to a...

b) Oscar can't go because he has to go ....

c) Oscar can go after..

d) Oscar will bring..

e) They will ....for dinner.

CONVERSATION 2
WHY DON'T WE MEET THERE?

Is it all right for a woman to ask a man for a date?
Do women ask men for dates very often?
Are there any special days when women ask men out?

Karen: Hello. Could I speak to Justin, please?

Justin: Speaking.

Karen: Oh, hi Justin. This is Karen Hepburn. We met at Chris and Jim's party.

Justin: Of course. How're you?

Karen: Great. Uh, Justin, would you like to see Otis Isley on Thursday night? He's at the Kangaroo Club.

Justin: I'm sorry, Karen, but I can't. I have to work late this Thursday.

Karen: Oh… that's too bad.

Justin: Yeah. I really like Isley.

Karen: Actually, are you doing anything on Friday or Saturday? He's playing those two nights as well.

Justin: Well, I can't make it on Friday either, but I'm free on Saturday night. What time does it start?

Karen: At eight sharp. How about meeting in front of the club at about a quarter after seven?

Justin: That sounds perfect. And let's go out for coffee after the show.

Karen: Sure!

Justin: OK, see you at 7:15, Saturday.

Pronunciation Focus

Often one word in a sentence is more important than others and is stressed more heavily than the other words in the sentence. Listen.

Could I speak to Jústin please?

I have to work láte this Thursday.

Listen to the conversation again and mark the stressed words. Then practice the conversation.

CONVERSATION 2
WHY DON'T WE MEET THERE?

Prelistening Questions

1. Have students open their books and cover the conversation and the prelistening questions.

2. Direct students' attention to the photograph. Ask students to speculate who the people are, what their relationship is, and what they are talking about. Ask volunteers for their ideas.

3 Read the title of the conversation and the prelistening questions.

4. Pair Work. Have students uncover the questions and take turns asking and answering them.

5. Elicit answers from several volunteers for each question.

Culture Note: In North America nowadays, women ask men out on dates more often than in the past. In addition, there are many dating traditions. On Sadie Hawkins Day, many high schools have a dance to which the girls must invite the boys. Tradition says that on February 29 of a leap year it's OK for a woman to ask a man to marry her. Valentine's Day is also a day that is rich in tradition. In North America, dating couples, family members, and friends give presents to each other. Chocolate is traditionally given. Cards, flowers, and jewelry are also exchanged. Ask students how this compares with their customs.

6. Ask students to look at the photograph again. Have them speculate:

- *Is she asking him for a date?*
- *What do you think she wants to do?*
- *Is he going to go out with her?*

Have students use information in the picture to support their answers.

Vocabulary

Introduce these words and phrases now or after the students listen to the conversation.

Uh, (Justin): a filler used to catch someone's attention and slow the conversation down.

By the way: used to change the topic in a conversation.

It's on me: an idiomatic way to say *I'm paying for it.* We can also say *It's my treat.*

Presentation

1. With books closed, play the recording or read the conversation at normal speed.

2. Ask the following general comprehension questions:
   Where does she want to go? (to a club)
   What day are they going to go? (Saturday)

3. Say: *Listen again. This time listen for details in their conversation.* Play or read the conversation again, pausing for choral repetition.

4. Ask the following questions:

- *What is his name?* (Justin)
- *What is her name?* (Karen Hepburn)
- *Where did they meet?* (at a party / at Chris and Jim's party)
- *Where does she invite him to go?* (The Kangaroo Club)
- *Why can't he go on Thursday night?* (He has to work late.)
- *What night is he free?* (Saturday)
- *What time does the show start?* (at eight o'clock sharp)
- *Where are they going to meet?* (in front of the club)
- *What time are they going to meet?* (a quarter after seven)

Elicit answers from volunteers or have students tell their partners the answers.

5. Pronunciation Focus. Explain that one word in a sentence is often more important than others and is therefore stressed more heavily. Go over the examples:
Could I speak to Justin please?
I have to work late this Thursday.

6. Play or read the conversation again. Have students mark the word in each sentence that receives the most stress.

7. Paired Reading. Have students read the conversation, switching roles. Circulate and make sure students are paying attention to the stress.

8. For extra pronunciation practice, model the conversation again one line at a time, emphasizing the stress. Have the students repeat chorally.

GIVE IT A TRY

1. SUGGESTING ANOTHER DAY

1. Direct students' attention to the function box. Give students time to read over the examples.

2. Model the examples; have students repeat.

Pronunciation Note: Stressed and reduced forms of *can't* and *can*. Although auxiliaries are generally not stressed, when they are negative they receive stress: *I can't make it.* Note how this contrasts with *We can do it.* When the auxiliary *can* is not stressed, it is reduced to */kin/*. Model the examples, emphasizing the difference.

Language Note: The two-word verb *to make it* has a combined meaning of *to arrive* and *to attend.* Present the following examples: *Can you make it? / I'll try to make it by 5:00. / I can't make it. / I didn't make it to class yesterday.* Prompt students to use it by asking: *Did you make it to class on time yesterday? How about having dinner at 6:30 tonight? Can you make it then?* Continue with other questions if time permits.

3. Pair Work. Have students practice the exchanges, switching roles. Circulate and assist with pronunciation.

Practice 1

1. Explain the activity. Have students think of things to do. Make a list on the board.

2. Pair Work. Have students take turns making, refusing, and accepting the refusal of invitations. They can either use the activities on the board or make up their own.

3. Check by having two pairs demonstrate for the class.

Practice 2

1. Explain the activity. Have students add a few more ideas to the list on the board.

Note: For variety and fun, encourage students to come up with some unusual activities such as skydiving, or hot-air balloon racing.

2. Pair Work. Have students take turns making the invitations. This time have them suggest another time to do the activity.

3. Check by having two pairs demonstrate for the class.

2. SETTING THE TIME AND PLACE

1. Direct students' attention to the function boxes. Give students time to read over the examples.

2. Model the examples; have students repeat chorally.

Pronunciation Note: Review of English as a stress-timed language. Review how the stress in English occurs at regular intervals by clapping out the rhythm or tapping on the table as you model the examples:

Where do you want to meet?
How about meeting in front of the club?
Why don't we meet at 7:15?
See you then.

Practice

1. Explain the activity. On the board, help students list a few activities they might do.

Note: To make this more realistic, look at a copy of the local newspaper before class and find out what movies, plays, or other cultural events are going on in town. Put this information on the board for the students to use.

2. Pair Work. Have students take turns practicing making invitations and setting the place.

3. Ask several pairs to demonstrate for the class.

1. SUGGESTING ANOTHER DAY

✦ I'm really sorry. I can't make it.

| ✧ OK. Maybe we can do it some other time then. | ✧ Well, how about *Friday*, then? |
| ✦ Yes, I'd really like to. | ✦ Great! That sounds good. |

Practice 1

Invite your partner to do something. He/she is busy and can't accept. Respond to the refusal.

Practice 2

Invite your partner to do something. He/she is busy and can't accept. Suggest another time.

2. SETTING THE TIME AND PLACE

✦ Where do you want to meet?

✧ How about meeting | *in front of the club?*
Why don't we meet | *at the restaurant?*
Let's meet *at the restaurant.*

✦ Great. What time?

✧ How about meeting | at | *7:15?*
Why don't we meet |
Is *7:15* OK?
Let's meet at *7:15.*

✦ Fine.
OK. See you | *at 7:15.*
| *then.*

Practice

Invite your partner to do something. He/she accepts. Set the time and place.

3. CHANGING PLANS

> ◆ Could we meet | *at the subway instead?*
> | *at 7:00?*
> | *a little later?*
> | *earlier?*
>
> ◇ Sure. That's no problem.

Practice

Invite your partner to do something and arrange a time and place to meet. Your partner will suggest a different time or place. Then reverse roles.

4. ADDING TO PLANS

> ◆ We could | *go for coffee after the show.*
> Let's | *go out dancing after dinner.*
>
> ◇ Do you want to | *have dinner before the movie?*
> Why don't we | *go swimming after we play tennis?*

Practice

Student A invites **Student B** to do two of the following. **Student B** suggests adding to the plan. Then reverse roles. Add some ideas of your own.

A's invitations:

1. go sailing
2. go for a drive in the country
3. meet downtown for lunch
4. come over and watch videos

B's suggestions:

1. have lunch first
2. stop somewhere for brunch
3. do some shopping afterward
4. order a pizza for dinner

LISTEN TO THIS

🔊 Barry is arranging an evening out with his friend, Andrew. Listen and answer the questions.

1. What does Barry want to do? ....
2. What time does Barry suggest? ....
3. What else does Andrew want to do? ....
4. What time are they going to meet? ....
5. Where are they going to meet? ....

3. CHANGING PLANS

1. Direct students' attention to the function box. Give students time to read over the examples.

2. Model the examples; have students repeat.

Pronunciation Note: Review of stress on content words. Here the speakers have already established that they are going to meet. Stress is placed on the content word regarding what in the plan the speaker wants to change: *Could we meet at the SUBWAY instead?* (change of place) *Could we meet at 7:00?* (change of time) *Could we meet a little EARLIER?* (change of time). This is also a good opportunity to demonstrate how stress is used to emphasize new information. Additional work can be done by writing examples on the board in which other parts of the plan are changed: *Could we get PIZZA instead?* (change of type of food) *How about going to a MOVIE instead?* (change of activity).

Language Note: Speakers often shorten *That's no problem* to *No problem*.

Practice

1. Explain the activity. Either make a list of activities or have students think up their own.

2. Pair Work. Have students practice inviting their partners to do things, making the arrangements, and changing the plans. Have students switch roles.

3. Ask several pairs to demonstrate for the class.

Language Note: If time permits, present some of the expressions used to negotiate plans. In response to *Could we meet at 7:00 instead of 7:30?* someone might say *I'm sorry I can't make it then* or *I'm afraid I can't get there by then. How about 7:15, instead? / Could we meet at 7:15 instead?*

4. ADDING TO PLANS

1. Direct students' attention to the function box. Give students time to read over the examples.

2. Model the examples; have students repeat.

Practice

1. Explain the activity. Divide the students into pairs. Give students time to read the information for their parts.

Culture Note: *Brunch* is a meal usually eaten in late morning. The name comes from the combination of the words *breakfast* and *lunch*. Some hotels and restaurants have brunch buffets at which someone pays a set price and can eat whatever he or she wants. Brunch menus often include typical breakfast food as well as salads, meats, and other lunch type of foods.

2. Pair Work. Have students practice the invitations, reversing roles.

3. Ask several pairs to demonstrate for the class.

LISTEN TO THIS

1. Explain the activity. Give students time to read the questions. Remind students that they do not need to answer in full sentences; it will slow them down.

2. Play or read the conversation as students answer the questions.

3. Play or read again as students check their answers.

4. Pair Work. Have students check their answers by asking and answering the questions.

5. Ask volunteers for the answers.

Answers: 1. *play tennis,* 2. *7:00,* 3. *have dinner first,* 4. *7:30,* 5. *at the restaurant*

6. Play or read the conversation again as a final check if necessary.

OPTIONAL ACTIVITY 6: More Invitations. *See Teacher's Notes, page 124, and Activity Sheet, page 132.*

PERSON TO PERSON

Practice 1

1. Divide the class into pairs and have students decide who will be Student A and who will be Student B.
2. Have students listen to the introduction. Then give them time to read the directions and look at what is already written in the appointment book for their parts.
3. Play or read the conversation as the students fill in the appoinment books (Student A: Carmen's book, Student B: Yoshiko's book).
4. Have students listen again to check their answers.
5. Pair Work. Have students check their answers with someone from their own part, not with their partner. Circulate and help students resolve any differences.

Answers:

Carmen's schedule: Sunday: *Mom's for dinner, 4:30,* Monday: *study for final exam,* Tuesday: *free,* Wednesday: *dinner with Emma,* Thursday: *free,* Friday: *class party at 8:00,* Saturday: *free*

Yoshiko's schedule: Sunday: *packing all day, 4:30,* Monday: *study for final exam,* Tuesday: *dinner with Nancy, 6:30,* Wednesday: *free,* Thursday: *free,* Friday: *class party at 8:00,* Saturday: *disco with friends*

Practice 2

1. Have students read the directions.
2. Pair Work. Have students review the times Carmen and Yoshiko are both busy (every night except Thursday night). Have them discuss their schedules and figure out when they are both free. Next have them decide what type of restaurant they will go to and make plans.
3. Check by calling on various pairs to tell the class what they arranged to do.

LET'S TALK 6

Student Book, page 103.
1. Give students time to read the directions. Explain that *enjoy each other's company* means *enjoy being together.*

2. Model the opener: *We should get together some time. What do you like doing outside class?* Have students repeat.
3. Separate the students into pairs.
4. Pair Work. Have students work together to decide on a plan and make the arrangements. Circulate and assist with vocabulary as neeeded.

Note: If students have been working with the same partners throughout the unit, have them change partners for this exercise. Point out that people can go out together just as friends.

5. Ask volunteers to explain to the class where they will go and what they will do. Encourage classmates to ask questions and seek clarification as needed *(What time are you going? Where are you going to meet?).*

REVIEW (UNITS 4–6)

Student Book, page 104.
1. Give students time to read the situation and the directions. Explain that a "Getting To Know You" party might take place at the beginning of a school year or at a company where there are new employees.
2. Direct students' attention to the art. Ask students to describe what activities they see.
3. Model an example opener: *Hi. This party is a great idea, isn't it? I'm* (your name), *and I really like* (going to the movies).
4. Ask the students to stand up and prepare to circulate around the classroom as if they were at a party.
5. Class Work. Have students circulate around the room, find a partner, introduce themselves, and try to make arrangements to go somewhere together. Remind students that if they can't find something they and their partners both like, they should change partners.

Note: Students should do this exercise based on their true interests.

6. Have pairs report to the class on the activites they have chosen and the time and place they are going to meet.

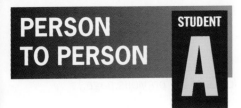

PERSON TO PERSON

STUDENT A

(Student A looks at this page. Student B looks at the next page.)

📼 Carmen and Yoshiko want to get together sometime this week, but they're having difficulty finding a time when both of them are free.

Practice 1

Listen and fill in Carmen's appointment book.

Practice 2

Review the times that Carmen and Yoshiko are both busy. Then continue their conversation. Find out when they are both free. Decide what type of restaurant they'll go to, and arrange a place and a time to meet.

PERSON TO PERSON

STUDENT B

(Student B looks at this page. Student A looks at the previous page.)

Carmen and Yoshiko want to get together sometime this week, but they're having difficulty finding a time when both of them are free.

Practice 1

Listen and fill in Yoshiko's appointment book.

J A N U A R Y

Monday 10

Tuesday 11

Wednesday 12

Thursday 13

J A N U A R Y

Friday 14

Saturday 15

Cleaning and packing — all day! **Sunday 16**

January

S	M	T	W	T	F	S
2	3	4	5	6	7	1 8
9	10	11	12	13	14	15
16	17	18	19	20	21	22
23	24	25	26	27	28	29
30	31					

Practice 2

Review the times that Carmen and Yoshiko are both busy. Then continue their conversation. Find out when they are both free. Decide what type of restaurant they'll go to, and arrange a place and a time to meet.

COMPONENTS

Student Book, pages 49–56
Let's Talk 7, Student Book page 105
Cassette/CD
Optional Activity 7, page 133

OBJECTIVES

Functions: Talking to salespeople, getting and giving help, getting information about items in a store, asking prices and colors, comparing things

Topics: types of stores, refund/exchange policies, cash or charge, trying on clothes

Structures:

- Can/Could: Can I help you with something?/ Could you help me? / What can I do for you?
- Count nouns: a cup of coffee / a movie ticket / a golf bag
- *Yes/No* questions: Do you have this in size 10? Do you carry this in a medium?
- This/that/these/those: How much is this radio? / Could you tell me the price of these speakers?
- This/that comes in a medium. These/those come in black and white.
- Comparatives: Which hat do you like better? / I like the red boots better than the white ones. The green hat is fancier than the yellow one.

Pronunciation Focus: In American and Canadian English, *r* is pronounced after a vowel; for example, *sweater.*

Listen to This: Listening for specific information; listening to fill in a chart

CONVERSATION 1
COULD YOU HELP ME?

Prelistening Questions

1. With books closed, read the title of the conversation and the prelistening questions. Elicit an answer to each question from a student volunteer.

2. Pair Work. Have students open their books and take turns asking and answering the questions. Have them cover the photograph and the conversation first. Circulate and assist with vocabulary as needed.

3. Elicit answers from several volunteers. Develop this into a whole-class discussion of shopping in department stores vs. specialty shops. Make a chart on the board in which you write the advantages and disadvantages of each. Next, discuss paying in cash vs. using a charge card, following the same procedure.

Culture Note: There are many ways to pay for things. *To pay cash* usually means to use currency or a personal check. *A charge card* means a bank card such as Visa or MasterCard, which can be used at many places, or a charge card for a specific store such as a *Sears* charge card, which can only be used at a Sears store. A common question in stores is: *Will that be cash or charge?*

4. Have students uncover the photograph. Give students time to study it. Ask students to speculate:
   - *Where are these people?*
   - *What do they want to buy?*
   - *What is their relationship?*

Ask students to support their answers with specific information (e.g., *They want to buy something for him because they are in the men's department.*).

Vocabulary

Introduce these words and phrases now or after the students listen to the conversation.

have (it): alternative way to say *sell* (it) or *carry* (it)

What can I do for you?: alternative way to say *How can I help you?*

come (in): *made* (in); *Does this sweater come in red? / Is it made in red?*

take (it): *buy* (it)

Presentation

1. With books closed, play the recording or read the conversation at normal speed.

2. Ask the following general comprehension questions:
   - *What does he want to buy?* (a sports shirt)
   - *Does he find one he wants?* (Yes)

3. Say: *Listen again. This time listen for more details about the shirt.* Play or read again, pausing for choral repetition.

4. Ask the following questions:
   - *What department are they looking for?* (the men's department)
   - *Where is it?* (by the escalator)
   - *How much is the shirt?* ($19.98)
   - *Do they think it is too expensive?* (No)
   - *What size does the man need?* (medium)
   - *Does he decide to buy the shirt?* (Yes)

Elicit answers from various volunteers or have students tell their partners the answers.

Language Note: On the board write: *Does this shirt come in medium? / Here's a medium.* Point out that the article is optional here. We can say *come in a medium* or *come in medium*. We usually keep the article with *Here's a medium* because it is a short form of *Here's a medium (shirt).*

5. Paired Reading. Have students read the conversation, switching roles.

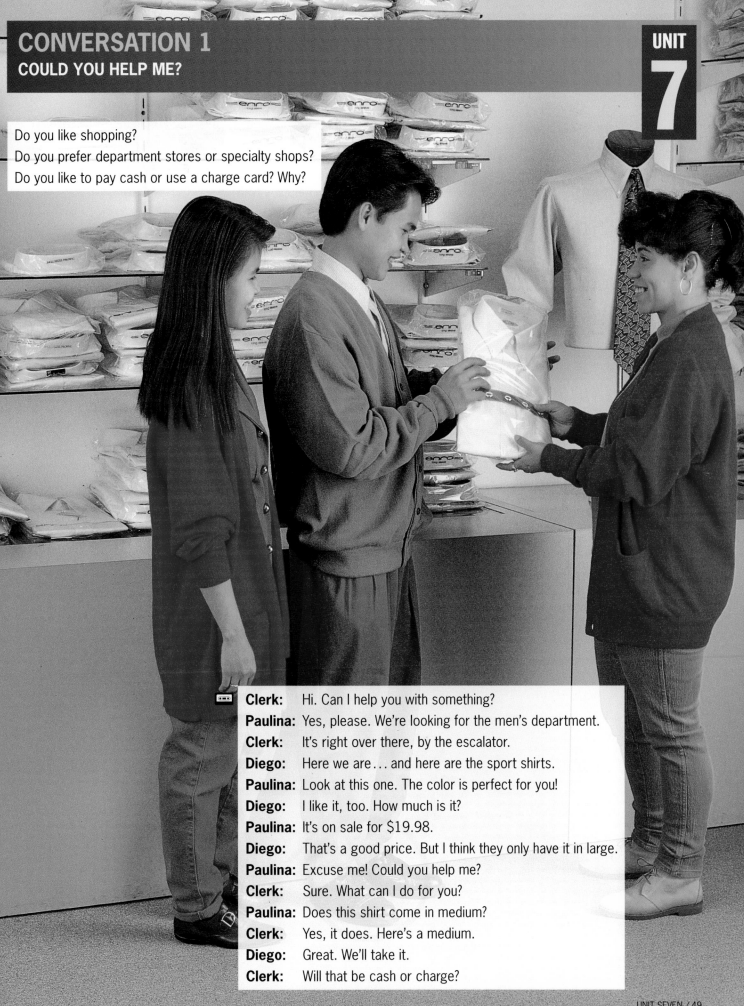

Do you like shopping?

Do you prefer department stores or specialty shops?

Do you like to pay cash or use a charge card? Why?

Clerk: Hi. Can I help you with something?

Paulina: Yes, please. We're looking for the men's department.

Clerk: It's right over there, by the escalator.

Diego: Here we are… and here are the sport shirts.

Paulina: Look at this one. The color is perfect for you!

Diego: I like it, too. How much is it?

Paulina: It's on sale for $19.98.

Diego: That's a good price. But I think they only have it in large.

Paulina: Excuse me! Could you help me?

Clerk: Sure. What can I do for you?

Paulina: Does this shirt come in medium?

Clerk: Yes, it does. Here's a medium.

Diego: Great. We'll take it.

Clerk: Will that be cash or charge?

1. GETTING AND GIVING HELP

◆ Excuse me. | Could | you help me?
| Can |

✧ Certainly. | What can I help you with?
Sure. | What can I do for you?

◆ Can I help you with something?
Is there something I can help you with?

✧ No, thanks. I'm just looking.
Yes, please. I'm looking for the *men's sweaters*.

Practice 1

You are shopping in a department store. Your partner is a sales clerk. Ask him/her for help.

Practice 2

You are a clerk in a department store. Your partner is a customer. Ask if he/she needs help.

2. GETTING INFORMATION

◆ Do you | have | this | in *size 10?*   ✧ Yes, we do.
| carry | these | in *green?*   No, I'm sorry. We don't.

◆ Does this | come in | *medium?*   ✧ Yes, | *it does.*
Do these | | *beige?* | *they do.*
| | *size 8?*
| | a | *larger* | size?   ✧ No, I'm sorry. | *It doesn't.*
| | | *smaller* | | *They don't.*

Practice

Your partner is a salesperson. Get his/her attention and ask for information about two of the items below. Then reverse roles.

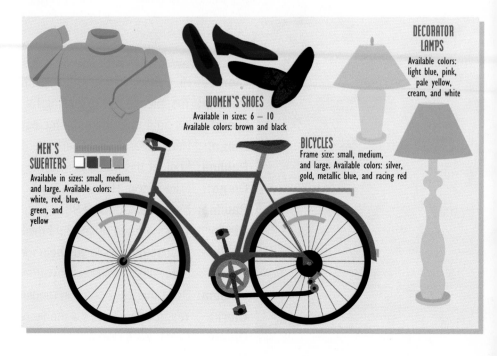

DECORATOR LAMPS
Available colors: light blue, pink, pale yellow, cream, and white

WOMEN'S SHOES
Available in sizes: 6 — 10
Available colors: brown and black

BICYCLES
Frame size: small, medium, and large. Available colors: silver, gold, metallic blue, and racing red

MEN'S SWEATERS
Available in sizes: small, medium, and large. Available colors: white, red, blue, green, and yellow

GIVE IT A TRY

1. GETTING AND GIVING HELP

1. Direct students' attention to the function box. Give students time to read over the examples.

2. Model the examples; have students repeat.

Pronunciation Note: Blending of *could you*. In rapid speech, *you* is often reduced to */yuh/*. *Could you* is often blended so that it sounds like */cu-juh/*. Write the following question on the board.

Could you help me?

Exaggerate the blending as you model the question.

3. Model the questions and answers in the function box again. Emphasize the regular rhythm by clapping your hands (*WHAT can I HELP you with? / WHAT can I DO for you? / Can I HELP you with SOMEthing?/ Is there SOMEthing I can HELP you with? / I'm looking for the MEN'S sweaters*, etc.).

Practice 1

1. Explain the activity. Ask students to name some things they might buy in a department store. Make a list on the board. Then make a list of the departments in which these items would be found. (*Department names: infants, boys, girls, women's, men's, shoe, sporting goods, jewelry, furniture, toys, housewares, appliances,* etc.)

2. Pair Work. Have students role-play getting and giving help in a department store. One student is the shopper, the other is the clerk.

Practice 2

1. Explain the activity.

2. Pair Work. Have students switch roles and continue practicing the role play.

3. Ask several pairs to demonstrate for the class.

2. GETTING INFORMATION

1. Direct students' attention to the function box. Give students time to read over the examples.

2. Model the examples; have students repeat.

Pronunciation Note: Stress on content words. Heavier stress is placed on the content words. As a result, the beginning of the question (*Do you have... / Does this come in...*, etc.) is reduced. Write the following questions on the board and mark the stress.

Do you have this in SIZE TEN?

Do you carry this in GREEN?

Do these come in BEIGE?

Do these come in SIZE EIGHT?

Model the questions, say the first part of the question softly and the content word(s) loudly to emphasize the stress. Continue with the other examples in the function box.

3. Ask pairs to model asking and answering the questions in the function box for the class. Point out that we use falling intonation in the responses (*Yes, it does. / Yes, they do*, etc).

Practice

1. Explain the activity. To demonstrate the gestures a shopper might use, pick up a student's jacket, point to it, look at the student and ask: *Does this come in medium?* Walk around the classroom and continue, asking about other personal belongings of the students. Tell students to use props as they do the role play. Emphasize that they should make eye contact as well.

2. Pair Work. Have students take turns asking for and giving information about different items in the department store. Circulate and assist students with the gestures as needed.

3. Ask several pairs to demonstrate for the class. Make sure they use gestures and props.

3. ASKING PRICES

1. Direct students' attention to the function box. Give students time to read over the examples.

2. Model the examples; have students repeat.

Culture Note: Give students a quick review of how to talk about prices. Write the following prices on the board: *$1.98, $100, $39.95, $250.* Model how these prices are usually said; have students repeat chorally. Point out that *$1.98* = A dollar ninety-eight, not ONE dollar and ninety-eight cents, *$100* = A hundred dollars, not ONE hundred dollars, *$39.95* = thirty-nine ninety-five, *$250* = two hundred and fifty or often two-fifty. Explain that we assume we know by the object we're talking about whether it is a $2.50 object or a $250 object. Some students may know the colloquial term *bucks*, which is used for *dollars.* Emphasize that they are better off not using *bucks* because they may use it in a context in which it is not appropriate.

Practice 1

1. Explain the activity. Model the prices listed under Student B; have students repeat chorally and individually.

2. Pair Work. Have students take turns asking about the prices of four of the items listed. Circulate and check pronunciation.

3. Check by having students do a chain drill. Select a student *(Hiroko)* to ask the first question. Tell *(Hiroko)* to direct the question to another student. *(How much are these shoes, Jiro?)* *(Jiro)* answers the question *(They're fifty-nine ninety-five)* and asks a third student about another item. Have students continue with the remaining items. Note: Having the students cue each other *after* they ask the questions, promotes active listening by all of the students.

Practice 2

1. Explain the activity. Ask volunteers to name items they often buy. Model an example: *How much is a cup of coffee?* Explain that they should use indefinite articles here *(a/an)* rather than *this/these* because these are general questions.

Note: Point out that students are to talk about the prices in the currency they normally use.

2. Pair Work. Have students ask their partners about the prices of four items they often buy, switching roles. Circulate and check students' pronunciation.

3. Check by calling on new pairs to demonstrate for the class. Do not have students perform with the partners with whom they have been practicing.

LISTEN TO THIS

1. Explain the activity. Give students time to look at the chart. Make sure students understand that *size available* means the sizes of that item that the store carries. *Color available* means the colors of that item the store carries. On the board, write: *S, M, L.* Tell students to abbreviate *small, medium,* and *large* as they fill in the chart.

2. Play the recording or read the conversations at normal speed as the students fill in the chart.

3. Play or read the conversations again as students check their answers.

4. Pair Work. Have students check their work by comparing their charts.

5. Ask volunteers for the answers.

Answers:

Ski jacket	Leather gloves	Golf bag
10	M	S
4, 6, 8, 10	S, M, L	L
pink	tan	not given
yellow, red, pink light blue, black	brown, black	red & black, white & red white & navy
$160	$25	$150
no	yes	no

Language Note: Point out that *I'll think about it* and *Thanks anyway* are common ways to say *I'm not going to buy it now.*

6. Play or read the conversations again for a final check.

3. ASKING PRICES

◆ How much	is *this (radio)/it?*		◇ (It's)	$59.98.
	are *these (speakers)/they?*		(They're)	$299.
Could	you tell me the price of	*this radio?*	(It's)	$129.
Can		*these speakers?*	(They're)	$600.

Practice 1

Ask your partner the price of four of the following items. Then reverse roles.

Student A
1. shoes
2. CD player
3. pen
4. postcards
5. silk jacket
6. T-shirts
7. cassette tape
8. silver picture frame

Student B
1. $59.95
2. $299
3. $1.59
4. 10 for $1
5. $235
6. 3 for $19
7. $7.99
8. $89.98

Practice 2

Ask classmates for the prices of four items that you often buy in your city. Use the list below or think of your own.

1. a cup of coffee
2. bus fare from home to school
3. a CD
4. a Coke

5. a movie ticket
6. an ice-cream cone
7. a video rental
8. a pack of gum

LISTEN TO THIS

A man and his wife are in a department store buying Christmas gifts for their three children. Listen and write down the information they get from the sales clerk. Put a check (✔) if they buy the item.

	Ski Jacket	Leather gloves	Golf bags
Size needed			
Size available			
Color wanted			
Color available			
Price			
Bought Item			

CONVERSATION 2
THAT COLOR LOOKS BETTER.

Why do you return things to a store?
What is an exchange?
What is a refund?

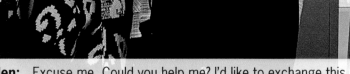

Allen: Excuse me. Could you help me? I'd like to exchange this sweater.

Clerk: What's the problem with it?

Allen: It was a birthday gift, but I don't really like it. I think I want something plainer.

Clerk: I see . . . Well, why don't you look around?

Marta: I like these two, Allen. Try them on.

Allen: OK. So, which one do you like?

Marta: I like the red one much better than the black one.

Allen: Really? How come? I kind of like the black one.

Marta: The red one is longer and a little looser so it will be more comfortable.

Allen: True . . . and it feels softer.

Clerk: And that color looks better on you. Actually, it's a better quality and it's the same price as the sweater you're exchanging.

Allen: You've talked me into it! I'll take this one instead.

Clerk: No problem. I'll switch them for you.

Pronunciation Focus

In American and Canadian English, *r* is pronounced after a vowel. Listen and practice these words.

sweater	more	birthday
plainer	looser	softer
longer	better	color

CONVERSATION 2
THAT COLOR LOOKS BETTER.

Prelistening Questions

1. Have students open their books and cover the conversation. Read the title of the conversation and the first prelistening question.

2. Direct students' attention to the photograph. Ask students to speculate why the man wants to return the sweater, who gave it to him, and for what occasion (a birthday, Christmas, etc.). Ask volunteers for their ideas.

3. Read the other prelistening questions. Elicit answers from volunteers for each question.

Culture Note: Explain that *to exchange* (a sweater) means to return it to the store and get another one in a different size or color, etc. It can also be returned for a *refund*. There are different types of refunds: cash, store credit, and a credit card credit. A store credit means you can buy something else in that store or have the price of the item credited to your store charge acount, whereas a credit card credit refunds the money to you on your credit card account. Most stores require a sales slip for a refund. There is also usually a time limit of 30 days on returning items. Ask students how this compares with the system in their culture.

Vocabulary

Introduce these words and phrases now or after the students listen to the conversation.

plainer: simpler. Clothes that are plain are sometimes described as quiet, whereas clothes that have a detailed pattern are described as busy.

talk me into it: to convince someone to do something

to switch: to exchange

Presentation

1. With books open, play the recording or read the conversation at normal speed.

2. Ask the following general comprehension questions:
   - *What does the man want to exchange?* (a sweater)
   - *Why?* (He doesn't like it.)

3. Say: *Listen again. This time listen for details about the sweaters he looks at.*

4. Play or read the conversation again, pausing for choral repetition.

5. Ask the following questions:
   - *What colors are the two sweaters the man tries on?* (black and red)
   - *Which one does the woman like better?* (the red one)
   - *Which one does he like better?* (the black one)
   - *Why does she like the red one?* (It's longer and looser / more comfortable)
   - *Which sweater is softer?* (the red one)
   - *Which color looks better on him?* (red)
   - *Which sweater is the same price as the sweater he is exchanging?* (the red one)
   - *Which sweater does he decide to take?* (the red one)

Elicit answers from volunteers or have students tell their partners the answers.

6. Pronunciation Focus. Explain that in American and Canadian English, *r* is pronounced after a vowel. Model the examples: *sweater, plainer, longer, softer, color, birthday.* Have the students repeat chorally and individually.

7. Play or read the conversation again as the students follow along in their books. Tell students to pay attention to the *r* sound.

8. Paired Reading. Have students read the conversation, switching roles.

9. Ask several pairs to demonstrate the conversation for the class.

GIVE IT A TRY

1. COMPARING THINGS (1)

1. Direct students' attention to the function box. Give students time to read over the examples.

2. Model the examples; have students repeat.

Pronunciation Note: Review of sentence stress. Speakers emphasize the words that are most important by stressing them. In comparisons, the qualities being compared receive the stress. On the board, write the following sentences:

> I like the GREEN hat better than the YELLOW one.
> I like the RED boots better than the WHITE ones.

As you model the statements, clap your hands on *green, yellow, red,* and *white.*

Language Note: Point out that a speaker can drop the second half of a comparison (*...than the yellow one.*) if the listener knows from the context what is being compared. A speaker can also delete the nouns on both sides of the comparison as in *I like these better than those* if it is obvious from the context what is being compared. Point out that in this case the stress falls on *these* and *those.* Model; have students repeat.

3. Pair Work. Have students practice the examples in the function box, switching roles.

Practice

1. Direct students' attention to the pictures. Explain the activity.

2. Pair Work. Have students take turns asking each other which items they prefer.

3. Ask several pairs to demonstrate for the class.

4. Expansion. Bring in pictures of items clothing from magazines or advertisements in the newspaper. Ask students to compare the items following the pattern in the activity.

2. COMPARING THINGS (2)

1. Direct students' attention to the function box. Give students time to read over the examples.

Pronunciation Note: Review of stress and rhythm. A speaker places stress on words that are most important. Here the speaker stresses *Why* in order to focus on the reason for the listener's preferences. As a result, *do you like* is reduced. On the board, write the following questions:

> WHY do you like the GREEN hat better?
> WHY do you like the RED boots better?

Exaggerate the stress by tapping out the rhythm as you model the questions. Have students repeat.

Language Note: Explain that *I like them* can be deleted because it is obvious from the context what is being compared.

2. Ask pairs to model the examples in the function box; have students repeat chorally.

Language Note: Remind students of the rules concerning the formation of comparative adjectives. All one-syllable adjectives (*old, small, big,* etc.) and two-syllable adjectives ending in -y (*pretty, heavy,* etc.) use *-er than* in forming the comparative (*This house is older than that one. / This dress is prettier than that one.*). Two-syllable adjectives not ending in -y (*crowded, polite,* etc.) and all adjectives with three or more syllables (*interesting, beautiful,* etc.) use *more than...* to form the comparative (*This book is more interesting than that one. / The pink dress is more beautiful than the white one.*).

Practice

1. Explain the activity. Give students time to look at the pictures.

2. Direct students' attention to the list of possible reasons. Give students time to read over the list. Model some of the pairs of adjectives; have students repeat chorally and individually. Ask students if they have any reasons they want to add to the list. Write them on the board.

3. Give students time to read over the example conversation. Ask a pair of volunteers to model the example, comparing two items in the pictures.

4. Pair Work. Have students take turns asking about and describing their preferences. Circulate and assist with pronunciation and vocabulary.

5. Ask several pairs to perform for the class.

1. COMPARING THINGS (1)

✦ Which | *hat* | do you like better?
| *boots* |

✧ I like | *the green hat* | better than | *the yellow* one.
| *this hat* | | *that one.*

✧ I like | *the red boots* | better than | *the white* ones.
| *these boots* | | *those.*

Ask your partner which one(s) he/she prefers.

2. COMPARING THINGS (2)

✦ Why do you like *the green hat* better?
✧ (I like it) because it's *fancier* than the *yellow* one.

✦ Why do you like the *red boots* better?
✧ (I like them) because they're *more stylish* than the *white* ones.

Look at the pictures above. Ask your partner which item(s) he/she prefers, and then ask why. Then reverse roles. Ask and answer like this:

Student A: Which .... do you like better?
Student B: I like the .... better than the .... one(s).
Student A: Why? / How come?
Student B: Because ....

Here are some possible reasons:

fancier/plainer, bigger/smaller, longer/shorter, looser/tighter,
more expensive/less expensive, more colorful, more comfortable, a nicer color,
brighter, softer, better quality

3. RETURNING THINGS

◆ I'd like | a refund, | please.
　　　　 | to get a refund,
　　　　 | to return this *(sweater)*,
　　　　 | to exchange this *(blouse)*,

◇ What's | the reason?
　　　　 | the problem with it?

◆ It's | *too big/small.*
　　　 | *the wrong color.*
　It doesn't fit.
　It was a gift. I already have one.
　I don't really like it.

◇ Of course. We can | exchange it.
　　　　　　　　 | give you a refund.
　I'm sorry. There are no refunds or exchanges.

Practice

Your partner is a sales clerk. Choose two of the items below and ask for a refund or an exchange. Then reverse roles.

LISTEN TO THIS

Three customers have items to return to a department store. Listen and write down the things they want to return, the reason, and the result.

	Item	Reason	Result
Customer 1			
Customer 2			
Customer 3			

3. RETURNING THINGS

1. Direct students' attention to the function boxes. Give students time to read over the examples.

2. Model the examples; have students repeat chorally.

Pronunciation Note: Review of rhythm. The rhythm in English is regular. In order to maintain the rhythm, some words are reduced. On the board, write the following statements:

> I'd like a refund.
> I'd like to get a refund.

Model, exaggerating the stress on *like* and *refund* and thereby demonstrating that *to get a* is reduced in the second statement.

Write additional examples on the board marking the stress:

> It's too big.
> It was a gift.
> I don't really like it.

Model, exaggerating the rhythm; have students repeat.

3. Pair Work. Have students practice the examples in the function boxes, switching roles.

Culture Note: Most items can be returned. The exceptions are items of clothing such as swimming suits or underwear. A store will usually post a sign stating that an item cannot be returned. In addition, some sale items and final markdown items cannot be returned. A final markdown item is an item whose price has been reduced more than once.

Practice

1. Explain the activity. Give students time to look at the pictures.

Language Note: *Not my style* means something doesn't fit with the person's personality or taste in clothing. The expression *It's not me* as in *This sweater is not me* has the same meaning.

2. Pair Work. Have students practice returning things, switching roles.

3. Ask several pairs to demonstrate for the class. Encourage students to use props if possible.

LISTEN TO THIS

1. Direct students' attention to the chart. Explain the activity. Check students' understanding of *result*.

2. Play the recording or read the conversations at normal speed as the students fill in the chart.

3. Play the recording or read the conversations again as the students check their answers.

4. Pair Work. Have students compare their answers.

5. Check answers by asking: *What did the first customer want to return?* (A coat) *Why?* (It is too small.) *What was the result?* (a refund) Repeat the questions for customers 2 and 3.

Answers:

Customer 1:	*A coat / too small / a refund*
Customer 2:	*A cassette tape / too noisy / no exchange*
Customer 3:	*A sweater / doesn't like the color / exchange made*

OPTIONAL ACTIVITY 7: I Want To Return It. See *Teacher's Notes, page 125, and Activity Sheet, page 133.*

PERSON TO PERSON

Practice 1

1. Divide the class into pairs and have students decide who will be Student A and who will be Student B.
2. Have students listen to the introduction. Then give them time to read over the items of clothing Kerry and Joan compare in the conversation.
3. Play or read the conversation as the students write down the comments. (Student A: Joan's comments, Student B: Kerry's comments)
4. Have students listen again to check their answers.
5. Pair Work. Have students compare what they wrote and decide which items they think Kerry will buy. Circulate and help as needed.
6. Check answers by asking one student to tell you Kerry's comments on each item of clothing and another student to tell you Joan's comments. Then have several volunteers explain which items of clothing they think Kerry will buy. Ask them to use specific information from the conversation to support their conclusions.

Answers:
Joan's comments:
Black pants: nice, go with everything
Pink pants: much nicer color
Purple sweater: too plain
White sweater: fancier, could wear in the evening
Suede jacket: beautiful, but too heavy
Cotton jacket: much lighter
Kerry's comments:
Black pants: too hot, already have black
Pink pants: feel like better quality
Purple sweater: likes it; looser / more comfortable
White sweater: agrees it's fancier, but already has fancy one
Suede jacket: too expensive
Cotton jacket: a lot more useful

Practice 2

1. Explain the activity. On the board, write: *H = High, L = Long, D = Deep, W = Wide*. If possible, explain using a piece of realia (a backpack, a briefcase, a handbag, etc.).

2. Pair Work. Have students take turns getting and giving information about the suitcase and garment bag. (Student A: gets information about the suitcase, Student B: about the garment bag.)
3. Check by asking volunteers the information: *What is the suitcase made of? What sizes does it come in?* etc.
Note: The sizes given are in inches. Below are the approximate measurements in centimeters.
Suitcase (Regular: 38 cm H x 55 cm L x 23 cm D)
     (Large: 50 cm H x 65 cm L x 23 cm D)
Garment Bag (Regular: 99 cm H x 61 cm W x 8 cm D)
     (Large: 119 cm H x 62 cm W x 9 cm D)

Practice 3

1. Explain the activity.
2. Pair Work. Have students work together to decide which piece of luggage Kerry should buy for the trip.
3. Ask volunteers what they decided and why.

LET'S TALK 7

Student Book, page 105.
1. Give students time to read the directions. Check students' understanding of the directions by asking: *Who is getting married? Who is going to get her a gift? What do you need to compare? What do you need to decide?*
Note: Discuss wedding gifts. Explain that in North America a typical wedding gift is usually something for the home, something meant to last a long time, such as kitchenware, linens, or a vase.
2. Model the opener *Which one of these gifts do you think is best? Does anyone have another idea?* Have students repeat.
3. Divide the class into groups of four.
4. Group Work. Have students work together to decide which gift to buy. Circulate and make sure students give reasons for their choices.
5. Group Work. Have two groups compare their decisions.
6. Ask volunteers from different groups to present their decisions to the class.

(Student A looks at this page. Student B looks at the next page.)

▭ Kerry is going to Europe this summer for two weeks and needs to buy some new clothes. Listen as she and her friend, Joan, compare each item.

Practice 1

Write down Joan's comments.

Black pants ....

Pink pants ....

Purple sweater ....

White sweater ....

Suede jacket ....

Cotton jacket ....

Discuss Joan and Kerry's comments with your partner. Which items do you think Kerry will buy?

Practice 2

Ask your partner questions to get information about the suitcase below. Your partner will ask you about the garment bag.

Suitcase
Materials: ....

Sizes: ....

....

Prices: ....

....

Colors: ....

....

Garment bag
Materials: Nylon and leather
Sizes: Regular (39"Hx24"Wx3"D)
        Long (47"Hx24.5"Wx3.5"D)
Prices: Regular $160
        Long $170
Colors: Burgundy, Navy, Green,
        Black

Practice 3

Kerry will be traveling by plane, train, and car. She only wants to carry one piece of luggage. Look at the descriptions above and decide with your partner which piece she should buy.

(Student B looks at this page. Student A looks at the previous page.)

▭ Kerry is going to Europe this summer for two weeks and needs to buy some new clothes. Listen as she and her friend, Joan, compare each item.

Practice 1

Write down Kerry's comments.

Black pants ....

Pink pants ....

Purple sweater ....

White sweater ....

Suede jacket ....

Cotton jacket ....

Discuss Joan and Kerry's comments with your partner. Which items do you think Kerry will buy?

Practice 2

Ask your partner questions to get information about the garment bag below. Your partner will ask you about the suitcase.

Suitcase
Materials: Nylon and leather
Sizes:　Regular (15"Hx21.5"Lx9"D)
　　　　Large (19.5"Hx25.5"Lx9"D)
Prices: Regular $84
　　　　Large $105
Colors: Burgundy, Navy, Green,
　　　　Black

Garment bag
Materials: ....
Sizes: ....
....
Prices: ....
....
Colors: ....
....

Practice 3

Kerry will be traveling by plane, train, and car. She only wants to carry one piece of luggage. Look at the descriptions above and decide with your partner which piece she should buy.

COMPONENTS

Student Book, pages 57–64
Let's Talk 8, Student Book page 106
Cassette/CD
Optional Activity 8, page 134

OBJECTIVES

Functions: Discussing the menu, ordering, specifying wants, asking about wants, offering service

Topics: ordering food in restaurants, restaurant menus, service

Structures:
- What are you going to have? / I think I'll have …
- Would you care for anything to drink? / Would you like something for dessert? / Would you like anything else?
- I'll have (a steak), please… / I'd like (soup), please.
- Shall I get (your coffee) now? / Would you like to have (your coffee) now?

Pronunciation Focus: Reduced form of *would you*: *wouldya*.

Listen to This: Listening for specific information; filling in charts

CONVERSATION 1
AND WHAT WOULD YOU LIKE?

Prelistening Questions

1. With books closed, read the title of the conversation and the prelistening questions. For each question, elicit an answer from a student volunteer.

2. Ask: *What kinds of restaurants are there?* On the board, help students make a list (*Greek, French, Italian, Japanese,* etc.).

Culture Note: In North America, there is a wide range of restaurants, from fast-food resturants such as McDonalds to very formal restaurants. Some restaurants have all-you-can-eat buffets where the customer pays a set price and eats whatever he or she chooses. Some places are self-service, some have table service only, and others have a combination of the above; for example, the customer might order at a window, then go to a table where the food is served by a waitperson.

3. Pair Work. Have students open their books, cover the conversation, and take turns asking and answering the questions. Elicit answers to the questions from various volunteers.

Note: If time permits, hold a class discussion on the criteria the students use for choosing a restaurant (type of food, atmosphere, cost, reputation, etc.).

4. Direct students' attention to the photograph. Ask students to speculate:

- *What kind of restaurant is this (formal/informal)?*
- *What type of food does it serve?*
- *Who are these people?*
- *What is their relationship?*

Elicit answers from several volunteers for each question. Maintain a rapid pace.

Note: Encourage students to study the photograph carefully and use their imaginations here.

Vocabulary

Introduce these words and phrases now or after the students listen to the conversation.

(What are you) having: ordering, eating

I feel like a steak: short form for *I feel like having a steak.*

medium-rare: instruction for how meat is to be cooked. Ranges from *rare* to *well-done*

clam chowder: a type of soup made with clams and potatoes, usually in a milk base

Presentation

1. Ask the following prelistening questions:

- *What do you think the woman is going to order?*
- *What do you think the man is going to order?*

Emphasize that they should focus on the main course only (for example, *chicken, pizza,* etc., and not the food that comes with it).

2. With books closed, play the recording or read the conversation at normal speed.

3. Ask the following general comprehension questions:
What is she going to have as a main course? (spaghetti)
What is he going to have as a main course? (a steak)

4. Say: *Listen again. This time listen for what else they order.* Play or read again, pausing for choral repetition.

5. Ask the following questions:

- *What else does she order?* (a salad)
- *What kind of dressing?* (oil and vinegar)
- *What kind of soup does he want?* (clam chowder)
- *What else does he order?* (a baked potato and carrots)
- *Do they order anything to drink?* (No)

Elicit the answers from various volunteers or have students tell their partners the answers.

6. Paired Reading. Have students read the conversation, switching roles.

Culture Note: *I'll be right back with your soup and salad.* It is customary to bring soup, salad, and drinks first. Point out that as a waitperson takes an order he or she will usually ask *Do you want that now or with your meal?* The customer then can decide when to be served.

CONVERSATION 1
AND WHAT WOULD YOU LIKE?

How often do you eat out at restaurants?
What is your favorite kind of restaurant?

Ted: Everything looks good. What are you going to have, Julie?

Julie: I think I'll have the spaghetti and a salad. How about you? What are you having?

Ted: Spaghetti sounds good, but I feel like a steak. I guess we're ready to order. Excuse me!

Waitress: Good evening. Have you decided yet?

Julie: Yes. I'll have the spaghetti and a salad.

Waitress: And what kind of dressing would you like on your salad?

Julie: I'd like oil and vinegar.

Waitress: OK. And what would you like, sir?

Ted: I'd like a steak, medium-rare, please.

Waitress: Would you like soup or salad with that?

Ted: What kind of soup do you have tonight?

Waitress: Cream of mushroom and clam chowder.

Ted: Clam chowder, please. And I'll have a baked potato and carrots.

Waitress: I'll be right back with your soup and salad.

Julie: Thank you.

1. DISCUSSING THE MENU

✦ What are you | going to have, | *Julie?*
| having, |

✧ (I think) I'll have *the spaghetti* and a *salad*.

You're at a restaurant having breakfast with a friend. Ask what he/she wants to eat and drink. He/she answers using the cues below.

1. scrambled eggs, home fries, and wheat toast/tea
2. a cheese omelette and sausages/a large glass of milk
3. some cereal/a small glass of orange juice/some cocoa
4. fried eggs and bacon/a large glass of apple juice
5. the blueberry pancakes/coffee

Try it again. This time, choose from the menu below.

GOOD MORNING MENU

Breakfast served from 7:00 to 11:30 A.M.

EGGS & OMELETTES

Eggs (2) **$3.95**
Fried, Scrambled, Poached or Boiled

Omelettes **$4.95**
Fluffy 3 egg omelette-Ham, Cheese or Western

All egg orders are served with bacon or toast.

OTHER SPECIALTIES

Pancakes **$5.25**
Waffles **$5.25**
French Toast **$4.75**

FROM OUR BAKE SHOP

Fresh Muffins **$1.50**
Bran, Blueberry, or Oatmeal

Croissant **$2.50**
Served with jam

Toast **$1.25**
Served with jam

BEVERAGES

Juice ....
*small... .75 large... $1.25
Orange, Apple, Tomato or Grapefruit*

Milk ....
small... .85 large... $1.50

Pot of Tea.................... **$1.25**
Coffee.......................... **$1.00**
Cocoa.......................... **$1.75**

2. ORDERING

✦ What | would you | like, *ma'am?*
| will | have, *sir?*
Are you ready to order, | *miss?*
Have you decided yet, |

✧ I'd like | *a steak, medium-rare*, please.
I'll have |
Could we have a few more minutes, please?

Look at the menu again. Choose something and the waiter/waitress will take your order.

GIVE IT A TRY

1. DISCUSSING THE MENU

1. Direct students' attention to the function box. Give students time to read over the examples.

2. Model the examples; have students repeat.

Pronunciation Note: Blending of *going to*. In rapid speech, *going to* is often pronounced /gonna/. Write the following question on the board:

What are you going to have, Julie?

Model; have students repeat chorally.

Language Note: There are various ways to talk about the future in English. Here, *What are you having?* (present continuous) has the same meaning as *What are you going to have?*

3. Pair Work. Have students practice the example in the function box, switching roles. Circulate and assist with the pronunciation.

Practice 1————————————

1. Explain the activity. Give students time to read over the list of cues. Check understanding of vocabulary: *home fries* are fried potatoes; *toast* is typically made with white bread unless the customer specifies wheat or rye; *cereal* can be hot or cold.

2. Pair Work. Have students practice discussing the menu, switching roles.

3. Ask several pairs to role-play for the class.

Practice 2————————————

1. Direct students' attention to the menu. For scanning practice and to familiarize students with the menu, ask the following questions: *When is breakfast served?* (from 7:00–11:30 A.M.) *What is served with eggs?* (bacon and toast) *How many kinds of muffins do they have?* (3) *How many kinds of juice do they have?* (4) *How much is the french toast?* ($4.75) *How much are the waffles?* ($5.25) *Which is more expensive, coffee or tea?* (tea) *Which is more expensive, an omelette or two eggs?* (an omelette)

Culture Note: When an order automatically comes with certain foods, a customer sometimes prefers substitutes. A customer might ask: *Can I have a muffin instead of (the) toast?* Usually a restaurant will let a customer do this, although sometimes there is an extra charge.

2. Pair Work. Have students continue discussing the menu, using the menu in the book.

3. Have students switch roles and comtinue.

4. Ask several pairs to role-play for the class. As they speak, make sure they use gestures, such as pointing to the menu.

2. ORDERING

1. Direct students' attention to the function box. Give students time to read over the examples.

2. Model the examples; have students repeat.

Pronunciation Note: Rising intonation at the end of a sentence. Intonation usually falls at the end of a sentence. However, in this context rising intonation is used to signal a request in sentence form. On the board, write the following statement, marking the intonation:

I'd like a steak, medium-rare, please.

Model; have students repeat. Explain that this means *Could I have a steak, medium-rare, please?* and therefore the intonation rises.

Language Note: The use of *Would* and *Could* is considered polite and appropriate in restaurants. The response using *will* as in *I'll have a (steak), please.* is particularly appropriate for restaurants.

3. Pair Work. Have students practice the examples in the function box, switching roles. Circulate and help with pronunciation.

Practice————————————

1. Explain the activity.

2. Pair Work. With one student the customer, the other the waiter/waitress, have students role-play ordering in a restaurant, using the menu in the book.

3. Have students switch roles and continue.

4. Ask pairs to demonstrate for the class. Make sure students use gestures and props and establish eye contact.

3. SPECIFYING WANTS

1. Direct students' attention to the function box. Give students time to read over the examples.

2. Model the examples; have students repeat chorally.

Pronunciation Note: Blending of *would you*. In rapid speech the words *would* and *you* are frequently blended to sound like */wu-juh/*. On the board write the following questions, drawing a line to connect *would* and *you*.

What kind of dressing would you like?

Would you like soup or salad?

Model; have students repeat chorally.

3. Pair Work. Have students practice the examples in the function box, switching roles. Circulate and draw attention to the pronunciation of *would you* as students practice.

Practice 1

1. Divide the students into pairs and have them read the directions for their parts. Explain that Student B should choose one of the lunch specials to order and then decide what he or she wants with it from each category.

2. To help students get started, ask a volunteer to model each of the questions (*Would you like soup or salad?* etc.). Explain that a waiter/waitress often presents the category, then the choices as in *For your vegetable, do you want buttered peas or glazed carrots?*

Language Note: Point out the importance of looking at the conjunctions in a menu very carefully. A dinner that comes with soup *or* salad means the customer can have either one, but not both. A dinner that comes with salad, vegetable, *and* potatoes includes all three.

3. Pair Work. Have students practice asking for and specifying wants, switching roles.

4. Call on various pairs to ask and answer about each item on the list. Make sure students are comfortable formulating the questions before continuing.

Practice 2

1. Explain the activity. Model the beginning of the conversation. Model again, have students repeat chorally and individually.

2. Pair Work. Have students role-play a restaurant scene, taking turns being the waiter/waitress and the customer. Students should continue working with the menu of Today's Lunch Specials.

3. Call on pairs to perform for the class. Encourage students to use gestures and a book or notebook to represent a menu.

4. Expansion: Group Work. In groups of three or four, have students role-play the same restaurant scene. Have the students who are the customers first discuss what each is going to order, then have the other group member take their orders. If time permits, have students switch roles. Alternatively, use real menus and follow the same procedure.

LISTEN TO THIS

1. Explain the activity. Emphasize that they should focus on what each person orders.

2. Play or read the conversation as the students fill in the chart.

3. Play or read again as students check their answers.

4. Pair Work. Have students compare their answers by reading them aloud to each other.

5. Ask volunteers for the answers.

Answers:

Davey: *a cheeseburger / large French fries / a chocolate shake*

Father: *chicken nuggets / large fries / a coffee / sweet and sour sauce*

Mother: *a fish sandwich / a garden salad / a coffee / French dressing*

6. Play or read the conversation again as a final check.

Culture Note: Point out that at a fast-food restaurant a customer is often asked at the end of the order *Is that for here or is it to go?* This means will the customer eat there or take it out.

3. SPECIFYING WANTS

✦ What kind of *dressing* would you like?

◇ I'll | have | *creamy garlic* (please).
     | take
 I'd like

✦ Would you like *soup* or *salad*?

◇ I'd like *soup*, please.

·Menu·

TODAY'S LUNCH SPECIALS
Chicken Fingers
Juicy strips of tender white meat deep-fried in crispy batter
Crab and Asparagus Quiche
Made with real crab meat and tender, young asparagus tips
Hot Roast Beef Sandwich
Thick slices of beef, cut fresh from the roast
Breaded Filet of Sole
Fresh sole, rolled lightly in bread crumbs, and baked to flaky
perfection

All specials come with your choice of:
-Cream of Mushroom Soup or Green Salad
(French or Oil & Vinegar Dressing)
-Potatoes: Baked, Mashed or French Fries
-Vegetables: Buttered or Glazed Carrots
-Dessert: Vanilla Ice Cream or Fresh Fruit

Practice 1

Student A:
You are the waiter/waitress. Ask the customer about the following items.

1. soup or salad
2. dressing for your salad
3. potatoes
4. vegetables
5. dessert

Student B:
You are the customer. Choose from today's lunch specials.

Practice 2

Role-play a restaurant scene. Take turns being the waiter/waitress and customer. Begin like this:

A: Excuse me!
B: Yes, sir/ma'am. What would you like?

LISTEN TO THIS

📼 A family is having dinner at their local fast-food restaurant. Listen and write down what each person orders.

Davey	
Father	
Mother	

CONVERSATION 2
WOULD YOU CARE FOR ANY DESSERT?

Do you take a long time to decide what to order in a restaurant?

Do you like to try new foods?

What new foods do you want to try?

Waiter: OK, so that's one cheeseburger and one order of chicken wings, extra spicy. Would you like something to drink with that?

Carol: Do you have any diet Coke?

Waiter: I'm sorry, we don't. We have diet Pepsi.

Carol: I'll have that, then.

Linda: Make it two.

Waiter: Would you like to have your Pepsi now?

Linda: Yes, please.

Carol: No, thank you. I'll wait for my cheeseburger.

Waiter: And would you care for any dessert?

Linda: No thanks. I'm sure I'll be full.

Carol: They have fantastic chocolate cheesecake here...

Linda: They do? Well, maybe we could split some.

Waiter: Would you like me to bring two forks?

Carol: Yes, please. Good idea.

Pronunciation Focus

We pronounce *would you* like *wouldya*. Listen to these questions, then practice them.

Would you like something to drink?
Would you like to have your Pepsi now?
Would you care for any dessert?

Now practice the conversation. Pay attention to *would you*.

CONVERSATION 2
WOULD YOU CARE FOR ANY DESSERT?

Prelistening Questions

1. With books closed, on the board, write: *Would you care for any dessert?* Ask:
   - *Do you like to eat dessert?*
   - *What is your favorite dessert?*

Elicit answers from various volunteers. Maintain a rapid pace.

2. With books still closed, read the prelistening questions. Elicit answers from several volunteers.

3. Group Work. Have students open their books, cover the conversation and the picture, and take turns asking and answering the questions.

4. Ask volunteers to name what new foods they want to try. Make a list on the board.

5. Have students uncover the picture. Check that the text of the conversation is still covered.

6. Ask students to describe what they see. Point out that customers often signal to the waiter/waitress that they are ready to order by closing their menus.

Vocabulary

Introduce these words now or after the students listen to the conversation.

(I'll have that) then: in that case (i.e., if you don't have my first choice)

Make it two: colloquial way to say *Please bring two.*

to care for: polite way to say *want, would like to have*

to split some: to share something

Presentation

1. Ask the following prelistening questions:
   - *What do you think they are going to eat?*
   - *What do you think they are going to drink?*

2. With books closed, play the recording or read the conversation at normal speed. Elicit answers to the questions.

3. Say: *Listen again. This time listen for when they want their drinks and what they want for dessert.*

4. Play or read the conversation again, pausing for choral repetition.

5. Ask the following questions:
   - *What are they having to drink?* (diet Pepsi)
   - *When do they want their drinks?* (One wants her Pepsi now, the other wants it with her cheeseburger.)
   - *What are they having for dessert?* (chocolate cheesecake)
   - *Are they each going to order some?* (No, they are going to split some.)

Elicit answers from various volunteers or have students tell their partners the answers.

Culture Note: Point out that the waiter/waitress usually checks the order by saying *OK, so that's one (cheeseburger) and one order of (chicken wings)*, etc.

6. Pronunciation Focus. Explain that we pronounce *would you* like /wouldya/. The sounds are blended together and reduced. Model the examples: *Would you like something to drink? Would you like to have your Pepsi now? Would you care for any dessert?* Emphasize the reduction of /wouldya/ and the stress on *something to drink / Pepsi now / dessert.* Have students repeat chorally.

7. With books open, play or read the conversation again as the students follow along in their books. Tell students to pay attention to *Would you.*

8. Paired Reading. Have students read the conversation, switching roles. Circulate and check pronunciation.

9. Ask pairs to demonstrate the conversation for the class.

GIVE IT A TRY

1. ASKING ABOUT WANTS

1. Direct students' attention to the function box. Give students time to read over the examples.

2. Model the examples; have students repeat chorally.

Pronunciation Note: Review of English as a stress-timed language. The rhythm is very regular in English. This means some words are reduced in order to keep an even beat. On the board, write the following questions.

Would you care for something to drink?

Would you like something to drink?

Can I get you something to drink?

Do you have any iced tea?

Tap out the rhythm as you model the questions. Emphasize that the rhythm is very regular. Model again; have students repeat chorally.

Language Note: *Would you care for…?* is a polite way to ask: *Do you want to have…? We're all out* and *we've run out* are alternative ways to say *We don't have* … Point out that *I'd like some…* and *I'll have some* … have the same meaning.

3. Pair Work. Have students practice the examples in the function box, switching roles. Circulate and assist with pronunciation as needed, emphasizing the rhythm.

Practice

1. Explain the activity. Give students time to read over the list of drinks.

Note: Explain that *espresso* is a strong coffee that is usually served in a small cup. *Cafe au lait* is coffee served with warm milk.

2. Pair Work. Have students ask for and answer about the list of drinks, switching roles.

3. Ask several pairs to demonstrate for the class.

2. OFFERING SERVICE

1. Direct students' attention to the function boxes. Give students time to read over the examples.

2. Model the examples; have students repeat chorally.

Pronunciation Note: Review of blending of *would you*. In rapid speech *would you* is pronounced /wu-juh/. The emphasis is on the questions here, and therefore, the stress is on the content words. As a result, the beginning of the question is blended together. On the board, write the following questions.

Would you like me to bring your coffee now?

Would you like me to get your coffee now?

Would you like some more coffee?

Say: *Would you like me to bring.* Repeat this rapidly several times blending the words together. Have students repeat. Then say with rising intonation:

your coffee now? / more coffee?

Next put the question back together:

Would you like me to bring your coffee now?

Exaggerate the blending and emphasize the last part of the question. Model the other questions; have students repeat chorally.

Practice

1. Explain the activity. Give students time to read over the list.

2. Pair Work. With one student the waiter/waitress, the other the customer, have students take turns asking if the customer would like the items on the list.

3. Ask several pairs to demonstrate for the class. Encourage students to use props and gestures.

1. ASKING ABOUT WANTS

✦ Would you	care for	anything	*to drink?*
	like	something	
Can I get you			

✧ Do you have any *iced tea?*

✦ I'm	afraid	we don't.	✦ Yes, certainly.
	sorry,	we're all out.	
		we've run out.	

| ✧ (I'll have) a *Coke*, then. | ✧ I'd like some, \| please. |
| | I'll have that, \| |

Practice

Student A (customer)
Ask for the following drinks.
If they are not available,
choose something else.

1. iced tea/ice coffee
2. lemonade
3. 7 Up/Coke
4. milk/hot chocolate
5. ginger ale/Pepsi
6. espresso/cafe au lait

Student B (waiter/waitress)
To answer, look at this list.

NOT AVAILABLE TODAY

*Iced Tea
Ginger Ale
Cocoa
7-Up
Iced Coffee*

2. OFFERING SERVICE

✦ Shall I bring	your *coffee* (now)?
Would you like me to get	
Would you like (to have)	
Would you like some more *coffee?*	

✧ Yes, please.
No, thank you.

Practice

Ask if the customer would like the following:

1. some coffee/tea
2. a glass of water
3. an extra plate
4. two forks with the dessert
5. some ketchup
6. extra cream for the coffee

3. ASKING ABOUT OTHER WANTS

◆ Would you | like | anything else?
           | care for | some *dessert?*

◇ No, thank you.
  Not right now, thank you.
  Yes, could you bring me | some more *rolls?*
                           | some *chocolate cheesecake?*

  Just the | bill, | please.
         | check, |

Practice

Student A: Ask the customer **(B)** if he/she wants anything else.

Student B: You can choose a dessert from the list below or decline if you don't want one.

Desserts

Pies: apple, cherry, peach, pecan
Cakes: chocolate, carrot, cheesecake
Ice Cream: chocolate, vanilla, rum raisin, coffee
Mousse: double chocolate, strawberry, lemon

LISTEN TO THIS

🔊 Listen to the conversations. Write down the thing(s) that the waiter/waitress is going to bring.

Conversation 1 ....

Conversation 2 ....

Conversation 3 ....

3. ASKING ABOUT OTHER WANTS

1. Direct students' attention to the function box. Give students time to read over the examples.

2. Model the examples; have students repeat chorally.

Pronunciation Note: Review of intonation. The questions have rising intonation and the statements have falling intonation. On the board, write the following and mark the intonation lines.

> *Would you like anything else?*
> *No, thank you.*
> *Not right now, thank you.*
> *Yes, could you bring me some more rolls?*
> *Just the check, please.*

Move your hand along the intonation lines as you model. Have students repeat chorally.

Culture Note: Customers are expected to leave a tip in restaurants that have table service. The standard formula is 15% of the bill. Some people tip over or above that in response to the quality of the service. Students who come from cultures where a service charge is added instead need to be reminded of this practice.

3. Pair Work. Have students practice the examples in the function box, switching roles. Circulate and assist with pronunciation.

Practice

1. Explain the activity. Give students time to look at the list of desserts.

2. Pair Work. Have students take turns role-playing the customer and the waiter/waitress.

3. Ask several pairs to demonstrate for the class. Make sure students use props and gestures.

LISTEN TO THIS

1. Explain the activity. Tell the students to focus on what the waiter/waitress is going to bring.

2. Play the recording or read the conversations at normal speed as the students write their answers.

3. Play the recording or read the conversations again as the students check their answers.

4. Pair Work. Have students compare their answers.

5. Ask volunteers for the answers.

Answers:

Conversation 1: *a large orange juice*

Conversation 2: *pecan pie with vanilla ice cream*

Conversation 3: *more coffee and cream and the check*

Culture Note: In conversation 2, the customer says *Could I have pecan pie with vanilla ice cream on the side?* Point out that *on the side* means in a separate dish, not on top of the pie (*à la mode*). Customers also use *on the side* for sauces, salad dressings, toppings, etc., if they want it in a separate dish.

Language Note: Waiters and waitresses use *sir, ma'am,* and *Miss* to indicate politeness.

OPTIONAL ACTIVITY 8: What Are You Going To Have?

See Teacher's Notes, page 125, and Activity Sheet, page 134.

PERSON TO PERSON

Practice 1

1. Divide the class into pairs and have students decide who will be Student A and who will be Student B.

2. Have students listen to the introduction. Then give them time to read the directions and look at the menu for their parts.

3. Play or read the conversation as the students mark the menus (Student A: the woman's choices, Student B: the man's choices).

4. Have students listen again to check their answers.

5. Pair Work. Have students check their answers. Circulate and help students resolve any differences.

Answers:

woman's choices: *salmon teriyaki, baked potato, broccoli, salad with oil and vinegar, iced tea*

extra request: extra butter

man's choices: *a steak, mashed potatoes, asparagus, cream of cauliflower soup, iced tea*

extra request: none

Practice 2

1. Have students read the directions.

2. Group Work. Have two pairs role-play ordering in a restaurant using the menu given. Have the student who is the waiter/waitress write down the orders. Ask the other students to arrange their seats as though they are sitting in a restaurant. If time permits, have students switch roles.

3. Check by calling on one or two groups to role-play for the class.

4. Expansion. Bring copies of real menus to class. It is not necessary for the groups to have the same menu. Have students repeat the role play, using the menus.

LET'S TALK 8

Student Book, page 106.

1. Have students read the directions for the first part of the activity. Explain that *type of food* means Italian, Chinese, Japanese, etc. *Size of restaurant* means seating capacity or the number of tables. *Decor* includes the color scheme, artwork, and decorations. Point out that first deciding whether the restaurant is formal, informal, or a fast-food restaurant will help them decide the decor.

2. Give students time to read the directions for the second part of the activity. Check understanding by asking: *What are you going to do?* (Plan the menu.)

3. Model the opener *What kind of food do you think we should serve?* Have students repeat.

4. Separate the students into pairs.

5. Pair Work. Have students work together to plan the menu for their restaurants. Circulate and assist with vocabulary and prices as needed.

6. Ask pairs of volunteers to present their restaurants to the class.

PERSON TO PERSON

STUDENT A

(Student A looks at this page. Student B looks at the next page.)

🔊 You are going to hear a couple ordering dinner. As you listen, look at the menu.

Practice 1

Write (W) for woman next to the choices she makes. The man's choices are marked for you.

MENU
ENTREES

m **NEW YORK SIRLOIN STEAK**
broiled to sizzling perfection

___ **HALIBUT CREOLE**
fresh halibut cooked in a zesty sauce of tomatoes, onions, and green peppers

___ **SALMON TERIYAKI**
fresh Atlantic salmon with a taste of the Orient

___ **LOBSTER TAILS**
served with melted butter, lemon wedges and a bib

___ **BARBECUED CHICKEN**
tender breast of chicken with our spicy barbecue sauce from a secret family recipe

All of the above entrees are served with your choice of

Potato (*m* mashed, ___ boiled or ___ baked)
Vegetable (___ broccoli, *m* asparagus ___ peas & carrots)
and
Soup of the day (ask your server about today's soup)
or
Salad (___ French, ___ blue cheese or ___ oil & vinegar dressing)

Beverage (___ coffee, *m* iced coffee, ___ tea or ___ iced tea)
Dessert (___ ice cream, ___ French pastry or ___ fresh fruit)

What extra request does the woman have? ....

Check your answers with your partner.

Practice 2

Join another pair of students. Using the menu above, one of you will take the part of the waiter/waitress. The rest of you will look at the menu and discuss what you're going to have. Then call the waiter/waitress and place your order. If you have time, reverse roles.

Guest Check

Thank you – Call Again

TABLE	NO. PERSONS	WAITER / WAITRESS			

PERSON TO PERSON

STUDENT B

(Student B looks at this page. Student A looks at the previous page.)

📼 You are going to hear a couple ordering dinner. As you listen, look at the menu.

Practice 1

Write (M) for man next to the choices he makes. The woman's choices are marked for you.

MENU

ENTREES

—— **NEW YORK SIRLOIN STEAK**
broiled to sizzling perfection

—— **HALIBUT CREOLE**
fresh halibut cooked in a zesty sauce of tomatoes, onions and green·peppers

W **SALMON TERIYAKI**
fresh Atlantic salmon with a taste of the Orient

—— **LOBSTER TAILS**
served with melted butter, lemon wedges and a bib

—— **BARBECUED CHICKEN**
tender breast of chicken with our spicy barbecue sauce from a secret family recipe

All of the above entrees are served with your choice of

Potato (___ mashed, ___ boiled or *W* baked)
Vegetable (*W* broccoli, ___ asparagus ___ peas & carrots)
and
Soup of the day (ask your server about today's soup)
or
Salad (___ French, ___ blue cheese or *W* oil & vinegar dressing)

Beverage (___ coffee, *W* iced coffee, ___ tea or ___ iced tea)
Dessert (___ ice cream, ___ French pastry or ___ fresh fruit)

What extra request does the man have? ....

Check your answers with your partner.

Practice 2

Join another pair of students. Using the menu above, one of you will take the part of the waiter/waitress. The rest of you will look at the menu and discuss what you're going to have. Then call the waiter/waitress and place your order. If you have time, reverse roles.

Thank you – Call Again *Guest Check*

TABLE	NO. PERSONS	WAITER / WAITRESS		

COMPONENTS

Student Book, pages 65–72
Let's Talk 9, Student Book page 107
Cassette/CD
Optional Activity 9, page 135
Review (Units 7–9), Student Book page 108

OBJECTIVES

Functions: Making small requests, making larger requests, asking for favors, complaining politely, requesting action, accepting an apology

Topics: Lending and borrowing things, seeking favors, resolving problems in hotels

Structures:
- *Would you mind* + gerund: Would you mind lending me your car?
- *Could I/you* + simple form: Could I borrow your car?
  too + adjective: too hot / too noisy

Pronunciation Focus: Pronunciation of *can* and *can't*. When can you help me? / I can't come over until 10 o'clock.

Listen to This: Listening for specific information: complaints, matching pictures and conversations

CONVERSATION 1
COULD I BORROW YOUR CAR?

Prelistening Questions

1. With books closed, read the title of the conversation and the prelistening questions. Elicit answers to each question from several volunteers.

2. Group Work. In small groups, have students open their books and discuss the questions. Check that the photograph and the text of the conversation are covered. Ask each group to compile a list of three things friends sometimes borrow and three things they do not like to lend. Ask volunteers for their group's lists. Hold a brief discussion on the criteria they used for deciding what is acceptable / not acceptable to borrow and lend.

3. Direct students' attention to the photograph. Read the title of the conversation again. Ask students to speculate:

- *Who are these people? How is each of them feeling?*
- *Do you think these people are friends?*
- *One of them says, "Could I borrow your car?"*
- *Which one? Why?*

Elicit answers from several volunteers for each question. Encourage students to use their imaginations as they look at the expressions of the people in the photograph.

Vocabulary

Introduce these words and phrases now or after the students listen to the conversation.

Can you believe this?: a rhetorical question to show shock or surprise

to pick up: to get

spare keys: extra keys

Here you go: colloquial form of *Here you are*

Anything else?: short form of *Do you need anything else?*

Presentation

1. With books closed, play the recording or read the conversation at normal speed.

2. Ask the following general comprehension questions:

- *What's the problem?* (Paul locked his keys in the car.)
- *What does he want to borrow?* (his friend's car)
- *Does his friend lend it to him?* (No)
- *Does his friend help him?* (Yes)

3. Say: *Listen again. This time listen for more details.* Play or read again, pausing for choral repetition.

4. Ask the following questions:

- *Where does Paul need to go?* (to the airport)
- *Who does he need to pick up?* (his aunt)
- *How long does he want to borrow Andy's car for?* (a few hours)
- *Why doesn't Andy lend him his car?* (He really needs it.)
- *Why does Paul want to go home?* (He has spare keys there.)
- *Is Andy going to take him?* (Yes)
- *What else does Paul want to borrow from Andy?* (a quarter)
- *Why?* (He wants to make a phone call.)

Elicit answers from various students or have students tell their partners the answers.

5. Paired Reading. Have students read the conversation, switching roles.

Do friends sometimes borrow things from you? What things?
Are there some things you don't like to lend? What are they?

700

6'6" CLEARANCE

Andy: What's the matter, Paul?

Paul: Can you believe this? I locked my keys in the car, and I have to go to the airport to pick up my aunt.

Andy: So, what are you going to do?

Paul: I don't know… Hey, do you think I could borrow your car for a few hours?

Andy: I'm sorry, but I really need it this afternoon.

Paul: Well, could you drive me home? I have spare keys there.

Andy: Sure. That's no problem.

Paul: Oh, and Andy? Do you have a quarter for the phone? My wallet's in the car.

Andy: Here you go. Anything else?

Paul: No, that's it. Thanks. I really appreciate it.

1. MAKING SMALL REQUESTS

✦ Do you have an extra Could I borrow a	pencil? piece of paper? tissue? quarter?

✧ Sure. Here you	are. go.	✧ I'm sorry. I don't have	one. any.

Practice 1

Ask for four of the following items. Your partner can agree or refuse. Make sure to give reasons for refusals. Then reverse roles.

1. pen
2. pencil
3. dime
4. dictionary

5. piece of paper
6. ruler
7. quarter
8. eraser

Practice 2

Think of four small things you want to borrow. Move around the class and ask your classmates. When you have all four things, return to your seat.

2. MAKING LARGER REQUESTS

✦ Do you think I could borrow Would you mind lending me	$25 until Tuesday? your watch for a few hours?

✧ Sure. OK.	✧ I'm sorry.	I don't have $25. I need it right now. Can I let you know later?

Practice 1

Make four requests. Your partner can agree or refuse. Be sure to give reasons for refusals. Then reverse roles.

1. car for the afternoon
2. $100 until next Friday
3. computer for the weekend
4. sleeping bag for a week

5. videotape machine tonight
6. new motorcycle for an hour
7. lawnmower on Sunday
8. CD player for a party
   on Saturday night

Practice 2

Now practice the exercise again. This time, think of your own requests.

GIVE IT A TRY

1. MAKING SMALL REQUESTS

1. Direct students' attention to the function box. Give students time to read over the examples.

2. Model the examples; have students repeat chorally.

Pronunciation Note: Blending of *do you*. In rapid speech, *do you* is pronounced /d'yuh/. On the board, write the following questions.

Do you have an extra pencil?

Do you have a piece of paper?

Model; have students repeat chorally and individually.

Language Note: *Here you go* is a common expression used when someone agrees to lend something or when complying with a request (for example, between a store clerk and a customer).

3. Pair Work. Have students practice the examples in the function box in different combinations. Circulate and assist with pronunciation.

Practice 1

1. Explain the activity. Point out that we usually give a brief reason for refusing to lend something, but it is not necessary to give details.

2. Pair Work. Have students take turns asking to borrow four of the items listed.

3. Ask several pairs to demonstrate for the class.

Practice 2

1. Give students time to read the directions and list four small things they each want to borrow.

2. Class Work. Have students circulate around the class and find someone from whom they can borrow the items. Tell students to return to their seats as soon as they are finished.

Note: To control the amount of time spent on this activity and to make it more of a challenge, time it. Tell students they have five minutes to complete their requests and return to their seats.

3. Ask various volunteers what they borrowed and from whom. In addition, ask volunteers which classmates refused their requests and why.

2. MAKING LARGER REQUESTS

1. Direct students' attention to the function box. Give students time to read over the examples.

2. Model the examples; have students repeat.

Pronunciation Note: Review of intonation with *yes/no* questions. The intonation rises at the end of a question. On the board, write the following questions, marking the intonation.

Do you think I could borrow $25 until Tuesday?

Would you mind lending me your watch for a few hours?

Can I let you know later?

Model, emphasizing the intonation. Have students repeat chorally.

Language Note: *Do you think I could borrow…?* and *Would you mind lending me …?* are both polite ways to ask *Can I borrow / Can you lend me…?* The bigger the request the more polite we tend to be.

3. Ask pairs to model the conversational exchanges in the function box for the class.

Practice 1

1. Give students time to read the directions and the list of requests.

2. Pair Work. Have students practice making larger requests, switching roles. Circulate; check pronunciation.

3. Ask several pairs to perform for the class.

Practice 2

1. Explain the activity. Ask students to think of other possible requests. Make a list on the board.

2. Pair Work. Have students practice the activity again, using the requests on the board or other requests they think of.

3. Ask volunteers to demonstrate for the class. Discuss any of the requests that sound outlandish or socially inappropriate.

OPTIONAL ACTIVITY 9: Could I Borrow...? *See Teacher's Notes, page 125, and Activity Sheet, page 135.*

Culture Note: When making larger borrowing requests, it is a good idea to include when the thing/money will be returned or repaid. If time permits, discuss to whom it is appropriate to make larger requests. In addition, point out that people sometimes tell white lies when they are uncomfortable with a large request. For example, the response "I'm sorry, I don't have ($25)." may not be the truth, but it indicates an unwillingness to make the loan.

3. ASKING FOR FAVORS

1. Direct students' attention to the function box. Give students time to read over the examples.

2. Model the examples; have students repeat.

Pronunciation Note: Review of intonation. The intonation falls in short responses. On the board, write the following responses, marking the falling intonation.

Sure. No problem.

Of course.

I'd be glad to.

I'm sorry. I can't right now.

Model, emphasizing the falling intonation. Have students repeat chorally and individually.

Language Note: *Get* is used idiomatically in *get the lights* and *get the door* as follows. If the lights are on, turn them off. If the lights are off, turn them on. If the door is open, then close it. If the door is closed, then open it. *Favors* are usually small requests. The expressions *Can I ask you a big favor?* or *Can you do me a big favor?* are often used to preface a larger request.

Culture Note: If a favor is small, we may want to help, but be unable to do so at that moment. After *I'm sorry. I can't right now,* we can say *Hold on a second / Just a second / In a second* to signal our willingness to help as soon as we can.

Practice 1

1. Give students time to read the directions and the list of favors.

2. Pair Work. Have students practice asking for favors, switching roles.

3. Call on pairs to perform for the class. Encourage students to use gestures and props.

Practice 2

1. Explain the activity. Ask students to think of some interesting or unusual favors. Make a list on the board.

Note: Alternatively, have students get into small groups and generate their own lists. Members can then circulate and try to find classmates to agree to their requests. Students can then return to their groups and report how well they did.

2. Pair Work. Have students practice the activity again, using the favors on the board or other favors they think of.

3. If students generate the lists in small groups, have volunteers report their lists of favors.

LISTEN TO THIS

1. Direct students' attention to the pictures. Explain the activity. Give students time to look at the pictures.

2. Play the recording or read the conversations at normal speed as the students number the pictures 1–6.

3. Play or read the conversations again as students check their answers.

4. Pair Work. Have students exchange books and check their answers.

5. Ask volunteers for the answers.

Answers:

a. *3*, b. *5*, c. *1*, d. *2*, e. *6*, f. *4*

6. Play or read the conversations again as a final check. Pause after each conversation. Have students tell you what clues in each picture they used to decide their answers.

3. ASKING FOR FAVORS

✦ Would you (please) Could you	get the	*door?* *lights?*
	hold my coat for a minute?	

✧ Sure. (No problem.) Of course. I'd be glad to.	✧ I'm sorry. I can't right now.

Practice 1

Ask your partner to do three of these favors for you. Your partner agrees to do each favor. Use the following, and then reverse roles.

1. open the window
2. turn up the volume
3. carry my books

4. hold my books for a second
5. explain the homework after class
6. check my homework

Practice 2

Think of some interesting or unusual favors. Move around the room and ask your classmates. They can agree or refuse.

LISTEN TO THIS

🔲 Listen to the conversations. Put the number of the conversation on the correct line.

____   ____   1

____   ____   ____

Have you ever had problems at a hotel?
What happened?
What did you do?

Guest: Excuse me.

Clerk: Yes? What can I do for you?

Guest: I just checked in, and there's a problem with my room.

Clerk: And what is the problem?

Guest: I asked for a non-smoking room, and I don't have one. My room smells like cigarette smoke. I can't stand it. Could you change my room, please?

Clerk: Let me see... I'm sorry, but we don't have any more non-smoking rooms. We won't charge you for your room tonight.

Guest: Thank you.

Clerk: I'm very sorry about this.

Guest: That's OK. Thanks for your help.

Pronunciation Focus

Notice how we pronounce *can* and *can't*.

can [kən]
What can I do for you?

can't [kænt]
I can't stand it.

Now practice the conversation. Pay attention to *can* and *can't*.

CONVERSATION 2
COULD YOU CHANGE MY ROOM?

Prelistening Questions

1. With books closed, read the title of the conversation. Ask students to speculate where the conversation takes place (at a hotel).

2. With books closed, ask the prelistening questions. Elicit answers to each from student volunteers.

3. Group Work. In small groups, have students discuss any problems they have had at hotels and how they resolved them. Ask several volunteers to report their experiences.

4. Direct students' attention to the photograph in the book. Check that the text of the conversation is covered. Ask the following questions:

- *Why do you think the woman is talking to the clerk?*
- *What are possible problems she could have with her room?*
- *How do you think she feels?*

Elicit answers from volunteers. Maintain a rapid pace.

Vocabulary

Introduce these words and phrases now or after the students listen to the conversation.

check in: to register at a hotel

non-smoking room: room where no smoking is allowed

can't stand (it): can't bear or tolerate (it)

charge: to have someone pay for something

Presentation

1. With books closed, play the recording or read the conversation at normal speed.

2. Ask the following general comprehension questions:

- *What is the problem?* (She doesn't have a nonsmoking room.)
- *Is he going to change her room?* (No, they don't have any more nonsmoking rooms.)

3. Say: *Listen again. This time listen for more details about the problem.* Play or read the conversation again, pausing for choral repetition.

4. Ask the following questions:

- *What does her room smell like?* (cigarette smoke)
- *How does she feel about the smell?* (She can't stand it.)
- *If he can't change the room, what will he do instead?* (not charge her for the room)
- *Is that OK with the woman?* (Yes)

Elicit answers from various volunteers or have students tell their partners the answers.

5. Pronunciation Focus. Go over the examples: *What can I do for you? / I can't stand it.* Elicit additional examples if time permits.

6. Play or read the conversation again as the students follow along in their books. Tell students to pay attention to *can* and *can't.*

7. Paired Reading. Have students read the conversation, switching roles.

GIVE IT A TRY

1. COMPLAINING POLITELY

1. Direct students' attention to the function box. Give students time to read over the examples.

2. Model the examples; have students repeat.

Pronunciation Note: Review of sentence stress and blending of words. Heavier stress is placed on the content words. Introductory words are blended together because the focus (heavier stress) is on the content words. On the board, write the following statements and questions, marking the blending and stress.

> *Sorry to bother you, but I have a problem with my room.*
> *Could you help me? I have a problem with my seat.*
> *What's the problem?*
> *What seems to be the problem?*

Model; have students repeat chorally and individually.

Language Note: *What seems to be the problem?* is a more polite way to ask *What's the problem?* The introductory expressions *Sorry to bother you* and *Could you help me?* are used to soften a complaint and appear congenial.

Culture Note: Many short domestic flights in the United States now restrict smoking. However, many longer domestic flights and transcontinental flights still designate smoking and nonsmoking sections.

3. Pair Work. Have students practice the examples in the function box in different combinations. Circulate and check pronunciation.

Practice 1

1. Explain the activity.

2. Pair Work. Have students practice the role play, switching roles. Circulate and help with pronunciation.

3. Ask several pairs to demonstrate for the class.

Practice 2

1. Explain the activity.

2. Pair Work. Have students practice the role play, switching roles.

3. Ask several pairs to demonstrate for the class.

2. REQUESTING ACTION OR A CHANGE

1. Direct students' attention to the function box. Give students time to read over the examples.

2. Model the examples; have students repeat chorally.

Pronunciation Note: Review of rhythm. The rhythm is regular. As a result, some words are reduced. On the board, write the following statements and questions, marking the stress.

> *Could you change my room, please?*
> *I can change your room tomorrow.*
> *I'm sorry, I can't.*

Model; have students repeat chorally and individually.

3. Pair Work. Have students practice the conversational exchanges in the function box. Circulate and check pronunciation.

Practice

1. Explain the activity. Give students time to read the lists of problems and requests.

2. Ask students how they would do the first one. Call on a pair of volunteers to model it for the class.

3. Pair Work. Have students complete the activity, switching roles.

4. For each problem, ask a different pair to do the role play for the class.

1. COMPLAINING POLITELY

| ✦ Excuse me. Sorry to bother you, but Could you help me? | I have a problem with | *my room.* *my seat.* |

✧ What's the problem?
What seems to be the problem?

✦ *I asked for a non-smoking room.*
I requested the non-smoking section.

Practice 1

Student A is a hotel guest and **Student B** is the front desk clerk. **Student A** makes the following complaints.

1. asked for an ocean view/can only see the parking lot
2. asked for single beds/got a double bed
3. asked for a double room/got a single room

Practice 2

Student B is a passenger on a long flight and **Student A** is a flight attendant. **Student B** makes the following complaints.

1. asked for a seat in the non-smoking section/got smoking
2. asked for an aisle seat/got a window seat
3. asked to sit near the front of the plane/got the tail

2. REQUESTING ACTION OR A CHANGE

✦ Could you change *my room*, please?

| ✧ I can change *your room* tomorrow. I'd be glad to. | ✧ I'm sorry, I can't. |

Practice

Student A: You are staying in a nice hotel, but there are a few things wrong. Identify the problem and request action.

Student B: Agree to the request and say when the action can be taken.

Take turns role-playing.

Problem	Solution
1. not enough towels	1. send more towels
2. the room is too hot	2. fix the air conditioner
3. noisy people next door	3. ask them to be quiet
4. the toilet won't flush	4. send someone to fix it

3. ACCEPTING AN APOLOGY

◆ I'm (very) sorry about this.

◇ That's | OK. | Thanks for your help.
It's | | It wasn't your fault.
| | Don't worry about it.

Practice

Now put it all together. With your partner, choose one of the following problems, and prepare a conversation. One of you will complain, request action, and accept an apology. Then choose another problem and reverse roles.

1. at a dry-cleaners: your jacket still isn't clean
2. at a camera store: they reprinted the wrong photos
3. at a video store: the movie was blank in the middle
4. at a restaurant: the bill was added incorrectly

LISTEN TO THIS

⌨ You are going to hear conversations with two people who have complaints to make. Listen and answer the following questions.

Conversation 1
1. What is the woman's complaint? ....
2. What action does she request? ....
3. Where is the woman? ....

Conversation 2
1. What is the woman's complaint? ....
2. What action does she request? ....
3. How much is her new bill? ....

3. ACCEPTING AN APOLOGY

1. Direct students' attention to the function box. Give students time to read over the examples.

2. Model; have students repeat chorally.

Pronunciation Note: Review of statement intonation. The voice falls at the end of a statement. On the board, write the following statements, marking the intonation.

I'm very sorry about this.
Thanks for your help.
It wasn't your fault.
Don't worry about it.

Model, emphasizing the intonation. Have students repeat chorally and individually.

3. Pair Work. Have students practice the examples in the function box in different combinations. Circulate and assist with pronunciation.

Practice

1. Give students time to read the directions. Check understanding by asking *What should you do?*

2. Pair Work. Have students practice the role play.

3. Ask several pairs to role-play for the class.

4. Have students switch roles and continue practicing.

5. Expansion. Together make a list of other problems students might encounter in daily life. Have students practice these situations as well.

LISTEN TO THIS

1. Explain the activity. Give students time to read over the questions for each conversation.

2. Play the recording or read the conversations at normal speed as the students answer the questions.

3. Play the recording or read the conversations again as the students check their answers.

4. Pair Work. Have students compare their answers.

5. Check answers by asking: *What is the woman's complaint? What action does she request?* Continue asking the rest of the questions.

Answers:

Conversation 1

1. *There's a problem with the coffeemaker she just bought.*
2. *She wants a refund.*
3. *She's at a store.*

Conversation 2

1. *There's a problem with her telephone bill (a collect call from Finland).*
2. *She wants the charge taken off her bill.*
3. *Her new bill is $24.10.*

6. Play or read the conversations again as a final check.

PERSON TO PERSON

Practice 1

1. Divide the class into pairs and have students decide who will be Student A and who will be Student B.

2. Have students listen to the introduction. Then give them time to read the directions for their parts.

3. To help students get started, ask students to name some of the things Student B will need to borrow. Present example reasons students can give when they refuse (*I'm sorry, but I don't have an extra swimming suit. / I can't. I don't have another pair of shorts,* etc.).

4. Pair Work. Have students practice asking for the five favors and responding to the requests.

5. Call on various pairs to role-play for the class.

Practice 2

1. Have students read the directions. Check understanding by asking various students who are Student A: Why did you leave home in a hurry? What did you forget? What are you planning to do right after school? Then what are you going to do? Ask the class to name some things Student A might need to borrow.

2. Pair Work. Have students practice asking for five favors and responding to the requests.

3. Call on various pairs to role-play for the class.

LET'S TALK 9

Student Book, page 107.

1. Give students time to read the directions. Check student understanding of the directions by asking: *What is the problem?* To assist students with vocabulary, briefly discuss what the apartment looks like. Have students use the art to infer the meaning of *spotless.*

Note: One way to present the vocabulary is to put two columns on the board, one labeled *Complaint* and the other labeled *Action.* Write examples below: *dirty dishes / do the dishes; tennis gear by the front door / put in closet.* Elicit more examples from the students.

2. Model the opener: *I hate to mention this, but look at this apartment.* Have students repeat.

3. Separate the students into pairs.

4. Pair Work. Have students practice the role play.

Note: Have students first decide on the personalities of the roommates: Is the student who went away very angry? very neat? very particular about the way things are? Is the roommate who stayed home remorseful? always a slob? belligerent?

5. Ask pairs to perform their role plays for the class.

Note: If time permits, have students discuss what is a reasonable complaint and what isn't.

REVIEW (UNITS 7–9)

Student Book, page 108.

1. Give students time to read Situation 1 and the directions. Direct students' attention to the art. Ask them to speculate what a *fussy* shopper is. On the board, help students make a list of items of clothing they might ask for. Alternatively, suggest other items besides clothing: *bicycle, furniture, sports equipment, stereo equipment,* etc.

2. Model an example opener: *Can you help me? I'm looking for* (a blue sweater), *but I can't find one that I really like.*

3. Separate the students into pairs.

4. Pair Work. With one student the shopper, the other the salesclerk, have students role-play the conversation.

5. Ask one or two pairs to perform for the class.

6. Give students time to read Situation 2 and the directions. Direct students' attention to the art. Ask them to speculate what the problem is with the food. On the board, help students make a list of restaurant complaints: *overcooked, undercooked, not what I ordered, food is cold, cold drink is warm, food is too spicy, food is not spicy enough, service is too slow,* etc.

7. Model an example opener: *Excuse me! I'm sorry, but I can't possibly eat these things. First of all, my coffee is ice-cold. Second of all, this soup is much too salty!*

8. Pair Work. Have students reverse roles and role-play the conversation.

9. Ask pairs to perform for the class. Encourage them to use props and gestures.

PERSON TO PERSON

STUDENT A

(Student A looks at this page. Student B looks at the next page.)

Practice 1

You and your partner are on vacation in Hawaii for one week. Unfortunately, the airline lost your partner's luggage. Your partner will ask you for four favors. Agree to do some, but refuse to do others. Be sure to give reasons when you refuse.

Your information:

- you speak English very well
- your clothes won't fit your partner
- you didn't bring any suntan lotion
- you love shopping

Decide with your partner what actions you can take to solve any other problems you might have.

Practice 2

You're having a bad day today. You overslept, left home in a hurry, and forgot your book bag and wallet. You made plans to meet a friend right after school for a game of tennis and then dinner. Ask your partner to do these favors. Put a (✔) beside the ones he/she can help you with.

You want your partner to:

- lend you some paper and a pen (your supplies are all at home)
- drive you home at lunch (you can get the things you forgot)
- lend you his tennis racquet (you don't have your tennis equipment)
- lend you $25 to pay for dinner (you can pay it back tomorrow)

Decide with your partner what actions you can take to solve any other problems you might have.

PERSON TO PERSON

STUDENT B

(Student B looks at this page. Student A looks at the previous page.)

Practice 1

You and your partner are visiting Hawaii for a week. Your problem is that the airline lost your luggage. Everything you need is in your suitcases. Ask your partner to do these favors. Put a (✔) beside the ones he/she can help you with.

You want your partner to:

- call the airline for you (you're too shy)
- lend you some clothes (you're hot and uncomfortable)
- lend you some suntan lotion (yours is in the lost luggage)
- go shopping with you to buy clothes (you need something to wear)

Decide with your partner what actions you can take to solve any other problems you might have.

Practice 2

Your partner overslept today, arrived late, and forgot to bring his/her book bag and wallet. Your partner is going to meet another friend right after class for a game of tennis and then dinner. Your partner will ask you for four favors. Agree to do some, but refuse to do others. Be sure to give reasons when you refuse.

Your information:

- you have extra paper and pens
- you have only $20 but your bank is right around the corner
- you didn't bring your car today
- your tennis equipment is in your locker

Decide with your partner what actions you can take to solve any other problems you might have.

COMPONENTS

Student Book, pages 73–80
Let's Talk 10, Student Book page 109
Cassette/CD
Optional Activity 10, page 136

OBJECTIVES

Functions: Giving, getting, and clarifying personal information, being specific, discussing length of time, describing past experiences

Topics: personal history, childhood memories, school years, past accomplishments, work experience

Structures:

- Simple past: I went to college in Texas. / I traveled for a while in Europe.
- Used to: I used to hate cooking, but now I love it.
- Time expressions: for a while / in 1974 / six years ago / when I was six / right after college / after that / then

Pronunciation Focus: Reduced form of *you: did-juh*

Listen to This: Listening for specific information in a lecture; filling in a chart

CONVERSATION 1
SO, WHERE ARE YOU FROM?

Prelistening Questions

1. With books closed, read the title of the conversation and the prelistening questions. Elicit an answer to each question from a student volunteer.

2. Pair Work. Have students open their books, cover the photograph and the conversation, and take turns asking and answering the questions.

3. Class Work. On the board, write: *Advantages/Disadvantages.* Make a list of the advantages and disadvantages of moving from city to city and from country to country. Elicit ideas from as many students as possible. Introduce the concept of *weighing advantages/disadvantages.* The expression *weighing the pros and cons* can also be introduced here.

4. Group Work. In small groups, have students discuss the list. Ask them to decide if the advantages of moving outweigh the disadvantages or vice versa. Ask volunteers for their conclusions.

5. Direct students' attention to the photograph. Ask students to speculate:
   - *Where are these people?*
   - *Who are they?*
   - *Do these people know each other?*

Elicit answers from several volunteers for each question. Maintain a rapid pace.

6. Explain that the two people talking do not know each other. They have just met at the party. Ask students to briefly speculate what they might be talking about.

Note: If time permits, hold a brief discussion of *safe topics,* that is, topics that are culturally acceptable to discuss during a first encounter.

Vocabulary

Introduce these words and phrases now or after the students listen to the conversation.

originally from: the place a person was born

graduation: completion of a school

I bet (that was interesting): I feel very sure

that's enough about (me): let's stop talking about (me)

Presentation

1. With books closed, play the recording or read the conversation at normal speed.

2. Ask the following general comprehension questions:
   - *Where is she from?* (Canada)
   - *Where does she live now?* (Los Angeles)

Language Note: People who move often may use the expression *originally* to communicate the place they were born, but not necessarily the place they currently live. For example, *I'm from Massachusetts, but originally I am from Missouri* means *I live in Massachusetts now, but I was born in Missouri.*

3. Say: *Listen again. This time listen for details about what she did when she was younger.* Play or read again, pausing for choral repetition.

4. Ask the following questions:
   - *Where was she born?* (Montreal)
   - *When did she move to Los Angeles?* (when she was fourteen)
   - *Did she go to high school in Los Angeles?* (Yes)
   - *Where did she go to college?* (in Texas)
   - *Where did she travel after graduation?* (in Europe)
   - *When did she live in France?* (six years ago)
   - *What did she do in France?* (studied French)

Elicit answers from various students or have students tell their partners the answers.

5. Paired Reading. Have students read the conversation, switching roles.

6. Ask: *What lines tell you she is in Los Angeles now? (When did you <u>come</u> to Los Angeles? / We moved <u>here</u>... / Did you go to school <u>here</u>?*

Language Note: Some students have difficulty with *come* vs. *go.* This is a good opportunity to clarify the usage. Explain that if the question were *When did you go to Los Angeles?* we would know that they are not in Los Angeles now.

Do people in your country move around a lot?

Is it a good idea for families to move from city to city?

How about from country to country?

Brad: So, Paula, where are you from?

Paula: I'm from Canada, originally.

Brad: From Canada? Where were you born?

Paula: Montreal.

Brad: When did you come to Los Angeles?

Paula: We moved here when I was fourteen.

Brad: Did you go to school here?

Paula: Well, I went to high school here, but I went to college in Texas.

Brad: Did you get a job right after graduation?

Paula: No, I traveled for a while in Europe after college, and then I lived in France.

Brad: When was that?

Paula: Let's see... That was about six years ago.

Brad: I bet that was interesting. What did you do there?

Paula: I studied French. Anyway... that's enough about me. How about you? Were you born in L.A.?

1. GIVING AND GETTING PERSONAL INFORMATION (1)

◆ Where are you from?	✧ (I'm from) *Canada*, originally.
◆ Where were you born?	✧ (I was born in) *Montreal*.
◆ Were you born in | *Los Angeles?* *Hong Kong?*	✧ Yes, I was. No, | I was born in | *Canada*. I'm from

Practice

Ask your classmates where they were born. How many different cities did you find? Make a list.

2. GIVING AND GETTING PERSONAL INFORMATION (2)

◆ Did you *go to school* here?

✧ Yes. I *went to high school* here, but I *went to college in Texas*.
No. I *went to school in Boston*.

◆ Did you *get a job right after college?*

✧ No, I *traveled in Europe for awhile*.
Yes, I *started working right away*.

Practice 1

You and your partner are Brad and Paula. Brad asks and Paula answers. Use the cues below to make your questions and answers.
Follow this model:

Cue	**Question or Answer**
Brad: grow up in Los Angeles?	**Brad:** Did you grow up in L.A.?
Paula: No/Canada	**Paula:** No. I grew up in Canada.

Brad	**Paula**
1. go to high school here?	1. yes/high school in L.A.
2. go to college here?	2. no/college in Texas
3. travel after college?	3. yes/also lived in France
4. work in France?	4. no/studied French

Practice 2

Ask your partner these questions about his/her life. Ask more of your own, then reverse roles.

1. grow up around here?

2. study English in elementary school?

3. have teachers from the United States?

GIVE IT A TRY

1. GIVING AND GETTING PERSONAL INFORMATION (1)

1. Direct students' attention to the function box. Give students time to read over the examples.

2. Model the examples; have students repeat chorally.

Pronunciation Note: Review of stress on content words. Stress is placed on the content words. In addition, the other words are reduced. On the board, write the following questions.

Where are you from?
Where were you born?
Were you born in Los Angeles?

Model, emphasizing the stress and even rhythm. Have students repeat chorally and individually.

Language Note: *Where were you born?* and *Where are you from originally?* have the same meaning. With *Where are you from?* it is unclear as to whether the question is about where the person is currently from or where the person was born.

3. Pair Work. Have students practice the examples. Circulate and check their pronunciation.

Practice

1. Explain the activity. Divide the students into groups of four to six students, depending on class size.

2. Group Work. Have students circulate within their groups and find out where those classmates were born. Have each student make a list. Circulate and make sure students are practicing all of the example questions and answers.

Note: If you know in advance that most of the students are from the same city, teach them the additional question: *Where in (Tokyo) are you from?* Have students write down this information as well.

3. Have one student from each group report where the group members are from. Compile, or have a student compile, the information on the board. Have students discuss the results: *How many students are from (Kyoto)?*, etc.

2. GIVING AND GETTING PERSONAL INFORMATION (2)

1. Direct students' attention to the function box. Give students time to read over the examples.

2. Model the examples; have students repeat.

Pronunciation Note: Blending of *did you*. In rapid speech, *did you* is pronounced /did-juh/ or /did-ju/. On the board, write the following questions:

Did you go to school here?
Did you get a job right after college?

Model; have students repeat chorally and individually.

3. Pair Work. Have students practice the examples in the function box, switching roles.

Practice 1

1. Give students time to read the directions. Go over the model to make sure students know how to use the cues to formulate the questions.

2. Pair Work. Have students role-play the conversation between Brad and Paula, switching roles.

3. Ask different pairs to ask and answer each question.

Practice 2

1. Explain the activity. Give students time to read the questions and to write down questions of their own.

2. Pair Work. Have students take turns asking about each other's life.

3. Ask volunteers to tell the class what they found out about their partners.

3. BEING SPECIFIC

1. Direct students' attention to the function box. Give students time to read over the examples.

2. Model the examples; have students repeat chorally.

Pronunciation Note: Reduced form of *for*. In rapid speech, *for* is pronounced /fer/. On the board, write the following statement.

I traveled in Europe for a while.

Model; have students repeat chorally and individually.

Language Note: *Right* after college means *just* after or *directly* after college.

Practice 1

1. Give students time to read the directions. Go over the directions carefully. Check understanding by asking: *What is Paula going to do? What is Brad going to do?*

2. Go over the model to make sure students know how to use the cues to formulate the questions. Emphasize the three different ways Paula can respond to the question *When was that?* (in 1974 / 21 years ago / when I was six.).

Note: If time permits, an optional scanning activity can be done first. Rapidly ask students questions about the chart: *How old was Paula when she moved to Europe?* (21) *What year did she move there?* (1989) *When did she move to France?* (1990) *How many years ago was that?* (5) *How old was she when she got her first job?* (24) *When was that?* (1992–1995) Have students respond chorally and individually. Continue at a rapid pace.

3. Pair Work. Have students complete the activity, switching roles. Circulate and make sure they practice the different ways of responding to *When was that?*

4. Call on pairs to demonstrate asking and answering about the different points in Paula's life.

Practice 2

1. Explain the activity. Read the list of ideas aloud to help the students get started. Give students time to think about themselves and fill in the time line.

2. Pair Work. Have students take turns telling each other about their lives. Circulate and check that students are using all of the forms practiced.

3. Ask volunteers to report to the class one piece of information they learned about their partners. (*Two years ago Yuko went to France. / In 1994, Yuri got his first job. / When Hiro was six, he started karate lessons.*)

LISTEN TO THIS

1. Explain the activity. Give students time to look at the time line.

2. Play or read the conversation as the students fill in the events in the time line for Brad.

3. Play or read again as students check their answers.

4. Pair Work. Have students exchange books and compare their answers.

5. Ask volunteers for the answers.

Answers:

1. *moved to Japan / 2 years old (1957)*
2. *moved to Munich, Germany / 5 years old (1960)*
3. *moved to Middle East, Germany, Alaska, Hawaii / 10 years old*
4. *father retired in Hawaii / 17 years old (1972)*
5. *moved to Los Angeles / after college*

6. Play or read the conversation again as a final check.

3. BEING SPECIFIC

✦ I *traveled in Europe for awhile.*

✧ Did you? And when was that?

✦ That was │ *about six years ago.*
│ *in 1989.*
│ *when I was twenty-one.*
│ *right after college.*

Practice 1

Look at the time line below. You and your partner are Brad and Paula. Paula will make statements about her life using the cues. Brad will ask when she did the things she talks about.
Follow the model. Then reverse roles. This time, Paula tells how many years ago she did things, or how old she was at the time.

Paula's cues
1. began school/Montreal
2. moved/L.A./high school
3. college/Texas
4. travel/Europe
5. study/France
6. first job/translator

Example
Paula: I began school in Montreal.
Brad: When was that?
Paula: That was in *1974.*
That was *21 years ago.*
That was when *I was six.*

Age:	6	14	18	21	22	24
	Dorval Elementary School	Kennedy High School, L.A.	University of Texas	Europe	France	First Job: Translation Services
Year:	1974	1982	1986	1989	1990	1992...1995
Years Ago:	21	13	9	6	5	3

Practice 2

Now think about yourself. Fill in the time line below and tell your partner about your life. He/she will ask when each event happened. Try to use all of the forms practiced.

When:				

LISTEN TO THIS

▭ Now Brad is telling Paula about his life. As you listen, fill in the events in the time line for Brad. The first event is done for you.

When: *I was 2*	in 1960	I was 10	in 1972	after college
moved to Japan				

CONVERSATION 2
HOW LONG DID YOU DO THAT?

What activities from your childhood do you still enjoy today?
Are there any that you no longer enjoy?

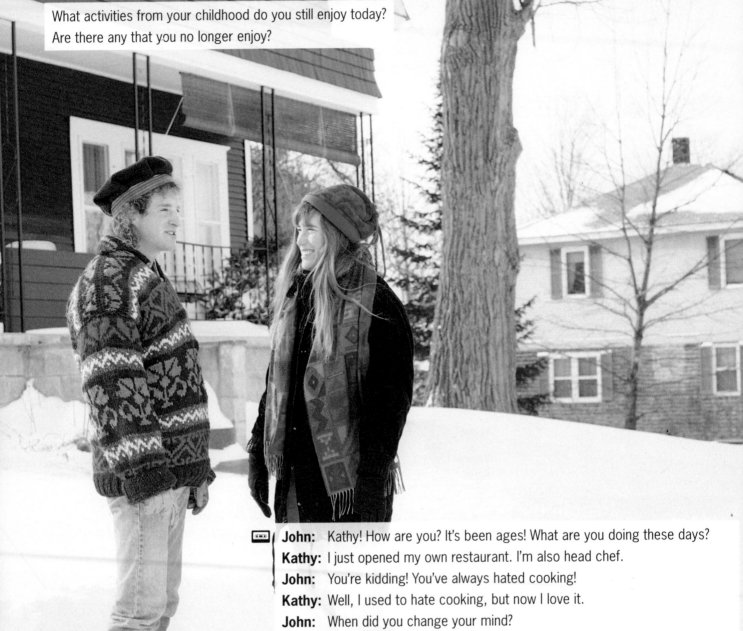

John: Kathy! How are you? It's been ages! What are you doing these days?

Kathy: I just opened my own restaurant. I'm also head chef.

John: You're kidding! You've always hated cooking!

Kathy: Well, I used to hate cooking, but now I love it.

John: When did you change your mind?

Kathy: After I tried French food. Before that, I used to cook really boring things for my family.

John: I still can't believe it! So, did you go to cooking school or something?

Kathy: Yeah. I went to California to study.

John: Really? How long did you stay there?

Kathy: I was there between '88 and '90.

John: And what did you do after that?

Kathy: Then I came back here. I worked for about three years to get some experience.

John: That's great! So, where is your restaurant? I'm going to eat there this weekend!

Pronunciation Focus

Did you is pronounced [didya]. Listen and practice these sentences.

When did you change your mind?
How long did you stay there?
What did you do after that?

Now practice the conversation. Pay attention to *did you*.

CONVERSATION 2
HOW LONG DID YOU DO THAT?

Prelistening Questions

1. With books closed, read the title of the conversation and the prelistening questions. Elicit answers to each question from various student volunteers. List on the board those activities students still enjoy and those they no longer enjoy. Talk about any patterns you see in the class (for example, many students rode bicycles when they were young, but few of them do today).

2. Direct students' attention to the photograph in the book. Check that the text of the conversation is covered. Ask the following questions:

- *What time of year do you think it is?*
- *Who do you think these people are?*
- *What is their relationship?*
- *Do they seem happy to see each other?*
- *What do you think they are talking about?*

Elicit answers from volunteers. Maintain a rapid pace.

Vocabulary

Introduce these words and phrases now or after the students listen to the conversation.

It's been ages!: It's been a very long time.

head chef: the chef (cook) who is in charge

You're kidding!: indicating surprise. Similar to expressions *I can't believe it!* and *You're joking!*

or something?: short form for *or something like that?*

Presentation

1. With books closed, play the recording or read the conversation at normal speed.

2. Ask the following general comprehension questions:

- *What has Kathy just done?*
  (opened her own restaurant)
- *Has she always liked to cook?* (No)
- *Where did she study cooking?* (California)

3. Say: *Listen again. This time listen for more details about Kathy's life.* Play or read the conversation again, pausing for choral repetition.

4. Ask the following questions:

- *What is Kathy's job?* (She is head chef.)
- *Why did she change her mind about cooking?*
  (She tried French food.)
- *When was she in California?*
  (between 1992 and 1994)
- *How long did she work after that?*
  (about three years)
- *What is her friend going to do this weekend?*
  (eat at her restaurant)

Elicit answers from various students or have students tell their partners the answers.

5. Pronunciation Focus: *Did you.* Model the examples: *When did you change your mind? / How long did you stay there? / What did you do after that?* Have students repeat chorally and individually.

6. With books open, play or read the conversation again as students follow along. Tell students to pay attention to *did you.*

7. Paired Reading. Have students read the conversation, switching roles.

8. Ask pairs to demonstrate the conversation for the class.

GIVE IT A TRY

1. DISCUSSING LENGTH OF TIME

1. Direct students' attention to the function box. Give students time to read over the examples.

2. Model the examples; have students repeat chorally.

Pronunciation Note: Review of *did you.* In rapid speech, *did you* is pronounced /did-juh / or /did-ju/. On the board, write the following questions:

How long did you stay in California?

How long did you stay there?

Model; have students repeat chorally and individually.

Language Note: The phrase *from 1992 to 1994* can also be *from 1992 until 1994.* The phrase *from 1992 to 1994* can also be *from '92 to '94.* In conversation, it is very common to say *'92* for *1992.*

Practice 1

1. Give students time to read the directions and look at Kathy's resumé.

2. For scanning practice, ask the following questions: *When did she start high school?* (9/84) *When did she graduate?* (6/88) *When did she start her first job?* (12/90) *Where was it?* (Gaston's Restaurant) *What did she do in 1993?* (opened her own restaurant) Continue. Maintain a rapid pace.

3. Pair Work. Have students complete the activity, switching roles. Circulate and make sure they practice using all three forms for expressing length of time.

4. Call on pairs to ask and answer the questions for the class.

Note: This can easily be expanded into a drill by calling on various students to give the different forms of the answer as different pairs demonstrate the activity. For example, one student responds *She stayed there between '92 and '94.* Indicate another student, who then responds *She stayed there from 1992 to 1994.* Indicate a third student, who then responds *She stayed there for two years.* Continue.

Practice 2

1. Explain the activity. Give students time to look at their partner's time line.

2. Pair Work. Have students complete the activity, switching roles.

3. Ask volunteers to report to the class how long their partners did various activities. To expand into a drill, see Practice 1.

2. ASKING "WHAT NEXT?"

1. Direct students' attention to the function box. Give students time to read over the examples.

2. Model the examples; have students repeat chorally.

Pronunciation Note: Blending of *what did you.* In rapid speech, *what did you* is pronounced /wu-did-juh/ or /wud-juh/. On the board, write the following questions:

What did you do after you left California?

What did you do after leaving California?

What did you do after that?

What did you then?

Model two times, emphasizing the blending. First use /wu-did-juh/. Then explain that in very rapid speech we use /wud-juh/. Model again. Have students repeat both forms chorally and individually.

Language Note: *After that?* and *then?* are interchangeable here.

Practice 1

1. Explain the activity.

2. Pair Work. Have students complete the activity, take turns role-playing Kathy. Circulate and make sure they practice the different forms presented.

3. Call on pairs to demonstrate for the class.

Practice 2

1. Explain the activity. Divide students into new pairs or have students select new partners.

2. Pair Work. Have students take turns asking each other about their lives, using the form *What did you do after...?* Circulate and check pronunciation.

3. Ask several pairs to demonstrate for the class. Maintain a rapid pace.

1. DISCUSSING LENGTH OF TIME

◆ How long did you stay | in California?
| there?

✧ I | stayed | there | between '92 and '94.
| was | | from 1992 to 1994.
| | | for two years.

KATHY SIMS

9/84.........Entered Lincoln High, Cleveland

6/88.........Graduated high school

6/88–9/88.........Summer job: Chef's helper

9/88.........Entered California School of Cooking

9/90.........Graduated with honors

9/90.........Returned to Cleveland

9/90–11/90.........Looking for work

12/90–1/91.........First job: Gaston's Restaurant

1/91–1/92.........Second job: Little Paris Cafe

1/92–12/92.........Third job: La Maison Restaurant

1/93.........Opened own restaurant

Practice 1

Look at Kathy's resume. Your partner is Kathy. Ask her how long she did these things. Kathy answers using all three forms above. Then reverse roles.

Student A asks:
1. go to Lincoln High
2. go to cooking school
3. look for work

Student B asks:
1. work as a chef's helper
2. live in California
3. work at Gaston's

Practice 2

Look at the time line that your partner did on page 75. Ask him/her about it, then reverse roles.

2. ASKING "WHAT NEXT?"

◆ What did you do | after you left California?
| after leaving California?
| after that?
| then?

✧ Well, then I came back here.

Practice 1

You are Kathy. Your partner will ask you about your education and work history, using the forms above. Then reverse roles.

Practice 2

Find a new partner. Look at the time line that he/she did on page 75. Ask him/her about it, then reverse roles.

3. DESCRIBING CHANGES

✦ I used to hate *cooking*, but now I love it.
I used to *cook really boring things* but now I don't.

Get into a small group. Tell the other group members three things that used to be true for you. Say how they have changed. Take turns.

▭ You are going to hear a college literature teacher talking about Ernest Hemingway. Answer the questions below.

1. When did Hemingway write *The Sun Also Rises*?

....

2. What is the subject of *A Farewell to Arms?*

....

3. What was his occupation the second time he went to Europe?

....

4. When did he write *The Old Man and the Sea*?

....

5. Why was this short novel so powerful and emotional?

....

6. When did Hemingway kill himself?

....

3. DESCRIBING CHANGES

1. Direct students' attention to the function box. Give students time to read over the examples.

2. Model the examples; have students repeat chorally.

Pronunciation Note: Review of stress, rhythm, and intonation. The emphasis here is on the contrast between a past action and a current one. Heavier stress is placed on the content words.

> I used to HATE COOKING, but now I LOVE IT.
> I used to cook REALLY BORING THINGS
>   (but now I don't).

Model emphasizing the rhythm and the stress. Have students repeat chorally and individually.

Language Note: *Used to* is used to describe an habitual action in the past that is no longer done. For this reason, *but ...* can be deleted. We can infer what the current situation is. For example, *I used to cook really boring things* means *Now I don't cook boring things.* If I say *I used to exercise every day,* you can infer that I no longer do this.

Practice 1————————

1. Have students read the directions. Give students time to each list three things that they used to do or that used to be true for them. Check understanding by asking: *What is one thing you used to do, (Hiromi)? How about you, (Shigeo)?*

2. Group Work. Have students take turns telling each other what they used to do and why they changed. Have students rotate turns, telling one thing at a time.

3. Call on several volunteers to tell the class information about themselves.

Language Note: It is very important that students understand that *used to* is used only for things that are no longer true, and that it is not used with a time marker. For example, we cannot say *I used to study English for three years.* We can say *I used to study English at a different school* or *I studied English for three years.* We cannot, however, combine the information in the same sentence. More importantly, we cannot say *I used to study English,* if I am currently studying it.

Practice 2————————

1. Explain the activity. Give students time to think of three more things that used to be true.

2. Model an example: *I used to play the piano. / How long did you play it? / For two years.*

3. Pair Work. With new partners, have students tell each other three other things that used to be true, and ask how long each thing was true.

4. Have students switch roles and continue.

5. Ask pairs demonstrate for the class.

LISTEN TO THIS

1. Explain the activity. Give students time to read over the questions.

2. Play or read the lecture. Have the students listen for general understanding only. Do not have them answer the questions at this time.

3. Play or read the lecture again as the students answer the questions.

4. Play or read again as students check their answers.

5. Pair Work. Have students compare their work by asking and answering the questions.

6. Ask volunteers for the answers.

Answers: 1. *1926*
　　　　　　 2. *It is a love story*
　　　　　　 3. *reporter*
　　　　　　 4. *1952*
　　　　　　 5. *It was based on his own personal experiences*
　　　　　　 6. *1961*

7. Play or read the conversation again as a final check.

8. Expansion. Hold a class discussion about any Hemingway books the students have read. Ask them to explain their favorite parts, etc.

OPTIONAL ACTIVITY 10: Who Am I? *See Teacher's Notes, page 125, and Activity Sheet, page 136.*

PERSON TO PERSON

Practice 1

1. Divide the class into pairs and have students decide who will be Student A and who will be Student B.

2. Have students listen to the introduction. Then give them time to read the directions for their parts. Make sure students understand what *suggest a new career* means.

Culture Note: A career counselor is a person whose job it is to help people figure out which job/career they are well suited for. The counselor considers the education, prior employment, activities and interests, as well as the personality of the individual. It is not uncommon for people in North America to switch careers. People switch careers for a number of reasons: the job market changes, they lose interest in what they have been doing, or they need to earn more money. Nowadays, it is rare for someone to work for the same company his/her whole life. If time permits, ask students how this compares with the situation in their country.

3. Direct students' attention to the resume worksheet. Check understanding of vocabulary by making model statements: *I was born in St. Louis, Missouri. My place of birth is St. Louis, Missouri. / The location of our school is… / My duties as a teacher include grading papers, giving exams, etc.* Continue.

Culture Note: A student receives a diploma, not a degree, upon graduation from high school. There are many types of degrees in higher education. For example, a B.A. is a Bachelor of Arts, a B.S. is a Bachelor of Science, an M.A. is a Master of Arts, an M.S. is a Master of Science. A bachelor's degree generally requires four years of study, a master's degree from one to two years. Times vary according to the field of study. Training can also be done in a nondegree program. This means the student receives a certificate of completion, but not a degree.

4. To help students get started, model some questions they might ask: *What is your place of birth? What is your date of birth? What was the name of your high school? Where was it located? When did you attend high school?* etc.

5. Pair Work. Have students practice the role play. Circulate and help students formulate their questions.

6. Call on several pairs to ask and answer questions for the class.

Practice 2

1. Explain that students are to switch roles and repeat the activity in Practice 1.

2. Pair Work. Have students practice the role play. Circulate and help students as needed.

3. Call on various students to explain to the class what new career they suggested for their partners and why.

LET'S TALK 10

Student Book, page 109.

1. Give students time to read the directions. Check understanding by asking: *Who are you? Who is your partner? What is your partner going to make? What is your partner going to do first?* Check vocabulary: *fictional, scriptwriter.*

2. Emphasize to the students that they don't need to know anything about the person they choose to be. Encourage them to use their imaginations when answering the questions. Model examples of details someone might make up *(I am Meryl Streep. I like to water-ski and watch horror movies. I became interested in movies when I was five years old.).* Elicit a few more suggestions of famous people they might be *(Mick Jagger, Mother Teresa, the prime minister of Japan).*

3. Model the opener *Before I can write this movie, I have to ask you a few questions about your life. First of all, …* Have students repeat.

4. Separate the students into pairs.

5. Pair Work. Have students role-play the interview, then switch roles and repeat.

6. Ask several pairs to perform their interviews for the class.

PERSON TO PERSON

(Student A looks at this page. Student B looks at the next page.)

Practice 1

Your partner is a career counselor who is helping you to write a new resume. Answer his/her questions.

Practice 2

You are a career counselor. You are helping your partner to write a new resume. If your partner has never worked before, get as much information as you can about his/her interests and hobbies. Complete the form below, look at it again, and suggest a new career for your partner.

RESUME WORKSHEET

Name: _____
Address: _____
Telephone: _____
Place of Birth: _____
Date of Birth: _____

Education

Name and Location	From Month/Year	To Month/Year	Degrees
High School			
College			
Other Education or Training			

Employment History

Name of Company	From Month/Year	To Month/Year	Duties

Activities, Interests, and Hobbies
(Please describe fully.)

_____
_____
_____

PERSON TO PERSON **STUDENT B**

(Student B looks at this page. Student A looks at the previous page.)

(Student B looks at this page. Student A looks at the previous page.)

Practice 1

You are a career counselor. You are helping your partner to write a new resume. If your partner has never worked before, get as much information as you can about his/her interests and hobbies. Complete the form below, look at it again, and suggest a new career for your partner.

RESUME WORKSHEET

Name: _____

Address: _____

Telephone: _____

Place of Birth: _____

Date of Birth: _____

Education

Name and Location	From Month/Year	To Month/Year	Degrees
High School			
College			
Other Education or Training			

Employment History

Name of Company	From Month/Year	To Month/Year	Duties

Activities, Interests, and Hobbies

(Please describe fully.)

_____

_____

_____

Practice 2

Your partner is a career counselor who is helping you to write a new resume. Answer his/her questions.

COMPONENTS

Student Book, pages 81–88
Let's Talk 11, Student Book page 110
Cassette/CD
Optional Activity 11, page 137

OBJECTIVES

Functions: Asking about past experiences, asking for a description or an opinion, comparing places

Topics: travel, unusual likes/dislikes

Structures:
- Present perfect: Have you ever been?
- Simple past: What did you think of Tokyo? / How was it?
- Comparatives: Montreal is more exciting than Ottawa. / Montreal is the most exciting city in Canada./ Vancouver has the most beautiful view.

Pronunciation Focus: Falling intonation with *Wh-* questions, for example, *Where did you* go *last night?*

Listen to This: Listening for specific information; filling in a chart

CONVERSATION 1
HAVE YOU EVER BEEN TO JAPAN?

Prelistening Questions

1. With books closed, read the prelistening questions. Ask some additional follow-up questions:

- *Where did you go?*
- *If you went to a city, how big was it?*
- *What was the weather like?*
- *What did it look like?*
- *What made it an interesting place?*

2. Pair Work. Have students open their books and take turns asking and answering the questions. Check that the text of the conversation is covered.

3. Direct students' attention to the photograph. Ask students to speculate:

- *Who are these people?*
- *Do you think these people know each other?*
- *Do you think they work together?*
- Say: *The title of the conversation is Have you ever been to Japan? One of them is going there. Why do you think he is going?*

Elicit answers from several volunteers for each question. Ask them to support their conclusions whenever possible. Maintain a rapid pace.

Vocabulary

Introduce these words and phrases now or after the students listen to the conversation.

fantastic: great; wonderful

kind of: fairly; sort of

temples: Buddhist and Shinto places of worship

historical: important in the history (of Japan); the former capital.

humid: containing a large amount of water vapor

humidity: the amount of water vapor in the air

sounds perfect: seems really great

Presentation

1. With books closed, play the recording or read the conversation at normal speed.

2. Ask the following general comprehension questions:

- *How many times has one of them been to Japan?* (twice)
- *Where did he go?* (Tokyo and Kyoto)
- *Did he like Japan?* (Yes)

3. Say: *Listen again. This time listen for what he says about Tokyo and Kyoto.* Play or read again, pausing for choral repetition.

4. Ask the following questions:

- *When is the first speaker going to Japan?* (in the fall)
- *Where did the second speaker go on his first trip to Japan?* (Tokyo)
- *What did he think of it?* (very big and exciting, but very crowded)
- *What did he think of the restaurants there?* (excellent, but expensive)
- *What did he think of Kyoto?* (beautiful)
- *What did he like there?* (the old temples and gardens)
- *When did he go to Tokyo?* (in August)
- *What was the weather like?* (really hot and humid)
- *When did he go to Kyoto?* (in October)
- *What was the weather like?* (hot and sunny, but no humidity)
- *Does the first speaker want to go?* (Yes)
- *How do you know?* (He says *Sounds perfect. I can't wait.*)

Elicit answers from various students or have students tell their partners the answers.

5. Paired Reading. Have students read the conversation, switching roles.

Where have you been on vacation?
How would you describe it to friends?

Jack: Have you ever been to Japan? I'm going in the fall.

Ted: Yeah, I've been there twice.

Jack: Really? Tell me about it. What's it like?

Ted: Oh, it's fantastic.

Jack: Where did you go?

Ted: On my first trip I went to Tokyo, and on my second trip I visited Kyoto.

Jack: What did you think of Tokyo?

Ted: Very big and exciting, but very crowded, too.

Jack: Yeah. I've seen pictures of the crowds!

Ted: And the restaurants are excellent… but they're kind of expensive.

Jack: And how about Kyoto?

Ted: Kyoto is lovely. It's full of beautiful old temples and gardens. It's a very historic city.

Jack: How was the weather?

Ted: I was in Tokyo in August, and it was really hot and humid. I went to Kyoto in October. It was hot and sunny, but there was no humidity.

Jack: Sounds perfect. I can't wait!

1. ASKING ABOUT PAST EXPERIENCES

✦ Have you ever been to *Japan?*

✧ Yes. | (I've been there) *twice.*
      | I was there *last summer.*

✧ No, never.

Practice 1

Combine a verb in the first column with an appropriate phrase from the second column and form a question like the example. (You may combine some verbs with several phrases.) Student A asks Student B four questions. Student B answers truthfully. Then reverse roles.

Example:
Have you ever been to a rock concert?

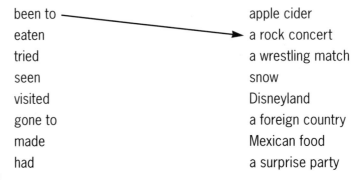

been to	apple cider
eaten	a rock concert
tried	a wrestling match
seen	snow
visited	Disneyland
gone to	a foreign country
made	Mexican food
had	a surprise party

Practice 2

Think of three more ideas of your own. Ask your partner and two other classmates.

2. ASKING FOR A DESCRIPTION OR OPINION

✦ What | did | you think of | *Tokyo?*
      | do | | *it?*
How was | *Tokyo?*
          | *it?*
What | was | *Tokyo* | like?
      | is | *it* |

✧ It was *very big* and *exciting*, but it was very *crowded*.
It's *quite old*, but *it has a lot of modern buildings*.

✦ What | was | the *weather* like?
      | is |

How | was | the *weather?*
     | is |

✧ It was *really hot and humid*.

GIVE IT A TRY

1. ASKING ABOUT PAST EXPERIENCES

1. Direct students' attention to the function box. Give students time to read over the examples.

2. Model the examples; have students repeat chorally.

Pronunciation Note: Review of stress, intonation, and rhythm. Write the following on the board, marking the intonation.

Have you ever been to Japan?

Yes, I've been there a few times.

No, never.

Move your hand along the intonation lines as you model the examples.

Language Note: *Have you ever gone to San Francisco?* vs. *Have you gone to San Francisco? Have you (ever) gone ...?* is used to inquire if someone has done the action *any time in his/her life* (the emphasis is on *up until now*). In contrast, *Have you gone...?* simply concerns an action in the past with no specific time mentioned. For example, it could be an inquiry related to a particular tour the person is on at the time of the conversation *(Have you gone to San Francisco yet? / No, we've been to L.A. and San Jose. We're going to San Francisco tomorrow.)*. Furthermore, *Did you ...?* also concerns an action in the past, but it is used to inquire about a past action at a specific time. *(Did you go to San Francisco when you were in California last year?)*

3. Pair Work. Have students practice the examples in the function box, switching roles. Circulate and assist with pronunciation.

Practice 1

1. Explain the activity. Emphasize that it is possible to combine some verbs with several phrases *(gone to: Disneyland / a wrestling match / a foreign country / a rock concert)*. Also point out that they should answer truthfully.

2. Model the example. Elicit answers from several students.

Culture Note: *Apple cider* is juice pressed from apples that is uncooked. It is very popular in the autumn in parts of North America where apples are grown. A *surprise party* is a party given for someone who doesn't know about the party in advance. Typically friends gather together at the appointed time and place, then the person walks in and everyone yells *Surprise!*

Language Note: To help students understand the difference between the *present perfect* and the *simple past,* have students continue the practice as follows: *Have you ever...? / Yes, I have. / When did you...? / I ... (last year)*. Write the pattern on the board to help students get started.

3. Pair Work. Have students complete the activity, then switch roles and continue. Circulate and assist as needed.

4. Ask several pairs to demonstrate for the class.

Practice 2

1. Explain the activity. On the board, help students make a brief list of other ideas to ask about.

2. Give students time to each write down three more ideas of their own.

3. Pair Work. Have students take turns asking about their own ideas or the ideas listed on the board.

4. Group Work. In groups of three, have students take turns asking about each other's ideas.

Note: The groups should not contain previous partners.

5. Ask various students to report what they found out about their classmates: *(Mariko), where has (Shigeo) gone? / He has gone to Thailand and the Philippines. (Yuri), tell me something about (Hiromi). / (Hiromi) has tried windsurfing.* Continue.

OPTIONAL ACTIVTY 11: Find Someone Who... *See Teacher's Notes, page 126, and Activity Sheet, page 137.*

2. ASKING FOR A DESCRIPTION OR OPINION

1. Direct students' attention to the function box. Give students time to read over the examples.

2. Model the examples; have students repeat chorally.

Pronunciation Note: Blending of *did you*. In rapid speech, *did you* often is blended to sound like */didju/.* Write the following questions on the board.

> What did you think of Tokyo?
> What did you think of it?

Model; have students repeat chorally and individually.

Language Note: All of these questions can be posed in the simple past. They are based on asking for one's opinion *at the time of the visit.* The simple present could be used in all of these questions except in *How was Tokyo?* There is a subtle difference, however, between *What was Tokyo like?* and *What is Tokyo like?* The former is an inquiry as to what Tokyo was like during the time you were there or what your experience of Tokyo was. The latter asks for a description of the city that would be true at all times. The same holds true regarding the question *What is/was the weather like?* (i.e., a truth statement vs. personal experience).

3. Model the examples in the function box again. Have students repeat chorally and individually. Tell students to pay attention to the stress and intonation.

Practice

1. Explain the activity. Have students each decide on a town or city they want to discuss.

2. Go over the example. Model a response: *It's clean.* Point out that the stress falls on the predicate adjective *(clean).*

Note: Students must first tell their partners the name of the city or town they want to discuss in order for the partners to be able to follow the example given.

3. Direct students' attention to the words in the box. Check understanding of *well-kept, inefficient, run-down,* and any other words that may be problematic for the class.

4. Ask various students about their hometowns: *Where are you from (Yuri)? What's the (weather) like there?*

5. Pair Work. Have students complete the activity, then switch roles and continue. Circulate and assist as needed.

6. Ask several students to report to the class what they discussed with their partners.

LISTEN TO THIS

1. Give students time to read the directions. Point out that they should focus on Minako's opinion of the four topics listed (*San Francisco, transportation, restaurants, hotel*). Also emphasize that they only need to write down a few key words for each topic and that they do not have enough time to write down everything she says.

2. Play the recording or read the conversation at normal speed as the students write down Minako's opinions.

3. Play or read the conversation again as students check their answers.

4. Pair Work. Have students check their work by comparing what they wrote down.

5. Ask volunteers for the answers.

Answers: *San Francisco: beautiful, wonderful; transportation: efficient, cheap, comfortable; restaurants: real variety, (Fisherman's Wharf, fresh and delicious, but expensive. Chinatown, spicy, but good); hotel: small, very old, not fancy, clean, well-kept, reasonable.*

Language Note: The *rates* for a hotel room are the cost of using the room. Rates can vary depending upon the time of year (off-season vs. peak season), the number of people occupying the room (single/double occupancy, etc.) and whether the cost is calculated as a nightly rate, or a weekly rate, etc.

6. If time permits, play or read the conversation again. This time ask students to listen for more details about each category; for example *What are the buses / subways / cable cars like?*

First choose a town or city to talk about. Your partner will ask you to discuss these and other similar topics. To answer, use words from the box and words of your own. Then reverse roles.

Example:
Let's talk about Chicago. What's the downtown area like?

the downtown area

the hotels

the restaurants

the public transportation

the weather

the stores

the food

the people

well-kept	attractive
small	inefficient
clean	expensive
big	uncomfortable
cheap	run-down
crowded	noisy
quiet	exciting
humid	rainy
spicy	boring
dry	inexpensive
cold	kind

LISTEN TO THIS

Minako has just come back from a vacation in San Francisco. She is telling her friend Lin about it. Listen and write down Minako's opinions on the following. One or two words are enough.

San Francisco.. restaurants..

transportation.. hotel ....

CONVERSATION 2
WHICH CITY DID YOU LIKE BETTER?

Think of two cities you have visited.
Which one did you like better? Why?

Dana: Oh, hi Pam. When did you get back from Canada? How was it?

Pam: The day before yesterday. I only visited Montreal and Ottawa, but I had a great time.

Dana: Which city did you like better?

Pam: That's hard to say… I think Ottawa is prettier. It has better sightseeing, too. A lot of museums and galleries.

Dana: And what's Montreal like? What did you think of it?

Pam: Montreal is more exciting. It has better shopping. The stores are cheaper and more interesting.

Dana: Which one has better nightlife?

Pam: Oh, Montreal for sure. It has more restaurants and clubs. They say Montreal is the most exciting city in Canada.

Dana: Well, I've always wanted to see Vancouver. I've heard it has the most beautiful views.

Pronunciation Focus

Wh- questions have falling intonation.
Listen and practice these questions.

When did you get back from Canada? ↘

Which city did you like better? ↘

What did you think of it? ↘

Which one has better nightlife? ↘

Now practice the conversation. Pay
attention to intonation.

CONVERSATION 2
WHICH CITY DID YOU LIKE BETTER?

Prelistening Questions

1. With books closed, read the title. Say: *What do you think the conversation will be about?* Elicit answers from several volunteers. Continue. *It's about a trip to two cities. Which two cities? San Francisco and Los Angeles? Rome and Paris? Vienna and Hong Kong?* Elicit ideas from other volunteers. Emphasize that it could be any two cities they can think of. Maintain a rapid pace.

Note: To help students learn the English pronunciation of the cities, write them on the board. Model; have students repeat chorally.

2. Ask the first prelistening question. Elicit answers from several students. Continue with the second prelistening question. Elicit answers from other students.

Language Note: It might be useful to go over making comparisons using but (for example, more exciting, but noisier / more fun, but more expensive, etc.).

3. Group Work. In small groups, have students discuss cities they have visited and which they liked better. Circulate and check that students are supporting their answers.

4. Direct students' attention to the photograph in the book. Check that the text of the conversation is covered. Ask students to speculate who the women are and what their relationship is.

5. Say: *One of them went to Canada. Do you know the names of any cities in Canada she might have visited?* Make a list on the board (*Ottawa, Montreal, Toronto, Calgary, Vancouver,* etc.). Ask volunteers to briefly tell the class anything they know about these cities.

Vocabulary

Introduce these words and phrases now or after the students listen to the conversation.

How was it?: Did you have a good time?

That's hard to say: That's difficult to decide.

nightlife: leisure activities at night; theater, shows, etc.

for sure: definitely

Presentation

1. With books closed, play the recording or read the conversation at normal speed.

2. Ask the following general comprehension questions:
   - *Who went to Canada?* (Pam)
   - *Which cities did she visit?* (Montreal and Ottawa)
   - *Did she have a good time?* (Yes)

3. Say: *Listen again. This time listen for how she compares Montreal and Ottawa.* On a piece of paper, have students make two columns: *Montreal* and *Ottawa.* Tell them to write down what Pam says about each city. Emphasize that one or two words is enough.

4. Play or read the conversation again at normal speed as the students take notes.

5. Ask the following questions:
   - *According to Pam, which city is prettier?* (Ottawa)
   - *Which city has better sightseeing?* (Ottawa)
   - *Which city is more exciting?* (Montreal)
   - *Which city has better shopping?* (Montreal)
   - *Which city has more restaurants and clubs?* (Montreal)
   - *Which city does she like better?* (It's hard to say.)
   - *Where does Pam's friend want to go?* (Vancouver)
   - *Why?* (It has beautiful views.)

Elicit answers from various volunteers.

6. Pronunciation Focus. Explain that *Wh-* questions have falling intonation. Model the examples: *When did you get back from Canada? Which city did you like better? What did you think of it? Which one has better night life?* Have students repeat.

7. With books open, play or read the conversation again, pausing for choral repetition. Tell students to pay attention to the intonation.

8. Paired Reading. Have students read the conversation, switching roles.

9. Ask pairs to demonstrate the conversation for the class.

GIVE IT A TRY

1. COMPARING PLACES (1)

1. Direct students' attention to the function box. Give students time to read over the examples.

2. Model the examples; have students repeat chorally.

Pronunciation Note: Review of sentence stress. Speakers emphasize words that are most important by stressing them. In comparisons such as those in the examples, the qualities being compared receive heavier stress. On the board, write the following statements.

　It's more exciting than Ottawa.
　It's prettier than Montreal.

Emphasize the modifiers as you model the examples. Have students repeat chorally.

Language Note: Students may need to be reminded of the rules concerning the formation of comparative adjectives. Most one-syllable adjectives (*old, small,* etc.) and two-syllable adjectives ending in *-y* (*pretty, heavy,* etc.) use *-er than* in forming the comparative. Two-syllable adjectives not ending in *-y* (*crowded, polite,* etc.) and all adjectives with three or more syllables (*interesting, beautiful,* etc.) use *more...than* to form the comparative.

3. Pair Work. Have students practice the examples in the function box, switching roles.

Practice

1. Explain the activity. With the class, make a list of cities on the board.

2. Group Work. Divide students into small groups. Have each group decide which two cities to compare.

3. Have groups brainstorm what each city is like and make a list of its attributes. Have one student in each group write down what the group says.

4. Have students compare the cities, using the words given, plus any others that are suitable.

5. Ask various volunteers to report what their groups decided.

2. COMPARING PLACES (2)

1. Direct students' attention to the function box. Give students time to read over the examples.

2. Model the examples; have students repeat chorally.

Pronunciation Note: Stress used to highlight important ideas. Each idea that a speaker wants to emphasize is stressed. Thus, nouns plus the words that describe them receive stress if the speaker wishes to emphasize these ideas. On the board, write the following statements.

　Ottawa. There are more museums.
　Montreal. The stores are more interesting.

Emphasize the stress as you model the statements. Have students repeat chorally.

3. Pair Work. Have students practice the examples, switching roles. Circulate and check pronunciation.

Practice

1. Explain the activity. Give students time to each think of a city or area they have visited and how it compares with their hometown in terms of weather, transportation, restaurants, etc.

2. Model the first question: *Which has nicer weather?* Remind students to give reasons for their comparisons *(My hometown. It is warmer in the winter and cooler in the summer.).*

3. Pair Work. Have students take turns asking their partners to compare their hometown and another city or area. Encourage students to think up more questions of their own. Circulate and check that students give reasons for their comparisons.

4. Ask pairs to demonstrate for the class.

Note: To encourage active listening, tell the class to listen carefully to what each pair says and then decide where the most desirable place for them to live might be based on the information given.

1. COMPARING PLACES (1)

◆ What's | Montreal | like?
| Ottawa |

◇ It's *more exciting* than Ottawa.
It's *prettier* than Montreal.

Practice

As a class or in a small group, choose two cities and compare them. Make statements using these words.

older	more expensive
newer	more interesting
busier	more attractive
quieter	more exciting
cleaner	more crowded

2. COMPARING PLACES (2)

◆ Which city has | more interesting | sightseeing?
| better | shopping?

◇ *Ottawa*. There are more *museums*.
Montreal. The *stores* are more *interesting*.

Practice

Think of a city or area that you have visited. Your partner will ask you to compare it to your hometown. Give reasons for your comparisons. Think of more questions of your own. Then reverse roles.

Ask which has:

1. nicer weather
2. newer buildings
3. cheaper restaurants
4. bigger hotels

5. better sightseeing
6. older neighborhoods
7. better public transportation
8. friendlier people

3. COMPARING PLACES (3)

> ✦ Which *city* is the most *exciting?*
> ✧ *Montreal* is the most *exciting city in Canada.*
>
> ✦ Which *city* has the *best scenery?*
> ✧ *Vancouver.* It has the most *beautiful views in Canada.*

Practice 1

You want to find out what people think is best about your city. With a partner, on a separate piece of paper, write four questions. You need two questions for each of the models above. Ask other classmates for their opinions and write down their answers.

Examples:
Which shopping area is best?
Which restaurant has the best food?

Practice 2

With your partner, look at the answers. Then discuss the results with the class.

LISTEN TO THIS

🔲 Susan is going on a business trip to Boston. She is asking her secretary, Elaine, about hotels there. Listen and fill in the chart below.

❓	The Midtown	The Boston Bay	The Fairfield
Best location			
Newest			
Most expensive			
Cheapest			
Best restaurant			

3. COMPARING PLACES (3)

1. Direct students' attention to the function box. Give students time to read over the examples.

2. Model the examples; have students repeat chorally.

Pronunciation Note: Review of stress, intonation, and rhythm. Heavier stress is placed on the words of comparison. The rhythm and intonation pattern change accordingly. On the board, write the following, marking the stress and intonation.

Which city is the most exciting?
Montreal is the most exciting city.
Which city has the best scenery?
Vancouver. It has the most beautiful views in Canada.

Model, exaggerating the stress and intonation. Have students repeat chorally.

Language Note: For comparisons among three or more things, most one-syllable words and those two-syllable words ending in *-y* take *the -est.* Two-syllable words not ending in *-y* and all words of three or more syllables take *the most … .*

2. Pair Work. Have students practice the exchanges in the function box, switching roles. Point out that *in Canada* can be deleted when it is obvious from the previous part of the conversation what the topic (geographic location) is.

Practice 1

1. Explain the activity. To help students get started, list some topics they can ask about (theaters, parks, recreation areas, schools, transportation, etc.).

Note: *Their city* is the city in which the class is being held.

2. Pair Work. Have students work together to write four questions about the city (two of each type: *is the… / has the …).*

3. Class Work. Have pairs circulate and ask other classmates (three) about their opinions. Tell pairs to return to their seats when they are finished.

Note: The number of classmates can be varied according to how much time is available. This can also be done as a timed activity in which students have a fixed amount of time (5–10 minutes) to ask their questions.

Practice 2

1. Explain the activity.

2. Pair Work. Have students discuss their classmates' answers.

3. Class Work. Have various volunteers report their findings to the class. Talk about any patterns that emerge (for example, 80% think The Viking is the best restaurant).

LISTEN TO THIS

1. Explain the activity. Direct students' attention to the chart. To focus their listening, ask: *What are the names of the three hotels you will hear about? What is the first category in the chart?* (Best location) *What is the second category?* (Newest) Continue asking about the remainder of the chart. Tell students to fill in the chart by making a check mark in the appropriate box.

2. Play the recording or read the conversation at normal speed as the students fill in the chart.

3. Play the recording or read the conversation again as the students check their answers.

4. Pair Work. Have students compare their answers.

5. Check answers by asking: *Which hotel has the best location?* (The Midtown) *Which hotel is the newest?* (The Boston Bay) Continue asking about the remainder of the chart.

Answers:

Best location: *The Midtown*
Newest: *The Boston Bay*
Most expensive: *The Boston Bay*
Cheapest: *The Fairfield*
Best restaurant: *The Fairfield*

6. Ask: *Where is Susan going to stay? Why?* (The Midtown. It sounds the best.)

7. Read or play the conversation again as a final check.

PERSON TO PERSON

Practice 1

1. Divide the class into pairs and have students decide who will be Student A and who will be Student B.
2. Have students listen to the introduction. Then give them time to read the directions. To help students get started, ask students to tell the class what they know about Paris, London, and Rome. Steer them away from talking about the topics listed. Focus them on sharing any specific information they know about these cities.
Note: Do not spend a lot of time on this. The purpose here is to get them to think about what they know about Paris, London, and Rome. If students cannot think of anything to share, move on to the book activity.
3. Give students time to think about their own opinions and check the appropriate boxes.

Practice 2

1. Have students read the directions for their parts. Emphasize that those who are Student A should listen for Bob's opinions about *London and Paris*; those who are Student B should listen for Ruth's opinions about *Paris and Rome*.
2. Read or play the conversation as the students check the appropriate boxes.
3. Read or play again for students to check their answers.
4. Ask volunteers for the answers.
Answers:
Bob's opinion (London or Paris):
Worse traffic: *Paris*
Noisier: *Paris*
Better art galleries: *Paris*
More interesting restaurants: *Paris*
Better nightlife: *London*
Ruth's opinion (Paris or Rome):
Worse traffic: *Rome*
Noisier: *Rome*
Better art galleries: *Paris*
More interesting restaurants: *Rome*
Better nightlife: *Paris*

Practice 3

1. Have students read the directions.
2. Pair Work. Have students compare Bob's and Ruth's opinions with their own as well as their partner's.
3. Ask volunteers to report their findings to the class. To help them get started, model an example: *I think the traffic in London is worse than in Paris and so does (Yumi). Bob also thinks the traffic is worse in Paris, but Ruth thinks Rome is worse than Paris.*
Pronunciation Note: This is a good opportunity to show how stress is placed for emphasis. Here there is heavier stress on *Paris/London/Rome* and on *worse.* Emphasize the stress as you model the example.

LET'S TALK 11

Student Book, page 110.
1. Give students time to read the directions. Emphasize that it is important to give reasons to support their answers.
2. Model the opener *What do you think is the largest country in the world?* Have students repeat.
3. Divide the students into small groups.
4. Group Work. Have the class discuss their answers to the questions.
Note: If time permits, ask students to think of more questions on their own. Questions can be general *(What do you think is the best way to learn English?)* or specific *(What do you think is the best restaurant near here?).*
5. Ask volunteers to present their opinions to the class.
6. Variation: Have pairs of students select five of the opinion questions and interview as many of their classmates as possible. Ask volunteers to share the results with the class.

PERSON
TO PERSON

STUDENT
A

(Student A looks at this page. Student B looks at the next page.)

Bob and Ruth have just returned from Europe. You are going to hear their opinions about Paris, London, and Rome.

Practice 1

Before you listen, check whether you think London or Paris is noisier, has worse traffic, and so, on. Use the boxes below.

Practice 2

Now listen to Bob's opinions about London and Paris, and check the appropriate box.

	Your opinion		Bob's opinion	
	London	Paris	London	Paris
Worse traffic				
Noisier				
Better art galleries				
More interesting restaurants				
Better nightlife				

Practice 3

Compare all four opinions: yours, your partner's, Bob's, and Ruth's.

PERSON TO PERSON

STUDENT B

(Student B looks at this page. Student A looks at the previous page.)

Bob and Ruth have just returned from Europe. You are going to hear their opinions about Paris, London, and Rome.

Practice 1

Before you listen, check whether you think Paris or Rome is noisier, has worse traffic, and so on. Use the boxes below.

Practice 2

Now listen to Ruth's opinions about Paris and Rome, and check the appropriate box.

	Your opinion		Ruth's opinion	
	Paris	**Rome**	**Paris**	**Rome**
Worse traffic				
Noisier				
Better art galleries				
More interesting restaurants				
Better nightlife				

Practice 3

Compare all four opinions: yours, your partner's, Bob's, and Ruth's.

COMPONENTS

Student Book, pages 89–96
Let's Talk 12, Student Book page 111
Cassette/CD
Optional Activity 12, page 138
Review (Units 10–12), Student Book page 112

OBJECTIVES

Functions: Discussing future plans, discussing future wants, hopes, and possible plans

Topics: careers, hopes, and dreams; business trip itinerary

Structures:

- Future with plan to / going to / planning to: What do you plan to do? / are you going to do? /are you planning to do?
- Future with present progressive: What are you doing after that? / I'm going back to school after that.
- Expressing possibility: I might go fishing. / I hope to get a promotion. I hope I get (I'll get) a promotion. / I'd like to lose some weight. / I want to start getting more exercise.
- Will vs. going to: How long will you be there? / How long are you going to be there?

Pronunciation Focus: Stressed words in a sentence usually have a regular beat; for example, *I'd like to see a movie.*

Listen to This: Listening for specific information, filling in an appointment book

CONVERSATION 1
WHAT ARE YOU GOING TO DO?

Prelistening Questions

1. With books closed, read the title of the conversation and the prelistening questions. Introduce the difference between *plans* and *dreams* by explaining that a *plan* is something we intend to do in the future, while a *dream* is indefinite. Elicit answers to each question from several volunteers.

2. Have students open their books. Check that the photograph and the text of the conversation are covered.

3. Group Work. In small groups, have students take turns asking and answering the questions. Tell each group to select one person to write down what each group member plans to do.

4. Ask each group to report some of the things they plan to do *(Mayumi is going to get married next year. / Yuko is going to Thailand during school vacation,* etc.). Maintain a rapid pace.

5. Direct students' attention to the photograph. Tell students the high school guidance counselor is talking to students who are in their last year of high school. Explain that a guidance counselor helps students figure out what to do after they graduate.

6. Ask students to speculate:
   - *What do you think the guidance counselor is saying to them?*
   - *What are some things they might do after graduating from high school?*

Elicit answers from several volunteers for each question.

Vocabulary

Introduce these words and phrases now or after the students listen to the conversation.

to major in: to study in a concentrated way in college

field: an area of knowledge; someone majors in (medicine) to work in the field of (medicine) after graduation

the basics: fundamental knowledge

practical: useful

to take it easy: to relax

Presentation

1. With books closed, play the recording or read the conversation at normal speed.

2. Ask the following general comprehension questions:
   - *Are all the students going to go to college right after graduation?* (No)
   - *How many plan to work?* (one)
   - *How many plan to travel?* (one)

3. Say: *Listen again. This time listen for details about what each student plans to do.* Play or read again, pausing for choral repetition.

4. Ask the following questions:
   - *What is Donna going to do after she graduates?* (go to college)
   - *Where?* (in Ohio)
   - *What is she going to major in?* (engineering)
   - *What is Simon going to do?* (work for his father)
   - *How long is he going to work?* (about a year)
   - *What is he going to do after that?* (go back to school)
   - *What is he going to study?* (business)
   - *What is Fong planning to do?* (travel in Europe, then come back to study)
   - *How long is he going to travel?* (for about six months)

Elicit answers from various students or have students tell their partners the answers.

5. Paired Reading. Have students read the conversation, switching roles.

What plans do you have for the future?
Are you going to graduate soon? Get a job? Get married? Travel?

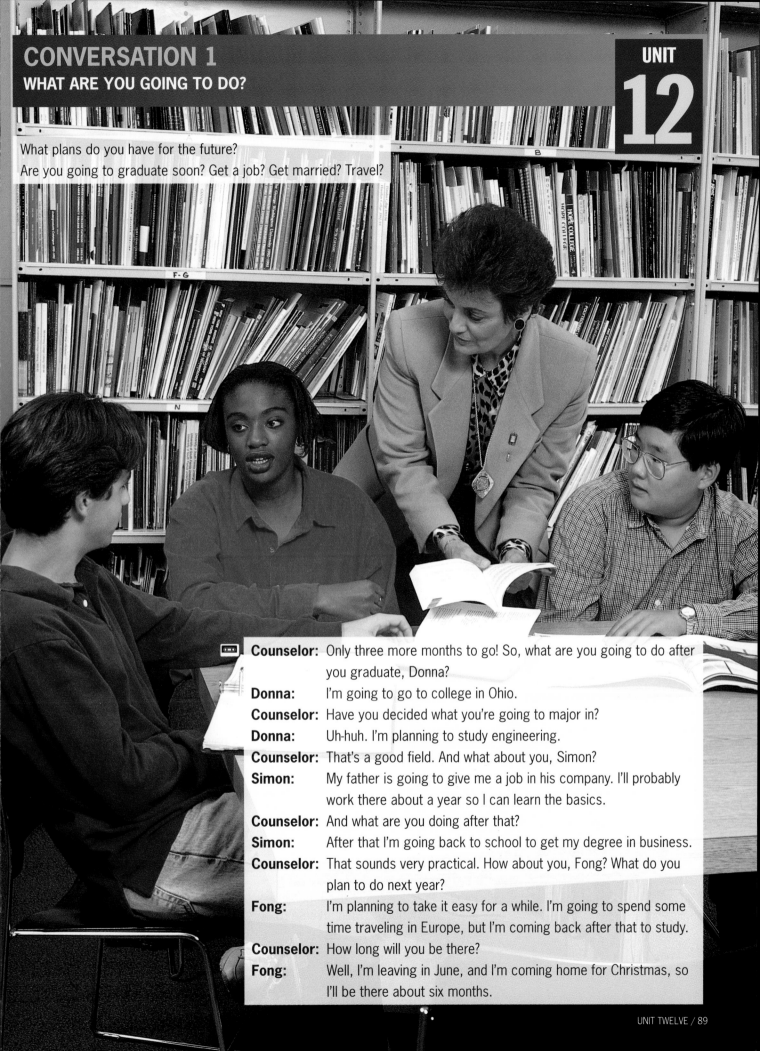

Counselor: Only three more months to go! So, what are you going to do after you graduate, Donna?

Donna: I'm going to go to college in Ohio.

Counselor: Have you decided what you're going to major in?

Donna: Uh-huh. I'm planning to study engineering.

Counselor: That's a good field. And what about you, Simon?

Simon: My father is going to give me a job in his company. I'll probably work there about a year so I can learn the basics.

Counselor: And what are you doing after that?

Simon: After that I'm going back to school to get my degree in business.

Counselor: That sounds very practical. How about you, Fong? What do you plan to do next year?

Fong: I'm planning to take it easy for a while. I'm going to spend some time traveling in Europe, but I'm coming back after that to study.

Counselor: How long will you be there?

Fong: Well, I'm leaving in June, and I'm coming home for Christmas, so I'll be there about six months.

1. DISCUSSING FUTURE PLANS (1)

✦ What do you What are you	plan to going to planning to	do	after you graduate? in the fall? next year?	
✧ I'm	going to planning to	go to college. take it easy.		✧ I don't know yet. I haven't decided yet.

Practice

Find a partner. Take turns asking each other about future plans. Use the cues below to ask. Then add two questions of your own.

1. after you finish this class
2. after school/work tonight
3. for your next vacation
4. the day after tomorrow
5. this weekend
6. on Friday night

2. DISCUSSING FUTURE PLANS (2)

✦ What are you doing after that?	
✧ I'm going back to school after that. working for my father next year.	✧ I'm not sure yet. I'm still not sure.

Practice 1

Student A: Ask your partner what he/she is doing at the following times.
Student B: Answer using one of the choices below.

Student A

1. next summer

2. on the weekend

3. for your birthday

4. on New Year's Eve

Student B

1. visit California
   relax and take it easy
   get a part-time job

2. go to the beach
   stay home
   have friends over for dinner

3. have a small party
   go out to a nice restaurant
   not do anything special

4. go to a dance
   watch TV
   go to a party

Practice 2

Repeat Practice 1, but this time answer using your own plans. Think of other times to ask about. Then reverse roles.

GIVE IT A TRY

1. DISCUSSING FUTURE PLANS (1)

1. Direct students' attention to the function box. Give students time to read over the examples.

2. Model the examples; have students repeat chorally.

Pronunciation Note: Blending of *going to.* In rapid speech, *going to* is often blended so that it sounds like /gonna/. Write the following on the board:

What are you going to do in the fall?
I'm going to go to college.

Exaggerate the blending *(gonnado/gonnago)* as you model the examples.

Language Note: *Plan to, going to,* and *planning to* are all used to talk about the future. The use of *going to* + infinitive is used to indicate that an event is under way *(It is going to rain. / I am going to get married.)*. *Plan to* and *planning to* are used when the plan is less definite or not quite finalized *(I'm planning to go to Europe next summer, but I don't know when I'm going.)*. Both *going to* and *will* are used to make factual statements regarding future activities. *Going to* is used more often than *will* in spoken English. Since *will* is used in certain contexts to indicate a promise or willingness, students should be encouraged to use *going to* when simply setting plans.

3. Pair Work. Have students practice the questions and answers in the function box, switching roles.

Practice

1. Explain the activity. Give students time to read the cues listed and think about how they would respond to each.

2. Pair Work. Have students take turns asking each other about future plans, using the cues given.

Note: To expand this practice, say: *Get more information from each other when possible. Ask questions like: Who are you going with? / Are you going on your own?,* etc.

3. Ask several pairs to demonstrate for the class. Tell students to pay attention to their pronunciation.

4. Have students continue, using cues of their own.

2. DISCUSSING FUTURE PLANS (2)

1. Direct students' attention to the function box. Give students time to read over the examples.

2. Model the examples; have students repeat.

Pronunciation Note: Review of stress. Heavier stress is placed on the content words. Write the following on the board:

What are you doing after that?
I'm going back to school after that.
I'm working for my father next year.
I'm not sure yet.

Exaggerate the stress as you model the examples.

Language Note: The present progressive (continuous) is used in a similar way to *going to* to talk about the future. It can be used to talk about a plan for a future happening that is anticipated in the present. *(He is leaving on Thursday. / She is seeing her dentist on Friday. / I am taking the bus to the airport.)*

3. Pair Work. Have students practice the questions and answers in the function box, switching roles. Circulate and check their pronunciation.

Practice 1

1. Explain the activity. Divide the students into pairs. Have them choose parts.

2. Give students time to read over their cues.

Language Note: *Have friends over for dinner* is a colloquial way to say *invite friends to one's house for dinner.*

3. Pair Work. Have students complete the activity, then switch parts and repeat.

4. Ask one pair to demonstrate the conversation for each of the times given.

Practice 2

1. Explain the activity. Tell students to think about what they plan to do at each of the times listed. Have them each write down (three) other times to ask about.

2. Pair Work. Have students ask and answer questions about their own plans, switching roles.

3. Ask volunteers to demonstrate for the class.

3. DISCUSSING FUTURE PLANS (3)

1. Direct students' attention to the function box. Give students time to read over the examples.

2. Model the examples; have students repeat chorally.

Pronunciation Note: Review of stress on content words. In response to the questions *How long …?* or *When …?* the stress will be placed on the time markers. In response to the question *Where will you be?* the stress will be placed on the location. Write the following on the board:

How long will you be there?

I'll be there for about six months.

I'll be there a week from today.

I'll be there on the sixteenth.

Where will you be at six o'clock?

I'll be at home.

Exaggerate the stress as you model the examples. Have students repeat chorally.

Language Note: Future with *will*. When talking about plans, there is some overlap with *going to*. However, *will* in future carries the idea of a promise *(I'll be there at 8 o'clock.)*, a prediction *(He'll be late for class; he always is.)*, or certainty *(I'll be in Chicago next week.)*.

3. Pair Work. Have students practice the examples in the function box, switching roles. Circulate and check their pronunciation.

Practice

1. Explain the activity.

2. Pair Work. Have students ask and answer questions about the schedule for next week, using the information in the appointment book.

3. Ask several pairs to demonstrate for the class.

4. Have students switch roles and continue.

LISTEN TO THIS

1. Explain the activity. Give students time to look at the appointment book.

2. Play the recording or read the conversation at normal speed as the students fill in the appointment book.

3. Play or read again for students to check their answers.

4. Pair Work. Have students check their work by comparing what they have written in the appointment book.

5. Call on various students to give parts of Irene Reynolds's schedule. To encourage active listening, vary the questions. For example, ask: *What is she doing first, (Yumi)? What is she doing at 10:00 A.M., (Hiro)? What time is her tour of the new building, (Maeko)?* Continue asking about the remainder of her schedule.

Answers:

8:00–10:00 A.M.	*Breakfast with vice presidents*
10:00 A.M.	*Drive to new building*
10:30–11:30 A.M.	*Tour of the new building*
1:00 P.M.	*Monthly meeting, managers Chicago/New York*
7:00 P.M.	*Go to TV station for interview*
8:00 P.M.	*Business Club Dinner*
8:30 P.M.	*Dinner served*
9:30 P.M.	*Give speech*
11:00 P.M.	*Dinner meeting will end*

6. Play or read the conversation again for a final check.

3. DISCUSSING FUTURE PLANS (3)

✦ How long will you be there?
✧ I'll be there *for about six months.*

✦ When will you be *in Chicago?*
✧ I'll be there | *a week from today.*
　　　　　　　 | *on the sixteenth.*

✦ Where will you be | *at six o'clock?*
　　　　　　　　　 | *on Sunday afternoon?*
✧ I'll be *at home.*

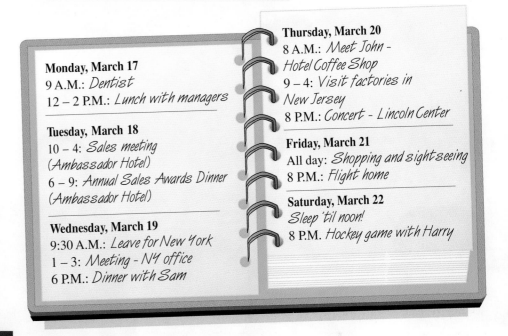

Monday, March 17
9 A.M.: *Dentist*
12 – 2 P.M.: *Lunch with managers*

Tuesday, March 18
10 – 4: *Sales meeting (Ambassador Hotel)*
6 – 9: *Annual Sales Awards Dinner (Ambassador Hotel)*

Wednesday, March 19
9:30 A.M.: *Leave for New York*
1 – 3: *Meeting - NY office*
6 P.M.: *Dinner with Sam*

Thursday, March 20
8 A.M.: *Meet John - Hotel Coffee Shop*
9 – 4: *Visit factories in New Jersey*
8 P.M.: *Concert - Lincoln Center*

Friday, March 21
All day: *Shopping and sightseeing*
8 P.M.: *Flight home*

Saturday, March 22
Sleep 'til noon!
8 P.M. *Hockey game with Harry*

Practice

Look at your appointment book for next week and answer your partner's questions. Your partner will ask you:

1. three *when* questions
2. three *where* questions
3. three *how long* questions

Then reverse roles.

LISTEN TO THIS

Irene Reynolds is the busy president of a large company. Listen as Jim, the assistant, gives Irene her schedule for Monday of next week. Fill in her appointment book.

MONDAY

APPOINTMENTS & EVENTS

Hours	Appointment	Hours	Appointment
8:00 am		4:00 pm	
9:00 am		5:00 pm	
10:00 am		6:00 pm	
11:00 am		7:00 pm	
12:00 pm		8:00 pm	
1:00 pm		9:00 pm	
2:00 pm		10:00 pm	
3:00 pm		11:00 pm	

CONVERSATION 2
WHAT DO YOU WANT TO DO?

What is a New Year's resolution?
Have you ever made one?
What are some typical resolutions?

Henry: Hi, Alice... have you made any New Year's resolutions yet?

Alice: Just the usual. I'd like to lose some weight, and I want to save some money.

Henry: Come on! Everybody makes those resolutions!

Alice: I know. Well, I hope I'll get a promotion at work, but that's not a resolution. I am going to work harder. How about you?

Henry: Hmm, I quit smoking last June. That was last year's promise to myself.

Alice: So, what do you want to do this year?

Henry: I want to start getting more exercise. I have to lose weight, so I'd like to join a health club. Jeff... what are you going to do?

Jeff: I'd like to treat myself to a really nice vacation.

Alice: Oh? Where do you think you'll go?

Jeff: I don't know. I might go to a quiet beach in Mexico, or I might go fishing up in Canada. I haven't made up my mind yet.

Pronunciation Focus

The stressed words in a sentence usually have a regular beat. Listen and practice.

I'd líke to lóse some wéight.

I wánt to sáve some móney.

Whát are you góing to dó?

Whére do you thínk you'll gó?

Now practice the conversation. Try to give stressed words a regular beat.

CONVERSATION 2
WHAT DO YOU WANT TO DO?

Prelistening Questions

1. With books closed, say: *Last New Year's I made a resolution.* Write *resolution* on the board. Continue: *I made a resolution to stop smoking. I also made a resolution to exercise more. My brother made a resolution to lose weight.*

2. Ask the prelistening questions. Elicit answers from various volunteers. Together make a list of typical resolutions.

Culture Note: A New Year's resolution is a promise made, usually to oneself, to do (or not do) something. Typical resolutions include: exercise more, quit smoking, lose weight, go to bed earlier, drink less coffee, and eat a better diet. This may vary from culture to culture.

3. Direct students' attention to the photograph. Check that the text of the conversation is covered. Say: *They are at the annual office holiday party. They are talking about their New Year's resolutions. What kind of resolutions might people in an office make to each other?* If students have difficulty responding, suggest: *Get to work earlier, work harder, take shorter coffee breaks.* Elicit answers from various volunteers. Maintain a rapid pace.

Vocabulary

Introduce these words and phrases now or after the students listen to the conversation.

the usual: whatever one usually does

promotion: a raise in position or rank (usually uncludes a salary increase)

treat myself: do something special for myself

made up my mind: decided

Presentation

1. With books closed, play the recording or read the conversation at normal speed.

2. Ask the following general comprehension questions:
   - *Have all of them made New Year's resolutions already?* (Yes)
   - *Are any of the resolutions unusual?* (No)

3. Say: *Listen again. This time listen for what each person plans to do. The woman's name is Alice. The first man's name is Henry. The second man's name is Jeff.*

Note: Knowing the speakers' names is not essential for understanding the conversation, but will facilitate understanding the conversation and the comprehension questions.

4. Play or read the conversation again, pausing for choral repetition.

5. Ask the following questions:
   - *What are the first two things Alice plans to do?* (lose some weight and save some money)
   - *What else is she going to do?* (work harder)
   - *Is Henry going to quit smoking?* (No)
   - *Why not?* (He quit last year.)
   - *What does he want to do this year?* (get more exercise)
   - *What is he going to join?* (a health club)
   - *What is Jeff going to do?* (go on a really nice vacation)
   - *Where is he going to go?* (He hasn't decided yet.)

6. Pronunciation Focus. Explain that stressed words in a sentence usually have a regular beat. Model the examples: *I'd like to lose some weight. / I want to save some money. / What are you going to do? / Where do you think you'll go?* Have students repeat.

Pronunciation Note: To emphasize the regular beat, clap your hands as you model the examples.

7. With books open, play or read the conversation again.

8. Paired Reading. Have students read the conversation, switching roles. Remind students to pay attention to the stressed word.

9. Expansion. If time permits, discuss how deciding to treat oneself to a really nice vacation could be a type of New Year's resolution. To help students get started, bring up how working less, taking time for oneself, and increasing leisure activities are all part of taking care of oneself. Students from cultures where increasing leisure activities is being promoted (for example, Japan) should be familiar with this concept.

GIVE IT A TRY

1. DISCUSSING THE FUTURE

1. Direct students' attention to the function box. Give students time to read over the examples.

2. Model the examples; have students repeat chorally.

Pronunciation Note: Review of rhythm and sentence stress. Heavier stress is placed on the content words. The rhythm is very regular. Write the following questions on the board:

What do you want to do?
What would you like to do?
What are you going to do?

Keep the rhythm very regular as you model the questions.

3. Pair Work. Have students practice the examples in the function box, switching roles. Circulate and assist with pronunciation.

Practice

1. Explain the activity. To help students get started, ask a student to choose a resolution from the list *(learn to play an instrument)*. Ask an appropriate follow-up question *(What are you going to learn to play?)*.

2. Pair Work. Have students practice telling each other their New Year's resolutions. Circulate and assist with the follow-up questions as needed.

3. Ask several pairs to demonstrate for the class.

2. DISCUSSING HOPES

1. Direct students' attention to the function box. Give students time to read over the examples.

2. Model the examples; have students repeat chorally.

Pronunciation Note: Blending of *what do you*. In rapid speech, *what do you* is often blended so that it sounds like */wuh-duh-ya/*. Write the following questions on the board.

What do you hope will happen?
What do you hope you'll do?
What do you hope to do?

Exaggerate the blending as you model the questions.

3. Pair Work. Have students practice the examples in the function box, switching roles. Circulate and assist with pronunciation.

Practice 1

1. Explain the activity. Model the example in the book. Repeat with a student, switching roles. Encourage students to ask follow-up questions.

2. Group Work. Have students discuss what they hope to do in the next five years.

3. Ask several pairs to demonstrate for the class.

Practice 2

1. Explain the activity.

2. Group Work. Have students discuss what they hope to do in the next ten years.

3. Ask several pairs to demonstrate for the class.

4. Expansion. Ask students to present some ideas about what they hope to do sometime in their lives.

1. DISCUSSING THE FUTURE

✦ What do you want to do?
What would you like to do?
What are you going to do?

✧ I'd like to | *lose some weight.*
I want to | *start getting more exercise.*

Practice

Make three New Year's resolutions. Your partner will ask you what they are. Choose from the list below or make up your own. Your partner will ask you for more information. Then reverse roles.

learn to play an instrument   get better grades

keep a diary   study more

read a book a month   take up a new hobby

2. DISCUSSING HOPES

✦ What do you hope | will happen?
| you'll do?
| to do?

✧ I hope | *I'll get a promotion.*
| *I get a promotion.*
| *to get a promotion.*

Practice 1

Form a small group to discuss your future goals. Ask and answer like this:

Student A: What do you hope to do in the next five years?
Student B: I hope to travel.

Practice 2

Repeat Practice 1, but this time ask about the next ten years.

3. DISCUSSING POSSIBILITIES

✦ *Where* do you think you'll *go?*
Where are you going to *go?*

✧ I might	go to Mexico. go fishing in Canada.	✧ I haven't made up my mind yet.

Practice 1

With your partner, discuss some possible choices for future plans. Answer each other's questions freely and reverse roles as you go along. Follow the example below.

Cue: college/apply to after high school
Question: Which college do you think you'll apply to after high school?

1. which subject/major in at university
2. which company/apply to after college
3. where/go on your vacation
4. when/take your vacation
5. how long/be in Europe
6. who/marry

Practice 2

Think of some more questions about the future to discuss with your partner. Try to use *which*, *where*, *when*, *who*, and *how long*.

LISTEN TO THIS

Alessandro is talking to his friend about what he wants to do this summer. He mentions all of the things below. Listen and put a question mark (**?**) beside the things he might do or wants to do. Put a check (✔) beside the things he will definitely do.

..........work in his father's restaurant

..........save money

..........take time off

..........read

..........rent movies

.........go to a friend's cabin

..........go waterskiing and swimming

..........help build a dock

..........visit uncle in Italy

..........go to Milan

..........go to Florence

..........move to a new apartment

..........organize new apartment

3. DISCUSSING POSSIBILITIES

1. Direct students' attention to the function box. Give students time to read over the examples.

Pronunciation Note: Stress on *might*. Heavier stress is sometimes placed on *might* to emphasize the uncertainty in the situation. Write the following statements on the board.

> I might go to Mexico.
> I might go fishing in Canada.

Exaggerate the stress on *might* as you model the statements.

Language Note: Review the difference between *will* and *going to*. *Will* asks for a prediction (*Where do you think you'll go?*) and *going to* asks what is planned (*Where are you going to go?*).

2. Pair Work. Have students practice the examples in the function box, switching roles. Circulate and assist with pronunciation.

Practice 1

1. Explain the activity. Model the example. Have students repeat. Emphasize that they are to answer each other's questions freely.

Note: Remind students to use the different ways to express uncertainty presented in the unit (*hope to / want to / would like to / might*) when they answer.

2. Pair Work. Have students practice discussing future plans, using the cues given.

3. Have students switch roles and continue.

4. Ask pairs to demonstrate using each of the cues provided.

Practice 2

1. Explain the activity. Emphasize that they should try to use *which, where, when, who,* and *how long*. Give students time to think up some questions to ask. Circulate and assist as needed.

2. Pair Work. Have students continue discussing future plans, using their own questions.

3. Ask several pairs to demonstrate for the class.

LISTEN TO THIS

1. Give students time to read the directions. Check understanding by asking: What are you going to write next to the things Alessandro might do or wants to do? (a question mark) What are you going to write next to the things he definitely will do? (a check mark)

2. Together read over the list of things Alessandro will talk about. Emphasize that he will mention all of these things. Their task is to listen for what he plans to do regarding each.

3. Play or read the conversation at normal speed as the students mark their answers.

4. Play the recording or read the conversation again as the students check their answers.

5. Pair Work. Have students compare their answers.

6. Check answers by asking: Is Alessandro going to work in his father's restaurant? (Yes, he is.) Is Alessandro going to save money? (He wants to.) Continue asking about the remainder of the things listed.

Answers: work in his father's restaurant (Yes, he is.); save money (wants to); take time off (Yes, he is.); read (maybe); rent movies (maybe); help build a dock (wants to); visit uncle in Italy (Yes, for two weeks); go to Milan (might go); go to Florence (might go); move to a new apartment (Yes, he is.); go to a friend's cabin (will definitely go); go waterskiing and swimming (wants to); organize new apartment (hopes to)

7. Play or read the conversation again as a final check.

OPTIONAL ACTIVITY 12: What Are Your Plans and Dreams? *See Teacher's Notes, page 126, and Activity Sheet, page 138.*

PERSON TO PERSON

Practice 1

1. Divide the class into pairs and have students decide who will be Student A and who will be Student B.
2. Have students listen to the introduction. Then give them time to read the directions. (Student A takes notes on Ben. / Student B takes notes on Jill.) Tell students to make their notes very brief.
3. Read or play the conversation as the students take notes.
4. Read or play again as the students check their notes.
5. Pair Work. Have students check their answers with their partner's information. Circulate and help resolve any inconsistencies.

Answers:

Ben: After high school: *work for a year, then go to college;* After college: *get an easy 9-to-5 job;* Future hopes: *a steady job and a nice family*

Jill: After high school: *go to Harvard;* After college: *go to law school;* Future hopes: *make a lot of money, be the president someday*

Language Note: Point out that *be the president someday* means *be the president of the United States.*

Practice 2

1. Explain the activity. To help students characterize Ben and Jill, ask how they would describe them. Make two columns on the board: *Ben* and *Jill*. List what students say in the appropriate column.

Note: The students are being asked to think about their own personalities and values. It is important that students feel that no judgment is being made on them as they do this activity.

2. Give students time to complete the activity. Circulate and help students decide where to put their X.

Practice 3

1. Explain the activity.
2. Pair Work. Have students compare their answers. Circulate and make sure students discuss the reasons for their answers.

LET'S TALK 12

Student Book, page 111.

1. Give students time to read the directions. Check understanding by asking: *Who has left you money? How much money? What do you have to do to get the money?*
2. Model the opener: *What things would make our community better?* Have students repeat. Elicit possible responses *(We could … / Why don't we …? / Let's …).* On the board, generate a list of community improvements. Some possibilities include: road improvements; recreational facilities: public swimming pool, or tennis courts; arts funding: youth orchestra, amateur drama group; day-care center; meals for the elderly; recycling programs.
3. Separate the students into pairs.
4. Pair Work. Have students work together to decide which community improvements to do and what they will cost. Make sure each student fills in the chart.
5. Group Work. Have partners split up and form new groups of three or four students. Have students report to each other on what they are going to do with the money.

REVIEW (UNITS 10–12)

Student Book, page 112.

1. Give students time to read the situation and the directions. Brainstorm some ideas to get the discussions going: trips; living abroad; a teacher, friend, or relative who was a big influence; a book; a stay in the hospital.
2. Model an example opener: *When I was 10, I had a very embarrassing experience. I woke up late for school and got to the school bus with my pajamas on!*
3. Divide the class into small groups.
4. Group Work. Have students discuss interesting or important experiences they have had. Encourage students to refer to Units 10, 11, and 12 for help.
5. Ask volunteers to report on their own experiences or on group members' experiences.

PERSON TO PERSON — STUDENT A

(Student A looks at this page. Student B looks at the next page.)

▭ Ben and Jill are high school friends who will be graduating soon. They are talking to each other about the future.

Practice 1

Listen and take short notes on Ben's future hopes and plans. Jill's are given to you.

	BEN	JILL
After high school		• go to Harvard • major in Business and Economics
After college		• go to law school • practice law
Future hopes		• go into politics • make a lot of money • be president of the U.S.

Practice 2

Check your answers with your partner's information.

Look at the information about Ben and Jill again and decide which of them you are more similar to. If you are more like Jill, put an X close to her name. If you are more like Ben, put an X close to his name.

More like Jill		More like Ben

Practice 3

Compare your X with your partner's. Start your discussion of the reasons like this: "I think I'm more like Jill/Ben because..."

PERSON TO PERSON

STUDENT B

(Student B looks at this page. Student A looks at the previous page.)

▭ Ben and Jill are high school friends who will be graduating soon. They are talking to each other about the future.

Practice 1

Listen and take short notes on Jill's future hopes and plans. Ben's are given to you.

	JILL	BEN
After high school		• work for Dad for a year • go to college • study literature or art
After college		• easy job • 9 to 5
Future hopes		• steady job • nice family

Practice 2

Check your answers with your partner's information.

Look at the information about Ben and Jill again and decide which of them you are more similar to. If you are more like Jill, put an X close to her name. If you are more like Ben, put an X close to his name.

More like Jill   **More like Ben**

Practice 3

Compare your X with your partner's. Start your discussion of the reasons like this: "I think I'm more like Jill/Ben because . . ."

Once every three years, the government does a survey about people and their occupations. Interview a classmate, and fill out the form below. Then find a new partner and reverse roles.

If you and your classmates are students, make up an occupation and employer that you think is interesting.

Start like this: "Could I ask you a few questions, please?"

SURVEY

NAME _____
         Last   *First*

ADDRESS _____

_____

_____

_____

TELEPHONE _____
              Area Code   *Number*

OCCUPATION _____

EMPLOYER _____

Someone you know is going to win an award today. You know who it is, but you can't tell anyone. However, the other members of your group might be able to guess from a description.

Get into groups of four people. Each member of the group thinks of a person who is well-known to all the other group members: a teacher? another student? a co-worker? Fill in one column of the chart below, but don't show it to anyone. The other group members will ask for information and fill in their charts. Then they will guess who you are describing. Take turns.

Start like this: "I can't tell you who it is, but I can answer questions."

Your names:				
Descriptions:				
Sex				
Age				
Height				
Weight				
Hair color				
Hair length				
Hair style				
Other details				
Person's name				

You and your partner are interior design students. Your homework is to decorate and furnish a one-bedroom apartment. Remember to think about sizes, shapes, and colors. This will be a model apartment, so you have to pay attention to details.

Start like this: "Which room do you want to talk about first?"

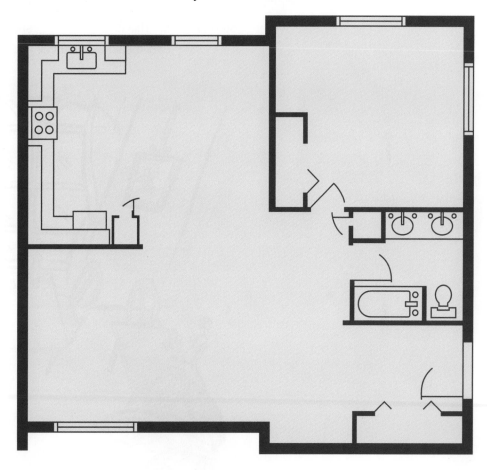

Situation:

You have just moved to a new city, and you don't know anybody. However, your cousin gave you the name and phone number of a friend. Call the friend, chat, and agree to meet.

Be sure to tell your partner what you look like. End the conversation by saying something like "Let's meet at the Cafe Coco. I'll be at the table in..."

With your partner, write the telephone conversation. Look at Units 1,2, and 3 to help you. Then join another pair of students and perform your conversation.

Start like this: "This is .... speaking. My cousin gave me your number and said I should call you..."

A group of six foreign students is coming to your city on an exchange program. You have been asked to plan their schedule for three days.

With a partner, decide where you want to take them, and when. Remember to think about when restaurants, stores, clubs, and sightseeing places open and close. Also, think about locations. Everyone will be walking or using public transportation.

Here is some information to help you plan.

- There are three male and three female students.
- They are all between 17 and 19 years of age.
- They are all staying in a college dormitory nearby.
- They get breakfast at the dorm, but not lunch or dinner.
- They asked for some free time.

Start like this: "Let's think of as many places as we can. Then we can choose some and arrange the schedule."

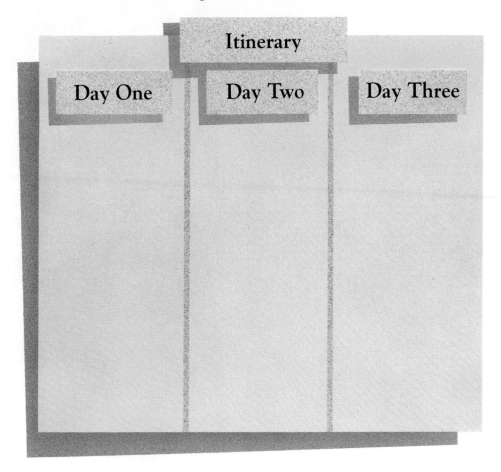

Itinerary

Day One	Day Two	Day Three

You and your partner are going on vacation for ten days. Try to reach an agreement about where you will go and what you will do. Discuss the things you like and dislike with your partner.

What things are there to do and see in these places?

Can you think of any that are not in the posters?

Start like this: "I like big cities. How about you?"

You and your partner enjoy each other's company, so you want to spend some time together outside of class.

Student A: Think of a place or activity that you like. Then, think of a time when you are free, and invite your partner.

Student B: Consider your partner's invitation. Do you like his/her suggestion? Are you free at that time? Do you want to change or add to the invitation? Decide on a plan that is good for both of you, and make all your final arrangements.

Start like this: "We should get together some time. What do you like doing outside of class?"

Situation:

Your school/company is having a "Getting To Know You" party. You want to find someone who likes some of the same things you do, and arrange to do them together.

Approach a classmate you don't know well. Introduce yourself and try to find activities you both like. If you find something, arrange a time and a place to meet and give directions to the place. If you can't find something you both like to do, approach another classmate. Look at Units 4, 5, and 6 for help or ideas.

Start like this: "Hi. This party is a great idea, isn't it? I'm .... , and I really like .... "

Anne-Marie is getting married, and you and your friends want to buy her a nice gift. You have enough money to get one of the choices below.
Get into a group of four people and compare the items below. If you have another idea, suggest it. Then, as a group, make a final decision about which gift you want to buy for her. Be sure to give reasons.

Start like this: "Which one of these gifts do you think is best?"

You and your partner are going to open a restaurant in San Diego, California. Plan your new restaurant.

Start like this: "What kind of food do you think we should serve?"

Type of food: ....
Size of restaurant: ....
Decor: ....

After you decide on the decor, the size of the restaurant, and the type of food you want to serve, plan your menu—including prices.

MENU

You are a college student. You were away visiting friends for the weekend. When you left on Friday afternoon, your apartment was spotless. When you got home on Friday evening, this is how you found the apartment and your roommate. Complain politely to your partner, and request action.

Start like this: "I hate to mention it, but look at this apartment!"

Situation 1:

Student A: You are a very fussy shopper. Nothing is ever 'just right.' Decide on an item to buy. See Units 7 and 9 for help and ideas.

Start like this: "Can you help me? I'm looking for a/an ...., but I can't find one that I really like."

Student B: You are the sales clerk who is helping Student A.

Situation 2:

Reverse roles.

Student A: You are a new waiter/waitress. Your partner will use a menu from Unit 8 to place his/her order. Use Unit 9 also, for more ideas and helpful language.

Student B: You are a very fussy customer. Nothing that you are served is ever 'just right.' Use the menu from Unit 8 to place your order. Also use Unit 9 for more ideas and helpful language. Then role-play the conversation with your partner.

Start like this: "Excuse me! I'm sorry, but I can't possibly eat/drink these things. First of all, . . . "

Imagine that you are a famous person, real or fictional. Your partner is a screenwriter who wants to make a movie about you. He/she is going to interview you about your life. (You don't have to know anything about the person you choose. Have fun making up the details.)
Your partner uses the chart below to write down your answers. Then reverse roles.

Start like this: "Before I can write this movie, I have to ask you a few questions about your life. First of all, . . . "

When:

What happened:

Get into a small group and exchange opinions with your classmates. Discuss what each of you *thinks* is the correct answer to these questions. Give reasons wherever possible.

What do you think is:

1. the best country to go to on vacation?
2. the worst country to go to on vacation?
3. the most dangerous city in (your country)?
4. the most dangerous city in the world?
5. the hottest country in the world?
6. the most interesting historical location in your country?
7. the most expensive country to visit?
8. the cheapest country to go to on vacation?

Start like this: "What do you think is the largest country in the world?"

A wealthy stranger has died and left you and your partner half a million dollars each – for your personal use. But. . . there's a catch. In order to get your money the two of you must spend two million dollars of the stranger's money to improve life in your community. Decide how the money will be spent. After the two of you make your final decision, discuss how each of you is going to spend your half million.

Use the chart below. (It isn't necessary to use all six spaces.)

Start like this: "What things would make our community better?"

COMMUNITY IMPROVEMENTS

AMOUNT:	PROJECT:

Situation:

People can learn from their own experiences. They can also learn from other people's experiences. Talk with your classmates about experiences.

Get into a small group and talk about an interesting or important experience you have had. Your classmates will ask you questions to get more details. Did anyone's experience give you an idea about something you want to do in the future? Talk about that, too. Check Units 10, 11, and 12 for help.

Start like this: "When I was young, I had a very funny/embarrassing/frightening/important experience. This is what happened..."

TAPESCRIPT

Conversation 1

Man: Great wedding, isn't it? Are you a friend of the bride or the groom?

Woman: The bride. We went to college together.

Man: Really? I work with the groom. Oh, by the way, my name's Bob...Bob Bradley.

Woman: Hi, Bob. I'm June Owens.

Man: I'm sorry. I didn't get your first name.

Woman: It's June. Nice to meet you.

Man: You, too. So, what do you do, June?

Woman: I'm a teller at the Bank of New York. How about you?

Man: I'm a computer programmer.

Conversation 2

Man: Tim always has good parties, doesn't he?

Woman: He sure does! Do you go to school with Tim?

Man: Yeah. We study law together at Princeton University. How about you?

Woman: I'm in the Fine Arts program at Smith College. My name's Kim Jackson, by the way.

Man: Nice to meet you, Kim. I'm John Hunt.

Woman: Well, John...would you like to dance?

Man: I'd love to.

Conversation 3

Woman: What did you think of the speeches?

Man: I learned a lot about international business.

Woman: Is this your first conference?

Man: Yes, it is. It's very nice to meet you. I'm Mario Pirelli. Please call me Mario.

Woman: Okay...Mario. My name's Mayumi Yamada.

Man: I'm sorry. I didn't catch your first name.

Woman: It's Mayumi. What company do you work for, Mario?

Man: I'm with Coca-Cola. How about you?

Woman: I work for the Sony Corporation.

Jean: I'd like to apply for a credit card.

Mr. Ames: All right. Please have a seat. Now...are you a regular customer at Darcy's Department Store?

Jean: Oh, yes. I love this store. I shop here all the time.

Mr. Ames: That's good. OK. Could I have your name, please?

Jean: Jean Sands.

Mr. Ames: How do you spell your first name?

Jean: It's J-E-A-N.

Mr. Ames: Thank you. And where do you live?

Jean: 30 Jackson Street.

Mr. Ames: I'm sorry. Did you say 13 or 30?

Jean: 30. Three zero.

Mr. Ames: Is that in Boston?

Jean: No, it's in Salem. The zip code is 01970.

Mr. Ames: I also need your telephone number.

Jean: It's 654-1315. (thirteen fifteen)

Mr. Ames: And what's your occupation?

Jean: I'm a chef at the Bayside Hotel.

Mr. Ames: Chef at the Bayside Hotel? All right. One more thing...do you have a local bank account?

Jean: Yes, I do...at East National Bank.

Mr. Ames: OK, Ms. Sands. I think that's everything. You'll receive your card in about a month.

Jean: Thank you very much.

Officer: Next please. Good afternoon, sir. May I have your disembarkation card?

Male: What?

Officer: Your landing card. Do you have one?

Male: No. I have no card.

Officer: Well, I'm afraid you need one. Here, let me help you. First of all, could I have your surname please?

Male: My name?

Officer: Yes...Your surname...last name...your family name.

Male: Ah, yes. Of course. It's Rosenzweig. R-O-S-E-N-Z-W-E-I-G.

Officer: R-O-S-E-N-Z-W-E-I-G. Thank you. And your first name?

Male: Albrecht.

Officer: I'm sorry, but you're going to have to spell that one, too.

Male: A-L-B-R-E-C-H-T.

Officer: All right. And what's your occupation, Mr. Rosenzweig? What do you do?

Male: I'm a businessman.

Officer: And when were you born? What's your birthday?

Male: 17 June, 1945.

Officer: June 17, 1945. And your nationality?

Male: My country? ...Austria.

Officer: So, you're Austrian. And are you here on business or pleasure?

Male: I'm sorry?

Officer: What is the reason for your trip? Why did you come to the United States?

Male: Why? To visit my brother.

Officer: Fine. And where will you be staying?

Male: With my brother, of course.

Officer: All right. What's his address, please? Where does he live?

Male: 238 East 82nd Street, New York, New York.

Officer: 238 East 82nd Street. OK, that's it. Thank you and have a nice stay.

1. This is me and my oldest son, Ted, with my two little granddaughters. They're twins, you know...just three years old. They were really excited when the cake came in. Of course, they had to help me blow out the candles!

2. Now, this man, this is my nephew. He played the piano when they sang "Happy Birthday". We're very proud of him. He's only 19 and he plays with the City Symphony Orchestra. That's his father, my youngest brother, standing behind him.

3. And this is my husband, Sam, with our youngest son. He's twenty-one and is in his last year of college. He wants to go to law school next year. I'm sure he'll make it. He's a straight-A student you know. Smart...just like his mother!

4. Here's the last one. This is my other brother with my nieces. The older girl is seventeen, and the younger one is fifteen, so they're both still in high school. It's impossible to call my brother because one of those girls is always on the phone!

Detective: OK. So everyone here actually *saw* the man riding his motorcycle through the flower beds at City Hall?

Chorus of Voices: Oh, yes! I did! I saw him!

Detective: Quiet, please! I can't listen to everyone talking at the same time! Thank you. I'll speak to each of you, alone, in my office.

Conversation 1

Detective: What did he look like?
Witness 1: Well, let me see...I think he was short, and very thin. He had, umm, light brown hair.
Detective: And what was his hair like?
Witness 1: It was medium length and curly.
Detective: Age?
Witness 1: I guess...early thirties.
Detective: So, he was between thirty-one and thirty-three years old?
Witness 1: Yes, that's right.
Detective: One more question. Do you remember what he was wearing?
Witness 1: He had on a blue and red golf shirt, shorts, and knee socks.
Detective: Well, thank you for coming in.
Witness 1: You're welcome.

Conversation 2

Detective: First of all, thank you for waiting.
Witness 2: Oh, no problem. I like to help the police when I can.
Detective: Fine. Now, what did the man look like?

Witness 2: He was pretty tall and thin. I think he was about twenty.
Detective: Good. And what about his hair? What was it like?
Witness 2: Oh. It was wavy and kind of short. It was blond or brown... Wait. It was blond.
Detective: And what about his clothes?
Witness 2: Tsk. Terrible. Not fashionable at all!
Detective: I mean...what did he have on?
Witness 2: Well. He was wearing a blue golf shirt with red stripes, and a pair of brown shorts. *And* he had on black socks. Can you believe it? Red *and* blue *and* brown *and* black? Terrible.
Detective: OK. That's everything. Thanks again, and could you send
in the next person, please?

Conversation 3

Detective: Come in please, and have a seat. So, can you describe the man for me?
Witness 3: OK. What do you want to know?
Detective: Let's start with clothes. What was he wearing?
Witness 3: Hmmm...Hmmm. I *think* it was a blue shirt.
Detective: Anything else?
Witness 3: Maybe... brown pants.
Detective: How about height? How tall was he?
Witness 3: I'm pretty sure he was tall, but he was sitting down. I remember he was pretty thin. And his hair...his hair was brown and curly. It was about medium-length.
Detective: Just one more question. His age...about how old was he?
Witness 3: I guess he was a teenager. In his late teens. He looked kind of young.
Detective: OK. Thank you for the information. I'm sure we'll catch him soon.

Conversation A

A: Hey Margo! Do you know where the scissors are?
B: Aren't they in the desk drawer?
A: No. That's the first place I looked.
B: Oh, I know. I was using them in the kitchen. Try beside the telephone.
A: Oh, yeah. I've got them. Thanks.

Conversation B

A: Mom...Do we have any ginger ale?
B: Yes. It's in the fridge.
A: No it isn't. Where in the fridge?
B: Look on the bottom shelf behind the juice.
A: Oh, I see it. Thanks.

Conversation C

A: What are you looking for?
B: My book. I can't find my book. Do you know where it is?
A: I saw it on the coffee table this morning.
B: You're right. Here it is. It was under the newspaper.

Conversation D

A: Excuse me. Do you sell computer disks?
B: Oh, yes. We sell all types of disks.
A: Great. And where do you keep them?
B: Do you see the computer section?
A: Uh-huh. Over there?
B: That's right. They're all on the middle shelf between the paper and the computer games.
A: I found them! Thanks for your help.

Speaker 1
Mine was the greatest invention ever! It's old, but people still need it today. It's round, and it comes in many sizes. Long ago, it was made of stone. It's also been made of wood. Then, people made it out of metal. Now, it's often made of rubber. It's used on cars, bicycles, and in machines.

Speaker 2
Well, my invention is more recent. It's long, narrow, and has a sharp point. It's usually made of plastic, but you can get expensive ones made of gold or silver. Everybody uses it. It's full of something called ink, and you write with it.

Speaker 3
The thing I invented has changed many times. Before, it was usually a wooden box with a big piece of ice in it. These days, it's a pretty big, rectangular box made of metal, and it has one or two doors. We have electricity now, so we don't need the ice. My invention keeps food cold or frozen.

Speaker 4
To tell you the truth, my invention isn't as important as those three, but it's still useful. My invention can be made of cotton, wool, silk, leather, or rubber. They're small, but they come in different sizes. You put them on your hands. Sometimes, they're used for fashion. But usually they're used to keep your hands warm, or to protect your hands when you work.

Speaker 5
My invention is very old. People use it to sweep their floors and keep them clean. Every house has one in it. It's very long and narrow. One end is much wider, and is usually made of straw.

Speaker 6
My invention is the newest. It's flat and round and has a very small hole right in the middle of it. It's quite small. In fact, it's usually smaller than your hand! You put it in a special machine and you can listen to music on it.

Speaker 7
You know, I'm very proud of my invention. I think it changed the world!
There are several in every house. They're also used outside. Now, they come in many sizes and colors, but they're always very small. They're usually round like a ball on top, and narrow at the bottom. My invention is made of glass and metal. People use them for light when it's dark.

Speaker 8
If you live in a cold place, you love my invention...especially at night. They're flat and usually square or rectangular. They're pretty big. Mostly, they're made of wool, but they can be made of cotton. You put one on your bed and it keeps you warm at night.

Ron: Well, Bruce. We're lucky we don't have to buy a whole lot of furniture.
Bruce: You're not kidding! So Ron, tell me what kind of stuff we're getting from your parents.
Ron: I think the best thing is probably the brown leather sofa. It's old, but it's in pretty good condition. Four people can sit on it comfortably.
Bruce: Fantastic.
Ron: They also gave us a wall unit. It's made of wood.
Bruce: How big is the wall unit?
Ron: It's tall, but it's not very long.
Bruce: Perfect! This summer I saved some extra money and bought a new CD player and some good speakers.
Ron: What size are the speakers?
Bruce: They're pretty small, but they sound great.
Ron: My mom also gave us two orange easy chairs. They're very wide and comfortable. They'll be perfect for studying.
Bruce: Yeah. Or for watching TV. My father said I could bring the old TV from home. It works well, and it has a big screen.
Ron: That's great! Our apartment is gonna be perfect.
Bruce: Really! I'm also bringing a glass coffee table and a floor lamp with a round shade.
Ron: Oh, good. Well, I also have two narrow lamps with square shades.
Bruce: I guess all we have to do now is decide where to put everything.

Conversation 1
A: City park swimming pool. Good morning.
B: Good morning. Could you tell me if the pool is open today?
A: Yes. The pool opens at 10:00 AM.
B: Oh, good. And what time does it close?
A: We have our summer hours now, so we close at 10:00 PM.
B: OK. Thank you very much.
A: You're quite welcome.

Conversation 2
A recorded voice says:
Hello. Thank you for calling The Golden Cinema Theater. Our specialty is movies from the good old days. Tonight we have two movies. The first is *Casablanca*, with Humphrey Bogart and Ingrid Bergman. It starts at 7:15 and ends at 9:00. Our second feature is *Breakfast at Tiffany's*, starring Audrey Hepburn. It starts at 9:30 and ends at 11:30. The admission price for members is $5.00, and $7.50 for non-members. Doors open at 6:45.

Conversation 3

A: Madison Square Garden. Can I help you?
B: Yes. Do you have any more tickets for the concert on Friday night?
A: Do you mean the Rock 'n' Roll Revival show? Yes, we still have some $25.00 tickets left.
B: Great. OK, and is the box office open now?
A: Yes, the box office is open from 10:00 to 8:00.
B: Oh, by the way, what time does the show start?
A: It starts at 8:00.
B: And what time does it end?
A: Well, there are four bands, so it'll probably end about midnight.
B: Thanks a lot.
A: No problem.

Location 1

A: It's about a five-minute walk from here. It's on Fourth Avenue, just past the post office.
B: So I walk up this street?
A: That's right. It's at the end of the third block, on the corner, across from the Sportsmen's Hotel.
B: I've got it. Thanks.
A: No problem.

Location 2

A: Just walk up Fourth one block to Twentieth Street. Turn left and walk one block to Third Avenue. Go up two more blocks, and you'll see it on the left, across from the day-care center.
B: Let me see... up Fourth to Twentieth, left on Twentieth to Third, up Third about two blocks. It's on the left side of the street?
A: That's it. Just past the park.
B: Great. Thanks for your help.
A: Sure.

Location 3

A: Go up this street and take the second right — that's at Twenty-First Street. Stay on the right side of the street. It's in the middle of that block, between the hardware store and the men's shop.
B: OK...so I want the second right, and it's in the middle of that block between what and what?
A: Between the hardware store — I think it's called Mel's — and a menswear place. You can't miss it.
B: I'm sure I'll find it. Thanks a lot.
A: OK.

Location 4

A: I'm sorry, but I don't know. We're not from around here.
B: Well, thanks anyway.
C: Wait! I saw it when we came out of that restaurant beside the hotel. Do you know the Tenth Inning Bar and Grill?
B: No, I don't.
C: It's easy. You walk up this street three blocks and turn right. Walk over one more block. You'll be at the corner of Fifth and Twenty-Second. You'll see it on Fifth Avenue, on the other corner across the street from the Tenth Inning.

B: So, I have to get to the corner of Fifth and Twenty-Second, and it'll be on my right?
C: Uh-huh. Across from the restaurant.
B: Thank you.
C: My pleasure. I'm always happy to help another tourist.

Stan: Thanks for coming out with me tonight.
Mary: Thanks for asking!
Stan: So. Dinner first. We could go out for a nice Chinese meal. I love the food at the Golden Dragon!
Mary: Oh, Stan. I don't really like Chinese food. I really just want a hamburger and french fries.
Stan: Oh, I see. I guess a hamburger and french fries will be OK tonight.
Mary: What do you want to do after dinner? There's a new musical at the State Street Cinema. I really love musicals.
Stan: Sorry, Mary. I hate musicals. But, you know...I want to see the documentary at the Triplex Theater. Do you like documentaries?
Mary: Documentaries usually put me to sleep. I can't stand them. Hmmm. Well, I have one more idea. We can go bowling. I like to bowl.
Stan: That *is* a good idea! I like bowling, too.

Conversation 1

A: Do you know why I love Sundays?
B: Sure. You don't work today.
A: That's true, but also, there are sports on TV all day.
B: Oh...yeah.
A: So... What do you want to watch? Football? Basketball? Golf? Which one do you like?
B: To be honest, I don't really like watching sports. Maybe I'll read.

Conversation 2

A: Do you know any good places for dinner around here? I want to go somewhere new and different.
B: Well, I really like the Cafe Pronto. They have fantastic Italian food.
A: Do they? I love Italian food! Is it very expensive there?
B: That's another good thing about it. It's not expensive at all.
A: Sounds perfect.

Conversation 3

A: This book is just excellent. I'm really enjoying it.
B: What is it?
A: *2001: A Space Odyssey*, by Arthur C. Clarke. Have you read it?
B: No, but I saw the movie a couple of times.
A: Do you want to read it when I'm finished?
B: No, thanks. I love watching science fiction movies, but I don't like reading sci-fi books.
A: You're kidding.

Conversation 4

A: What's the matter, dear?
B: I have a terrible headache. You know I took the kids shopping for clothes today.
A: That gave you a headache?
B: We went into one of the stores that sells mostly jeans, and they were playing that rock and roll music. And it was *loud!*
A: I can't stand loud rock and roll.
B: Neither can I! Where are the aspirin?

PERSON TO PERSON   UNIT 5/PAGES 39–40

Man: You really don't like Fellini? Or Kurosawa?
Woman: No. Not at all.
Man: How about Bergman? You must like his films.
Woman: I'm afraid not. I don't like any of his films.
Man: Oh, come on! Those men are the greats of modern cinema. I mean really...
Woman: I told you. I think they're boring. I can't stand them.
Man: Well, what movies do you like?
Woman: I like horror movies, as a matter of fact.
Man: Horror movies? You're kidding! I mean you can't be serious. Horror movies...they're so violent, so bloody, so, so, so...scary.
Woman: Well, you're obviously missing the point. You see, in horror movies you've got a classic conflict between the forces of good and the forces of evil.
Man: I just can't believe I'm hearing this. Now I suppose you'll tell me that you love heavy metal music.
Woman: No, I don't. I like classical music.
Man: You do? So do I, but I'll never watch a horror movie. You know? I also really like a good comedy, especially when I've had a hard day at the office.
Woman: Yes, I guess they're OK...but I really like a good horror movie better.

LISTEN TO THIS   UNIT 6/PAGE 43

Conversation 1

Diane: Here it is...Friday night. Do you want to go dancing?
Ted: Well, not really. I'm kind of tired. I had a pretty hard week. But, how about going out to listen to some music?
Diane: What kind of music?
Ted: How about a little light jazz?
Diane: Yeah. That sounds nice.
Ted: What about the Club Blue Note?
Diane: I've never heard of it.
Ted: My office manager was there last week. He said the food and the music are terrific.
Diane: Really? What kind of food do they serve?
Ted: Mostly sandwiches and salads.
Diane: Is it expensive?
Ted: He said the prices are very good. So, do you feel like trying it?
Diane: Why not? I'll just get my coat.

Conversation 2

Oscar: Hi, Ben. What's up?
Ben: What about coming over on Sunday afternoon for a baseball party?
Oscar: A baseball party? What's that?
Ben: This Sunday's baseball game is pretty important, so I'm inviting a bunch of people from our class over to my place to watch it.
Oscar: Who's coming?
Ben: So far, there's Han, Yuki, Stefan, Anna Maria, Ricardo, Lise, and Yong.
Oscar: I'd love to, but I'm afraid I can't. My brother-in-law is coming back from Mexico City. I have to pick him up at the airport.
Ben: That's too bad. Well, how about coming over after you get back from the airport?
Oscar: OK. That's a great idea. Can I bring anything?
Ben: Whatever you like to drink. We'll order pizza for dinner.

LISTEN TO THIS   UNIT 6/PAGE 46

Andrew: Hi, Barry. So, what's the plan?
Barry: Do you feel like playing tennis tonight?
Andrew: That's a good idea. I haven't played tennis in ages.
Barry : Great. Is 7:00 all right?
Andrew: Could we make it a little later? I have to work until 6:30.
Barry: That's no problem. What time do you want to meet?
Andrew: I'm sure I can make it to the tennis court by 7:30, but how about having dinner first? It's really busy around here today,and I didn't have time for lunch.
Barry: OK. I know a fantastic Mexican restaurant.
Andrew: I don't really like Mexican food. Could we go to a Chinese restaurant instead?
Barry: Yeah. The *Taste of Hong Kong* is really close to the courts.
Andrew: I've eaten there before. I liked it.
Barry: Then, why don't we meet at the restaurant?
Andrew: Sure. I'll see you there around 7:30. I'll try not to be late.

PERSON TO PERSON   UNIT 6/PAGES 47–48

Carmen: Yoshiko, I heard that you're going back to Japan pretty soon.
Yoshiko: That's right, and boy, I am *really* busy!
Carmen: I can imagine. But listen... I'd love to get together with you before you go. Would you like to go out for dinner one night?
Yoshiko: That's a great idea. Let's see... Monday night is no good. I have to study for that final exam.
Carmen: Me, too, but I'm free on Tuesday. How about going out that night?
Yoshiko: I'm afraid I can't. I'm going out for dinner with Nancy at 6:30. Hmmm... Are you going to the last class party on Friday night? Let's go out for dinner before the party. It doesn't start until 8:00.
Carmen: I know, but it's a potluck party, so we can't go out before that. I love to eat, but I can't eat two dinners!

Yoshiko: There's always Saturday night. Are you busy then?
Carmen: No... Saturday night I'm free.
Yoshiko: I'm going to a disco with a group of friends. Do you want to join us?
Carmen: I'd really like to have a quiet dinner instead. Oh! Can I call you back? Someone's at the door.
Yoshiko: Sure. I'll be home all afternoon.

LISTEN TO THIS　　　　　　　　UNIT 7/PAGE 51

Conversation 1

Wife: Excuse me. Could you help me?
Clerk: Certainly. What can I do for you?
Wife: We're looking for a girl's ski jacket. I like this style. Do you have it in size 10?
Clerk: Let me see...Size 4,6,8... Here we are. Size 10.
Wife: Oh. I don't really like yellow. What other colors does it come in?
Clerk: It comes in red, pink, light blue, and black.
Wife: The pink is nice. How much is it?
Clerk: It's $160.
Wife: Oh, well, we'll have to think about it.

Conversation 2

Clerk: Good afternoon. Is there something I can help you with?
Husband: Yes, there is. We'd like to see some men's leather gloves.
Clerk: Yes sir. Do you know what color or size you'd like?
Husband: What sizes do you carry?
Clerk: We carry small, medium, and large.
Husband: My son wears medium. This style is perfect. Do you have these in tan?
Clerk: I'm sorry, sir. They only come in black and brown.
Husband: Hmmm. And how much are they?
Clerk: They're usually $50, but they're on sale this week. Half price.
Husband: In that case, I think we'll take the brown.

Conversation 3

Clerk: Hi. Can I help you with something?
Wife: Yes, please. I'm interested in a golf bag for my daughter.
Clerk: Of course. I think this red and black one is very nice. It also comes in white and red, and white and navy. The quality is excellent, and it's only $150.
Wife: She's just a beginner. Do you have a smaller one?
Clerk: I'm sorry. This large size is the only size we have.
Wife: That's too bad. Well, thanks anyway.

LISTEN TO THIS　　　　　　　　UNIT 7/PAGE 54

Conversation 1

Clerk: Yes, miss. What can I do for you today?
Customer: I'd like to return this coat and get a refund, please.
Clerk: I see. And what is the reason?
Customer: I'll show you. It's too small.
Clerk: Oh, yes. I do see. Do you have your receipt?
Customer: Here it is.

Conversation 2

Customer: Pardon me. Could you help me?
Clerk: Sure. What can I do for you?
Customer: Well, I'd like to exchange this cassette.
Clerk: What's wrong with it?
Customer: My grandson gave it to me for my birthday. It's his favorite music...but it's too noisy for me. I want something quieter.
Clerk: I'm really sorry, but there are no exchanges on tapes after they've been opened.

Conversation 3

Clerk: Good morning, sir. What can I help you with today?
Customer: I'd like to exchange this sweater, please. I just bought it about half an hour ago. I have my receipt right here in the bag.
Clerk: What's the problem?
Customer: I decided that I don't really like the color. I think I like the orange one better.
Clerk: You're right. The orange one would look better than the brown one. I'll just switch them for you.

PERSON TO PERSON　　　　　　UNIT 7/PAGES 55–56

Joan: This is a really good store. I bet you can find everything you need for Europe right here.
Kerry: I hope so. I have a lot to do before the trip.
Joan: Do you know what you need?
Kerry: Not too much, really. Pants, a light jacket, and a sweater.
Joan: Here are the pants. Oh! This is a nice pair. They're black, so they'll go with everything.
Kerry: Except, if it's sunny, they'll be too hot. Besides, I already have black ones at home. How about these pink pants?
Joan: They're a much nicer color.
Kerry: And they feel like a better quality, too. I'll try them on later. Let's look for a sweater now.... I like this purple one.
Joan: Do you? I really think it's too plain. What do you think of this white one? It's fancier, so you could wear it in the evening.
Kerry: I know, but the purple one is looser. It'll be more comfortable.
Anyway, I have some fancy sweaters at home.
Joan: Well, try the purple, then.
Kerry: Let's see, I guess the last thing is the jacket.
Joan: Look at this beige suede jacket. It's beautiful, but I know it's too heavy for the summer.
Kerry: It's also too expensive! I don't want to spend that much money. Do you see any cotton jackets?
Joan: Right over here. Oh, these are much lighter.
Kerry: And a lot more useful!

LISTEN TO THIS　　　　　　　　UNIT 8/PAGE 59

Cashier: Hi. Is everybody ready to order?
Father: Yes, I think so. Davey? What are you going to have?
Davey: I want a cheeseburger, large french fries, and a chocolate milk shake.
Father: Davey...are you sure you can eat all that?

Davey: Sure, Dad! I'm starving!
Father: OK. How about you dear? What are you having?
Mother: I haven't decided yet. You go ahead.
Father: OK. I'll have the chicken nuggets, a large order of fries, and a coffee.
Cashier: What kind of sauce do you want for the chicken nuggets?
Father: Let's see...You have sweet and sour sauce and honey sauce...I'll take the sweet and sour sauce.
Mother: OK, well then... I think I'll have the fish sandwich, a garden salad, and a coffee.
Cashier: And what kind of dressing for your salad?
Mother: Oh, ummm. French dressing, please.
Cashier: All right. So... the little boy is having a cheeseburger, large fries, and a chocolate milk shake. You're having chicken nuggets with sweet and sour sauce, large fries and a coffee, and your wife is having a fish sandwich, a garden salad with French dressing, and a coffee.
Father: That's right.
Cashier: Is that for here or to go?

LISTEN TO THIS   UNIT 8/PAGE 62

Conversation 1
Waitress: Would you like something to drink?
Woman: Do you have apple juice?
Waitress: No, I'm sorry. We have orange, tomato, and cranberry.
Woman: OK. I'll take orange. A large one, please.

Conversation 2
Waitress: Would you care for some dessert?
Man: Well... What do you have?
Waitress: Tonight we have cheesecake, homemade pie, sherbet, and a fresh fruit salad with whipped cream.
Man: Do you have any ice cream?
Waitress: Yes, sir. We have vanilla, chocolate, and maple walnut.
Man: What kind of pie do you have?
Waitress: Pecan, peach, and apple.
Man: Could I have pecan pie with some vanilla ice-cream on the side?
Waitress: Certainly, sir.

Conversation 3
Waiter: Shall I bring you some more coffee?
Woman: Please. I'd love some.
Waiter: Here you are, ma'am.
Woman: And could I get a little more cream, please?
Waiter: Of course. Anything else?
Woman: I think...just the check, thanks.
Waiter: Right away.

PERSON TO PERSON   UNIT 8/PAGES 63–64

Waiter: Have you decided yet, sir?
Man: Yes, I think so. Marian?
Woman: Yes, I'll have the salmon teriyaki, please.
Waiter: And what kind of potatoes would you like with that?

Woman: Baked, please. For the vegetable, I'd like broccoli.
Waiter: And would you care for soup or salad to start?
Man: What is your soup today?
Waiter: We have cream of cauliflower and French onion.
Woman: Oh, they both sound heavy. I think I'll have a salad, please.
Waiter: Very good. With what kind of dressing?
Woman: I'd like blue cheese. Oh, wait, could you change that to oil and vinegar?
Waiter: Certainly. And you, sir? What will you have?
Man: Those lobster tails look pretty good.
Waiter: I'm very sorry, sir. We don't have any lobster tonight.
Man: No lobster? Well... I guess I'll take the steak then. Could you tell the chef I like my steak very rare?
Waiter: Of course. Mashed, boiled, or baked potatoes?
Man: Mashed, please.
Waiter: Vegetable?
Man: I'd like asparagus.
Waiter: And, soup or salad?
Man: I think I'm going to try the cream of cauliflower. I've never had that before.
Waiter: Dessert?
Woman: We'll decide later, if that's all right. But, could you bring me some extra butter with my potato?
Waiter: Certainly. Anything to drink while you wait?
Woman: An iced coffee, please.
Man: Make that two.

LISTEN TO THIS   UNIT 9/PAGE 67

Conversation 1
Woman: Oh no! The machine says, "Use correct change only." All I have is quarters.
Man: Don't worry. I have lots of change.
Woman: Do you have an extra dime?
Man: Sure. Here you go.

Conversation 2
Woman: OK... books, tape recorder, tapes, purse...let's see... yeah ...that's everything.
Boy: Can I carry something for you?
Woman: No. That's OK. I've got it all. But...could you please get the door and the lights for me?
Boy: Of course!

Conversation 3
Brother: Oh, wow. I'm exhausted!
Sister: Why?
Brother: I stayed up until 3:00 AM studying for that exam today. I was up at 7:00, at school by a quarter to nine...We took the exam from 9:00 to 11:30. Then we had basketball practice from 1:00 to 3:00.
Sister: That's a lot.
Brother: Yeah... Could you do the dishes tonight? I know it's my turn, but I'm just too tired.
Sister: Sure. You can do them for me tomorrow night.
Brother: It's a deal...and thanks. I appreciate it.

Conversation 4

Woman: Have you seen the rain? It's pouring out there!

Man: No, really? I have to walk to the bank on my lunch hour.

Woman: Did you remember your umbrella this morning?

Man: No. I forgot it. If you're not going outside at lunch, could I please borrow yours?

Woman: I'm sorry. I didn't bring mine today, either.

Conversation 5

Marge: Hi, Atsuko. How're you?

Atsuko: Great, Marge. What's new? Would you like to come in for coffee?

Marge: I'd love to, but to tell you the truth, I'm right in the middle of making Rachel's birthday cake, and I'm out of eggs. Do you think I could borrow a couple?

Atsuko: Oh, sure. No problem. How many do you need?

Marge: Just two.

Atsuko: Wait a minute. I'll get them.

Conversation 6

Woman: Oh... there they are. Of course they're on the top shelf. It's no use. Tsk!...Oh. Excuse me. Excuse me!

Clerk: Yes, ma'am. What can I do for you?

Woman: Hi. Sorry to bother you. Could you do me a favor? I need one of those jars of pickles on the top shelf, but I can't reach it. Could you please get it down for me?

Clerk: Sure. Here you go.

LISTEN TO THIS   UNIT 9/PAGE 70

Conversation 1

A: Excuse me!

B: Yes, ma'am? What can I do for you?

A: I have a problem with this coffee maker, and I want my money back.

B: Well, what seems to be the problem?

A: The problem is that it doesn't work! I've only used it three times.

B: I'd be happy to exchange it for you.

A: Thank you, but I'd like a refund, please. I invited six people to my place for dinner last night. After dinner, I plugged in the coffee maker, I put in the coffee and water, I turned it on, and nothing happened! I was very embarrassed. Now, I'd like my money back.

B: Of course. Here's your refund. And I'm really very sorry about all this.

A: That's OK. And thank you for your help.

Conversation 2

A: Next, please!

B: Yes, I just received my telephone bill, and there's a problem with it.

A: And what exactly is the problem?

B: There's a collect call from Finland on there, and I don't know anyone in Finland! I'm very upset. Could you please take the charge off my bill?

A: May I see your bill, please?

B: Certainly. There it is. On July 1st. I really don't know anybody in Finland.

A: OK, don't worry. I'll take the call off. Let's see... it was $42. Your bill was $66.10, minus $42, so your new total is $24.10. I'm very sorry about the mistake.

B: That's OK. It wasn't your fault.

LISTEN TO THIS   UNIT 10/PAGE 75

Paula: That's enough about me. How about you? Are you from Los Angeles?

Brad: No. Actually, I was born in Seattle, but I guess you could say I grew up all over the world.

Paula: Huh? What do you mean?

Brad: Well, my dad was in the Air Force, so we moved around a lot, starting when I was two. That was when we moved to Japan...just outside Tokyo.

Paula: Wow. Did you go to school there?

Brad: No. My father was sent to Germany after that. We moved to Munich in 1960, when I was five. I started elementary school there.

Paula: Where did you go after that?

Brad: Well! After Munich we lived in the Middle East, we moved there when I was ten, then Germany again, Alaska, and then Hawaii. In 1972 my father retired. Was it 1972? Yes...because I was seventeen.

Paula: Did you come to Los Angeles then?

Brad: No. My dad decided to retire in Hawaii. I really liked it there, so I went to the University of Hawaii.

Paula: So when did you come to Los Angeles?

Brad: Right after I finished college. I really feel like L.A. is my home now.

LISTEN TO THIS   UNIT 10/PAGE 78

When we think about Hemingway the writer, we also have to think about Hemingway, the man. In many ways, his life was as interesting as his work. Like many great authors, many of his books and stories were based on his personal experiences. Let's look at some of these books and see how his experiences influenced them.

In 1925, he published his first collection of short stories, called *In Our Time*. Most of the stories were really about his childhood. A year later, in 1926, his first two novels appeared — *Torrents of Spring*, and *The Sun Also Rises*. Remember, Hemingway lived in Paris during the early twenties. When he lived there, he knew many famous writers and artists. *The Sun Also Rises* is about some of those talented, but lonely and angry people.

Hemingway drove an ambulance during World War I — that was between 1914 and 1918. Many years later, in 1929, he used this experience when he wrote his fourth novel, *A Farewell to Arms*. This book, which was a love story about an American ambulance driver and a British nurse, made him famous throughout the world.

After that, during the 1930s, Hemingway continued to write short stories and also wrote two books about subjects he greatly loved. *Death in the Afternoon* was about bullfighting, and *The Green Hills of Africa* was about big game hunting. His father, a doctor, got him interested in hunting, fishing, sports, and the outdoor life when he was a child.

When the Second World War began, Hemingway returned to Europe. This time he was there as a reporter, so he was present at many of the most important battles of the war. He used these war experiences to write *Across the River and Into the Trees*. This book was not very successful, and people thought he was losing his magic.

But, in 1952, he wrote a short novel, *The Old Man and the Sea*. For this book, he won the Pulitzer Prize. And two years later, he received the Nobel Prize for Literature. The book tells the story of an old Cuban fisherman, but is really about man against nature. Why is it his best? As I said, when he was younger, he used to go fishing with his father, and in later years, deep-sea fishing remained his favorite hobby. He was able to write a powerful, emotional story because of his own personal experiences.

Sadly in 1961, sick and unable to live the active life he loved and wrote about, Hemingway killed himself with one of his own shotguns.

LISTEN TO THIS   UNIT 11/PAGE 83

Lin: Minako! How was your trip? I'm dying to hear all about it.
Minako: It was fantastic, Lin. I loved it.
Lin: So, what did you think of San Francisco?
Minako: Beautiful. Have you ever been there?
Lin: No, I haven't, but I've always wanted to go. So...convince me. Tell me all about it.
Minako: Hmmm. Where do I start? It really is a wonderful city. Mostly because it's so different, I think. Everywhere you look there are hilly streets, beautiful old Victorian homes and buildings, the bay, and of course the Golden Gate Bridge.
Lin: Was it easy to get around?
Minako: Oh, yeah. I walked a lot, but when I got tired it was easy to get a bus. The bus system is really efficient and inexpensive, but the buses are a bit run-down. I also took the subway a couple of times. It was cheap, fast, and comfortable.
Lin: How about the cable cars?
Minako: They were always packed with people, but they were really fun to ride.
Lin: What are the restaurants like?
Minako: There's a real variety. We had seafood at the Fisherman's Wharf. It was really fresh and delicious, but it was kind of expensive. And we went to Chinatown for dinner one night. The food there was really spicy, but good.
Lin: How was your hotel?
Minako: It was small and very old. I felt like I was in an old movie! It wasn't fancy at all, but it was clean and well-kept, and the rates were quite reasonable.
Lin: Sounds wonderful. San Francisco, here I come.

LISTEN TO THIS   UNIT 11/PAGE 86

Susan: Excuse me, Elaine, do you know any hotels in Boston? The boss is sending me there, and I have to find a place to stay.
Elaine: I know three... There's The Midtown, The Boston Bay, and The Fairfield.
Susan: What are the locations like? I'll be downtown most of the time.
Elaine: The Midtown has the best location, then. The Boston Bay is also good, but the Fairfield isn't downtown at all.
Susan: I've read about the The Boston Bay. It's also the newest hotel in Boston, isn't it?
Elaine: Yeah, I think so. It's the biggest, and it has a very good restaurant. But, I think it's the most expensive hotel in Boston.
Susan: I have to keep my expenses down. What about The Midtown?
Elaine: I have a hotel guidebook here someplace. Let me check. Here we are... The Midtown is cheaper than the Boston Bay. Oh, but it doesn't have a restaurant.
Susan: Could you look up The Fairfield?
Elaine: Sure. The room rates are the cheapest, probably because it's not downtown. My parents stayed at The Fairfield last year. It's a really nice, old hotel. They ate in the restaurant there. It's one of the best in Boston.
Susan: OK... Well, the Midtown sounds best. Could you reserve a room for me there?
Elaine: Sure. What days will you be there?

PERSON TO PERSON   UNIT 11/PAGES 87–88

Bob: Well, Ruth. It was great to get away, but it's good to be home again.
Ruth: It really was a wonderful trip. So, which city did you like best, Paris, London, or Rome?
Bob: That's hard to say. There were good things and bad things about all three cities.
Ruth: Wait a minute! What bad things?
Bob: Traffic, for one. The traffic in London was pretty bad, and the traffic in Paris was even worse! I was afraid to cross the street.
Ruth: That's true...and how about Rome? I thought Rome was worse than Paris. Those drivers are crazy! And always honking their horns! It was really noisy there.
Bob: Paris was noisy, too. A lot noisier than it was in London.
Ruth: You're right, but I still think Rome was noisier than Paris!
Bob: Well, all big cities have bad traffic and a lot of noise. Let's not think about the bad things. Think about all those art galleries we visited.
Ruth: Yeah, the art galleries in Rome were fantastic, but I thought the Paris art galleries were better. Of course, I've always dreamed of going to the Louvre.
Bob: Me, too. I loved the galleries in London, but I liked the ones in Paris even more. The restaurants in Paris were better than in London, too. I thought the food was more interesting. It had more flavor.
Ruth: And the food in Rome was incredible! I liked the Italian restaurants better than the French ones. I thought they were more interesting. Before we went to Rome, I thought Italian food was all pizza and spaghetti!
Bob: Really! I'm sure I put on weight in Rome.

Ruth: Maybe not. We did a lot of dancing at night. Those discos in Rome were great, but I think I liked the Paris nightlife better. It was more romantic.

Bob: You know where I had more fun in the evening? In London. Paris was good, but I thought the London nightlife was better.

Ruth: Yeah, we saw a couple of great plays. Oh, I'll never decide which city I liked best.

Bob: Me, neither.

LISTEN TO THIS   UNIT 12/PAGE 91

Jim: Good morning, Ms. Reynolds. I have your schedule for Monday of next week.

Irene: Thanks, Jim. Am I going to have any free time?

Jim: A little, but it's going to be a pretty busy day.

Irene: OK. Let's start with the morning.

Jim: All right. From 8:00 to 10:00 you're going to have breakfast with the vice presidents. Then you'll drive to the new factory. After you get there, around 10:30, there will be a tour of the new building.

Irene: How long is that going to take?

Jim: About an hour.

Irene: And after that?

Jim: At one o'clock, the managers from Chicago and New York will be here for the monthly meeting.

Irene: OK.

Jim: At seven o'clock, you're going to go to the TV station for an interview with a TV newswoman. Just a few questions about the new factory.

Irene: Anything else?

Jim: Just one more thing. The Business Club dinner.

Irene: Oh, right. And I've already written my speech for that.

Jim: So, you'll get there around 8:00. They're planning to serve dinner around 8:30, and you're going to give your speech at 9:30. The dinner meeting will end at eleven. By the way, I'm sure the food will be delicious.

Irene: Hmm. I'll go on a diet on Tuesday. And thanks for all your work, Jim.

Jim: My pleasure.

LISTEN TO THIS   UNIT 12/PAGE 94

Max: I can't believe it! The last day of school is finally here. What are you going to do this summer, Alessandro?

Alessandro: Well, starting tomorrow, I'm going to work in my Dad's restaurant.

Max: Really? Starting tomorrow? So soon?

Alessandro: I really want to save some extra money for college.

Max: Are you taking any time off?

Alessandro: Yeah. I'm not going to work weekends, and I'm going away the last three weeks of the summer.

Max: What are you going to do on the weekends? Just take it easy?

Alessandro: I don't know...maybe read a few books or rent some movies. Whatever.

Max: Sounds kind of boring.

Alessandro: Not really. I'm going to go to a friend's cabin by the lake most weekends. I want to do a little waterskiing and swimming. Let's hope for good weather!

Max: Now that sounds like fun!

Alessandro: Yeah. I'm looking forward to it. My friend and his dad are building a new dock this summer, and I'd really like to help them.

Max: How about the last three weeks? Are you going somewhere special?

Alessandro: I'm going to Italy to visit my uncle for two weeks. He lives in Rome. I'm also going to do a bit of traveling with my cousin while I'm there.

Max: What cities are you going to visit?

Alessandro: I've never been to Italy, so my cousin is deciding. We might go to Milan, we might go to Venice, or we might go to Florence. I'm not sure yet.

Max: And what are you doing the last week?

Alessandro: I'm moving to an apartment near the college, so I hope to get everything organized before school starts.

PERSON TO PERSON   UNIT 12/PAGES 95–96

Ben: You know what, Jill? You work too hard. Let's go and sit in the park.

Jill: I can't do that. I have to study. Final exams are next week.

Ben: But, Jill...You already know that you're going to go to Harvard! What are you going to major in, anyway?

Jill: I'm taking Business and Economics. How about you? Which school are you going to next year, Ben?

Ben: Actually, I'm going to work for my dad for a year. I'll go to college the year after that.

Jill: What do you want to study?

Ben: I'm not really sure. I'd like to study literature or art. So, do you want to work for a big company after college, or do you want to have your own business?

Jill: Neither. I hope to get into law school after I finish at Harvard.

Ben: Wow. You sure are ambitious!

Jill: What kind of job do you want to have after college?

Ben: Something easy. I'd like to work nine to five. I guess you'll be a lawyer.

Jill: Uh-huh. I'd like to practice law for a few years, and then I hope to go into politics.

Ben: Well, I just hope to have a steady job and a nice family.

Jill: Really? I want to make a lot of money.

Ben: Anything else?

Jill: Sure... I'd like to be president someday!

OPTIONAL ACTIVITIES TEACHER'S NOTES

OPTIONAL ACTIVITY 1:
Match the Occupation, *page 127.*

Preparation: Make copies of Optional Activity 1 for each student.

Procedure: Distribute one copy of the handout to each student. Explain the activity. Give students time to match each occupation from the list with the correct picture. In pairs, have students compare answers. Check answers as a class. For additional speaking practice, have students take turns describing to each other what each occupation involves. Help students get started by giving an example: *A mail carrier delivers letters.* Circulate and help with vocabulary as necessary.

Answers (Left to Right, Top to Bottom):

chef	mechanic	actress
waiter	photographer	optometrist
police officer	plumber	salesclerk
nurse	cashier	dentist
hairstylist	mail carrier	doctor

OPTIONAL ACTIVITY 2:
How Are They Different?, *page 128.*

Preparation: Make copies of Optional Activity 2, which consists of two similar pictures. Cut the copies to separate the pictures or leave intact (see below).

Procedure: Divide students into pairs. Distribute one picture to half of the class and the other picture to the other half of the class. If the handout is intact, tell students to cover their partner's picture. Give students time to study their pictures. Have students take turns describing or asking about various characteristics, items of clothing, etc., until they discover the differences between the two pictures. To maximize practice of the teaching points of the unit, have students also speculate about the age and marital status of the person in the picture. Afterwards, they can also speculate about what color the clothes might be (*She is wearing a light-blue T-shirt.*).

Answers:
Picture A: Woman, mid-twenties, tall and thin with medium-length straight dark hair. She is casually dressed: white shorts, T-shirt, dark jacket, athletic shoes, athletic bag or backpack, white baseball hat, watch on right arm

Picture B: Woman, mid-forties, tall and pretty heavy with short wavy dark hair. She is casually dressed: dark skirt, white sweater, high boots, dark shoulder bag (purse), wide brim hat, no watch on right arm, earrings, striped scarf at neck

OPTIONAL ACTIVITY 3:
What Is It?, *page 129.*

Preparation: Make one copy of Optional Activity 3 for each pair of students.

Procedure: Divide students into pairs. Distribute one copy of the handout to each pair. In pairs, have students find ten objects in the classroom and write down on the activity sheet what each object is made of and what it is used for. Then have each pair work with another pair of students. They can take turns describing and guessing the names of the objects on their lists. (*It's made of paper and it is used to look up new words. / Is it a dictionary?*) Encourage students to provide additional description if an object is not identified after the first clues. Circulate and assist with vocabulary.

OPTIONAL ACTIVITY 4:
Alibi, *page 130.*

Preparation: Make copies of Optional Activity 4. Cut into cards. Divide the students into groups of seven and distribute one of each of the seven cards to each group member. **Note:** the matches are: Card 1 and Card 4; Card 2 and Card 5; Card 3 and Card 6. *Card 7 has no match.* The holder of Card 7 is the robber.

Procedure: Announce to the class that several art and jewelry robberies have taken place. The police are trying to figure out who did them. Explain that each student has a card with four different days and dates. Have students move around the class and ask about the activities on their cards until they find another student with a card that has *three* matching dates, activities, and times. (See above for matches.) When students have found their partners, they have alibis. The student who cannot find someone with three matching dates, activities, and times (Card 7) is the robber. To help students get started, model an example question: *Where were you on Sunday, May 31?* (At a birthday party). *What time did the party begin? What time did it end?* Emphasize that the students must be very thorough and make sure *all* the information about a particular activity matches up. Allow ample time (10–15 minutes) for students to circulate and find their partners.

Note: This activity can also be done later, following **1. Describing Locations,** page 29. If it is done then, choose four places from the map (the video store, the supermarket, etc.) as the locations where the robberies occurred. Have some students in the class role-play conducting the investigation. In pairs, have one student role-play a local police officer, the other student a special investigator from another city. Have the local officer describe how to get to the places where the robberies occurred, starting from the police station.

OPTIONAL ACTIVITY 5:
What Do You Think Of...?, *page 131.*

Preparation: Make copies of Optional Activity 5. Make enough copies so that there is one set of topics for each group of three students. Cut each handout into individual strips along the dotted lines.

Note: The activity sheet consists of three columns of things and activities. They are marked **A, B,** and **C.** Some of the spaces in **B** and **C** have been left blank so that the names of activities, things, places, or people that are of particular interest to the students can be added either by you in advance or by the students as they do the activity.

Procedure: Divide the students into groups of three and distribute the sets of slips either in envelopes or face down. In each group, have one student take a slip and tell the other students how he or she feels about what is written there (*I love watching sports on TV.*). Tell the other students to each respond honestly, giving the appropriate short answer (*So do I. / You do? I can't stand it.*) Then, have another student take a new slip and continue. Tell the students to take turns in this way until the slips are all gone. Model an example with the students to help them get started. After students have used all the slips, ask several groups to demonstrate for the class.

OPTIONAL ACTIVITY 6:
More Invitations, *page 132.*

Preparation: Make one copy of Optional Activity 6 for each student. Divide the class in half. Half of the class will make the invitations; half will respond. Students can then switch roles. Have students fold their worksheets lengthwise with the appropriate side up.

Procedure: Have students who are doing the inviting choose five activities from the handout, then circulate around the room and invite classmates to join them in the activities. Tell students to try to find a *yes* for each invitation. Have the other students choose a response from their handouts. Tell them to use each response only once. Have the students who are inviting fill in the name, time, and meeting arrangement for each activity. Tell students to raise their hands to let you know they are finished. Then, have students switch parts and repeat the procedure above. Ask volunteers to tell the class what arrangements they made.

Note: This activity will take ten to fifteen minutes. If there are time constraints, reduce the number of invitations, do not have students switch parts, or do as a timed activity.

OPTIONAL ACTIVITY 7:
I Want to Return It, *page 133.*

Preparation: Make one copy of Optional Activity 7 for each student.

Procedure: Distribute one copy of the handout to each student. Explain the activity. Give students time to look over the pairs of pictures. Have students work in pairs. For each pair of pictures, have students compare the items and decide which they prefer. Next have students do a role play. One student is a shopper, the other is a clerk. For each pair of items, the shopper goes to the store to return the item in the pair he/she *does not* like and asks to exchange it for the item he/she *does* like. The shopper explains the reason he/she wants to make the exchange. Circulate and help as needed. If time permits, have students switch roles. As a final check, call on various pairs to perform for the class.

OPTIONAL ACTIVITY 8:
What Are You Going to Have?, *page 134.*

Preparation: Make one copy of Optional Activity 8 for each student. If possible, have students arrange their seats to appear like seating in a restaurant. Have students clear away their personal belongings.

Procedure: Distribute one copy of the handout to each student. Divide the students into groups of three. Two students are the customers, the other is the waiter/waitress. Have the customers decide what their relationship is (newlyweds, friends, a couple on their first date) and what their personalities are like (nervous, fussy, demanding, polite). Have the waiter/waitress decide if he/she is fast/slow/careless/attentive, etc. The customers are to do the following: discuss the menu and decide what they will order. The waiter/waitress should take their orders in the space provided, asking for specifics on the type of dressing, potato, etc., and what the customers want to drink. Tell one of the customers to keep asking for substitutions even though the menu says No Substitutions. The role play should end with the waiter/waitress asking

about other wants, and the customers can relate some problems that occur during the meal (e.g., the entree is overcooked, the coffee is cold, the ice cream is melted). Finally, the customers can request the bill. Ask one or two groups to perform for the class.

OPTIONAL ACTIVITY 9:
Could I Borrow...?, *page 135.*

Preparation: Make one copy of Optional Activity 9 for each student.

Procedure: Distribute one copy of the handout to each student. Divide the class into two groups: borrowers and lenders. The borrowers need to borrow things. The lenders have a list of things they have available. Tell students to fold their handouts in half so that the information they are using is face up. Check vocabulary before students begin. Have the borrowers circulate around the room and borrow the various items they need from their classmates. They can borrow only one item from each classmate. Have borrowers write down the name of the person they borrowed from beside the item borrowed. Emphasize that lenders may agree to lend only what is on their lists once and cross it off. If time permits, have students switch roles.

OPTIONAL ACTIVITY 10:
Who Am I?, *page 136.*

Preparation: Make one copy of Optional Activity 10 for each student. On a separate piece of paper, prepare a list of famous people from which students can choose who to be. Include local personalities familiar to the students. The list can be kept at the front of the class for students to refer to.

Procedure: Distribute one copy of the handout to each student. Divide the students into small groups. Have one member of each group think of a well-known person, living or dead. Tell students to pick someone who is very well known. The student can choose from your list or think of someone else. Have the rest of the group try to figure out who it "is" by asking the questions on the activity sheet. Tell group members to also make up questions of their own. They do not need to ask all of the questions on the activity sheet. The group members can ask up to 20 questions together. If no one in the group guesses the identity of the well-known person by the twenty-question mark, the answerer reveals the answer and thinks of another name. When a member of the group guesses the identity, that person then becomes the answerer. Each group member should have at least one turn being the answerer. To close the activity, ask various students to report to the class who they were.

OPTIONAL ACTIVITY 11:
Find Someone Who..., *page 137.*

Preparation: Make one copy of Optional Activity 11 for each student.

Procedure: Distribute one copy of the handout to each student. Explain that this is a class activity. They are to circulate around the room and ask their classmates about the activities on the sheet. When they find someone who answers *yes* to their question, they write down the person's name in the appropriate space. This can be played as a game in which students either see who can fill up the sheet first, or who can get the most names in a set amount of time. If played as a game, warn the students not to show their answers to their classmates.

Before students begin, model the question: *Have you ever...?* To check answers, ask various students: *Did you find someone, (Hiro), who has ridden a horse?* Continue.

OPTIONAL ACTIVITY 12:
What Are Your Plans and Dreams?,
page 138.

Preparation: Make one copy of Optional Activity 12 for each student.

Procedure: Distribute one copy of the handout to each student. Tell students to circulate around the room and interview four classmates. For each classmate, have them write down three things they definitely plan to do (PLANS) and three things they hope to do (DREAMS). Emphasize that "dreams" can range from *I want to see the new Tom Cruise movie this weekend* to *I want to go to Kenya someday.* Have students return to their seats when they are finished. Ask volunteers to report what they found out. See if there are any common "dreams."

Note: This can also be done in groups of ten to fifteen students if the class is very large.

OPTIONAL ACTIVITY 1: Match the Occupation.

Match the occupation from the list with the correct picture. Write the occupations under the picture.

a. photographer
b. hairstylist
c. optometrist
d. actress
e. mechanic

f. cashier
g. mail carrier
h. salesclerk
i. dentist
j. doctor

k. waiter
l. chef
m. plumber
n. nurse
p. police officer

1. _____

2. _____

3. _____

4. _____

5. _____

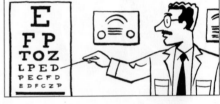

6. _____

7. _____

8. _____

9. _____

10. _____

11. _____

12. _____

13. _____

14. _____

15. _____

OPTIONAL ACTIVITY 2: How Are They Different?

Describe this woman to your partner.

Describe this woman to your partner.

OPTIONAL ACTIVITY 3: What Is It?

With your partner, find ten objects. Fill in the information about each object in the first two columns.
Then have other students guess what the objects are.

	It is made of	It is used for	Name of object
1.			
2.			
3.			
4.			
5.			
6.			
7.			
8.			
9.			
10.			

OPTIONAL ACTIVITY 4: Alibi

CARD 1

1. Sunday, May 31
   Birthday Party (2–6 p.m.)
2. Monday, June 1
   Family Reunion (6–11 p.m.)
3. Sunday, July 12
   Barbecue (2–9 p.m.)
4. Saturday, August 15
   Pub (8–midnight)

CARD 2

1. Sunday, May 31
   Birthday Party (2–6 p.m.)
2. Monday, June 1
   Family Reunion (6–11 p.m.)
3. Sunday, July 12
   Swimming (2–5 p.m.)
4. Saturday, August 15
   Baseball Game (8–10:30 p.m.)

CARD 3

1. Sunday, May 31
   Birthday Party (2–6 p.m.)
2. Monday, June 1
   Baseball Game (8–10:30 p.m.)
3. Sunday, July 12
   Barbecue (2–9 p.m.)
4. Saturday, August 15
   At the movies (7–9 p.m.)

CARD 4

1. Sunday, May 31
   Birthday Party (2–6 p.m.)
2. Monday, June 1
   Home watching TV (all night)
3. Sunday, July 12
   Barbecue (2–9 p.m.)
4. Saturday, August 15
   Pub (8–midnight)

CARD 5

1. Sunday, May 31
   Birthday Party (2–6 p.m.)
2. Monday, June 1
   Home watching TV (all night)
3. Sunday, July 12
   Swimming (2–5 p.m.)
4. Saturday, August 15
   Baseball Game (8–10:30 p.m.)

CARD 6

1. Sunday, May 31
   Birthday Party (2–6 p.m.)
2. Monday, June 1
   Baseball Game (8–10:30 p.m.)
3. Sunday, July 12
   Swimming (2–5 p.m.)
4. Saturday, August 15
   At the movies (7–9 p.m.)

CARD 7

1. Sunday, May 31
   Birthday Party (2–6 p.m.)
2. Monday, June 1
   Pub (7–10 p.m.)
3. Sunday, July 12
   Swimming (2–5 p.m.)
4. Saturday, August 15
   At the movies (5–7:15 p.m.)

OPTIONAL ACTIVITY 5: What Do You Think Of...?

A	B	C
getting up early in the summer	talking about politics	ice-cream sundaes
getting up late	dancing	doing housework
war movies	cooking	doing homework
singing	traveling	washing dishes
chocolate	opera	pizza
reading	airplane food	rap music
watching sports on TV	going for long walks	talking on the telephone
shopping for clothes	driving in the city	shopping for CDs and tapes
cats	spicy food	babysitting
thunderstorms	spending money	watching TV
sleeping until noon	your own idea: _____	your own idea: _____
window shopping	your own idea: _____	your own idea: _____
big dogs	your own idea: _____	your own idea: _____

OPTIONAL ACTIVITY 6: More Invitations

Invite someone to:	Response:
☐ see a movie	☐ Accept, but change the time.
☐ go out for dinner	☐ Accept, then set the time and place.
☐ go sailing	☐ You can't accept because you already have plans.
☐ play tennis	☐ Accept, then set the time and place.
☐ go to a museum	☐ Accept, then set the time and place.
☐ go for coffee	☐ You can't accept because you have work to do.
☐ go see a movie	☐ Accept, but suggest a different day.
☐ go dancing at a club	☐ Accept, then set the time and place.
☐ go shopping with you at the mall	☐ Accept, but suggest a different place.
☐ go swimming	☐ Accept, but change the day.
☐ go to the ballet	☐ Don't accept. Give a reason.
☐ go out for pizza after work	☐ Don't accept. You're going to get your hair cut then.
☐ go to the beach on Sunday	☐ Accept, then set the time and place.

OPTIONAL ACTIVITY 7: I Want to Return It.

You are a shopper. Your partner is a cashier. Choose the clothing you don't like and return it to the store. Describe what you would like to exchange it for. Then switch roles.

OPTIONAL ACTIVITY 8: What Are You Going to Have?

THE WALTZ CAFE

Relaxed Dining in a Casual Atmosphere

ENTREES	PRICE
Fried Shrimp	*$11.95*
Baked Garlic Lemon Chicken	*$12.95*
Broiled Salmon	*$14.95*
Grilled Lamb Chops	*$13.95*
Chopped Sirloin Steak	*$11.95*

served with your choice of:

French Fries, Baked Potato, or Rice

◆

Garden Salad or Soup of the Day*
*Salad Dressings: House Dressing,
Vinegar & Oil, Thousand Island*

◆

*Dessert: Apple Pie, Ice Cream,
Chocolate Cake, or Fruit Cup*

◆

Coffee, Tea, Soda, Lemonade

—— NO SUBSTITUTIONS ——

*Clam Chowder: $.50 extra

THE WALTZ CAFE

DATE		
ITEM	**PRICE**	
SUBTOTAL		
TAX		
TOTAL		

OPTIONAL ACTIVITY 9: Could I Borrow…?

Borrowers

You are making a cake.
You need:
> flour _____
> three eggs _____
> milk _____

You are writing a report.
You need:
> paper _____
> a book about China _____
> a dictionary _____

You are going camping.
You need:
> a tent _____
> a sleeping bag _____
> a large backpack _____

You are having a party.
You need:
> some glasses and plates _____
> a CD player _____
> some speakers _____

You are cleaning up your yard.
You need:
> a rake _____
> a lawnmower _____
> trash bags _____

You are fixing a window.
You need:
> a hammer _____
> a screwdriver _____
> a ladder _____

- Fold here. -

Lenders

You have:
> milk _____
> a tent _____
> a rake _____

You have:
> paper _____
> extra glasses and plates _____
> a hammer _____

You have:
> eggs _____
> a sleeping bag _____
> a lawnmower _____

You have:
> a book about China _____
> a CD player _____
> a screwdriver _____

You have:
> flour _____
> a large backpack _____
> trash bags _____

You have:
> a dictionary _____
> some speakers _____
> a ladder _____

OPTIONAL ACTIVITY 10: Who Am I?

INTERVIEW QUESTIONS	YES	NO
1. Are you living?	☐	☐
2. Are you a female?	☐	☐
3. Are you from North America?	☐	☐
4. Are you from Asia?	☐	☐
5. Are you from Europe?	☐	☐
6. Are you older than thirty?	☐	☐
7. Are you older than sixteen?	☐	☐
8. Are you older than sixty?	☐	☐
9. Are you a movie star?	☐	☐
10. Are you a politician?	☐	☐
11. Are you a singer?	☐	☐
12. Are you married?	☐	☐
13. Are you a parent?	☐	☐
14. Are you rich?	☐	☐
15. Are you from (name of city)?	☐	☐
16. _____	☐	☐
17. _____	☐	☐
18. _____	☐	☐
19. _____	☐	☐
20. _____	☐	☐

OPTIONAL ACTIVITY 11: Find Someone Who...

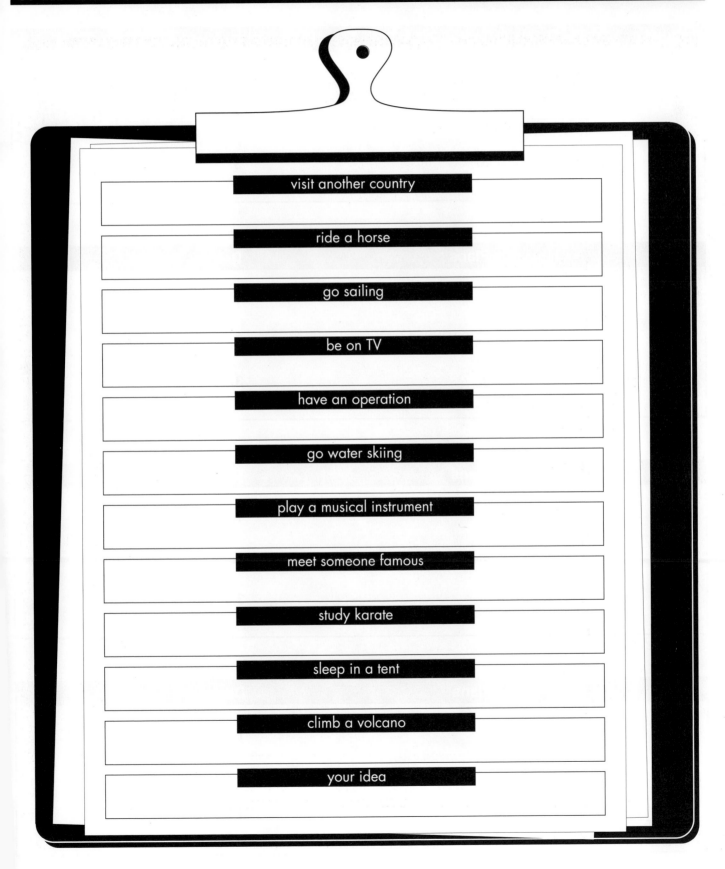

visit another country

ride a horse

go sailing

be on TV

have an operation

go water skiing

play a musical instrument

meet someone famous

study karate

sleep in a tent

climb a volcano

your idea

OPTIONAL ACTIVITY 12: What Are Your Plans and Dreams?

Name	Plans	Dreams
1.	1.	1.
	2.	2.
	3.	3.

Name	Plans	Dreams
2.	1.	1.
	2.	2.
	3.	3.

Name	Plans	Dreams
3.	1.	1.
	2.	2.
	3.	3.

Name	Plans	Dreams
4.	1.	1.
	2.	2.
	3.	3.